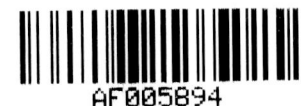

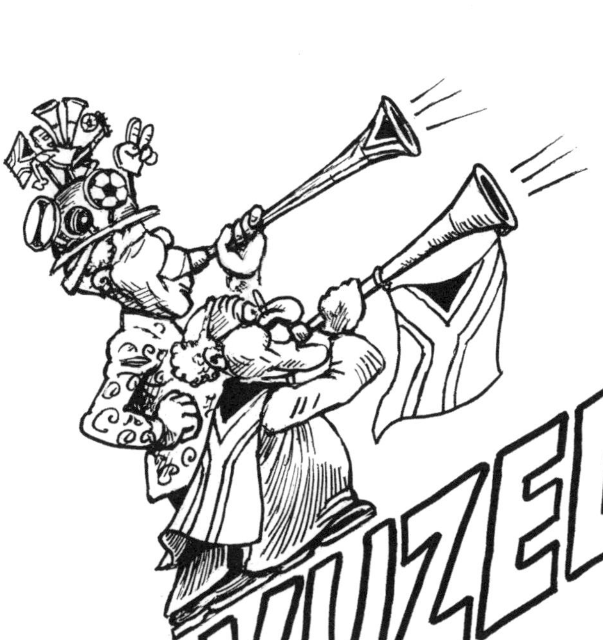

VUVUZELANATION

ZAPIRO

ON SA **SPORT** 1995 – 2013

TEXT BY MIKE WILLS

JACANA

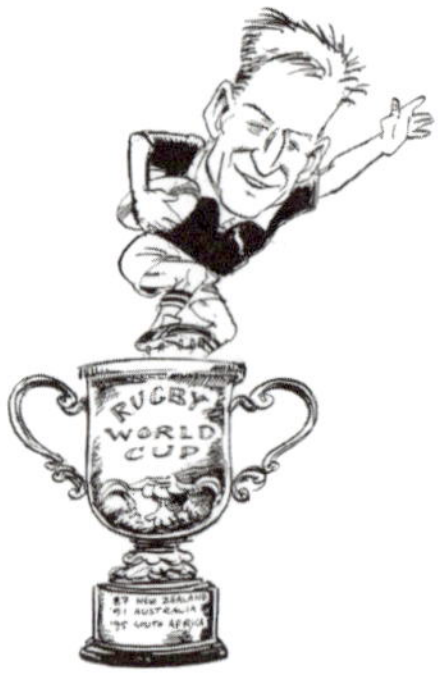
RUGBY WORLD CUP

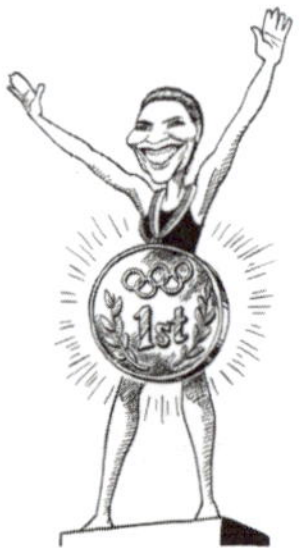

1st

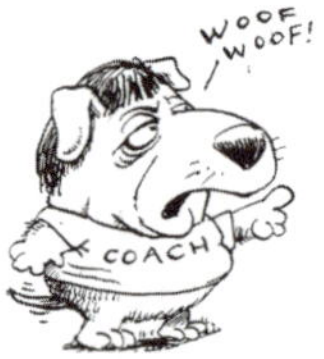
WOOF WOOF!
COACH

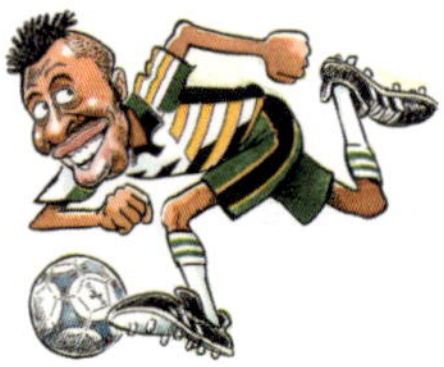

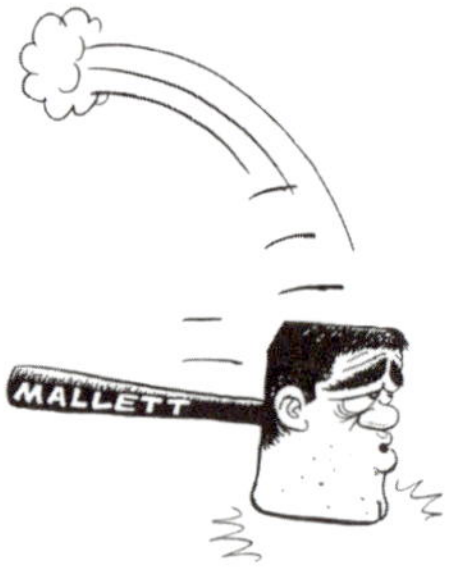
MALLETT

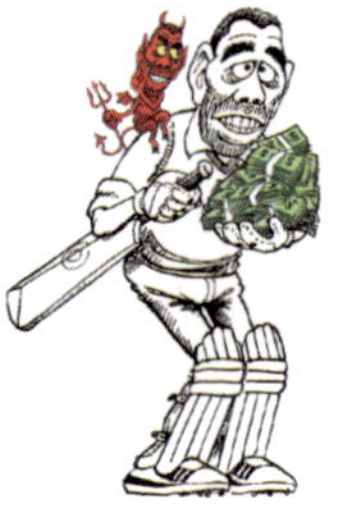

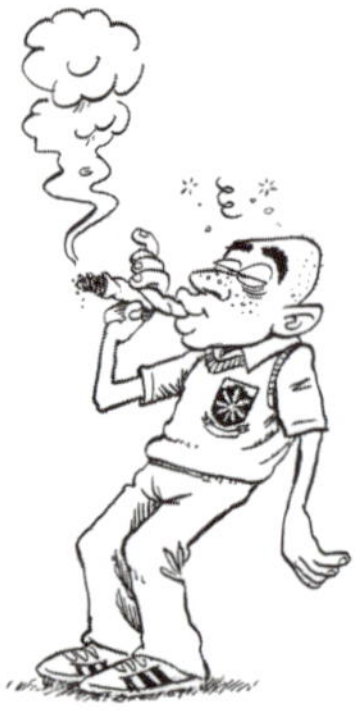

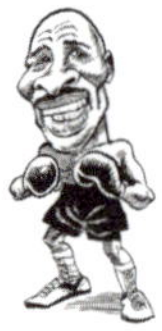

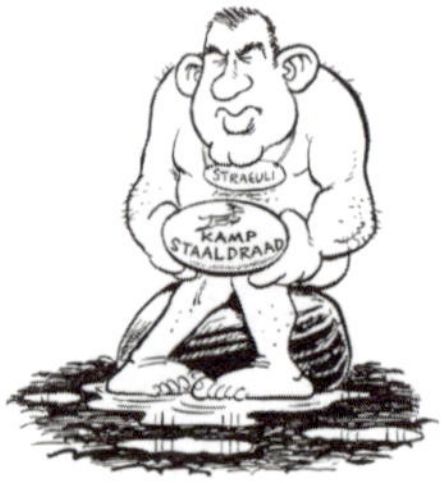
STRAEULI
KAMP STAALDRAAD

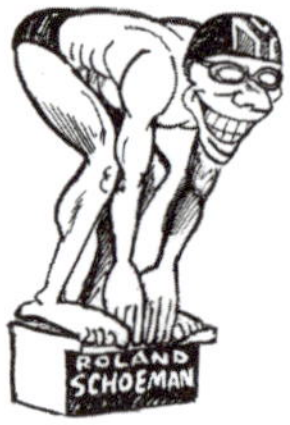
ROLAND SCHOEMAN

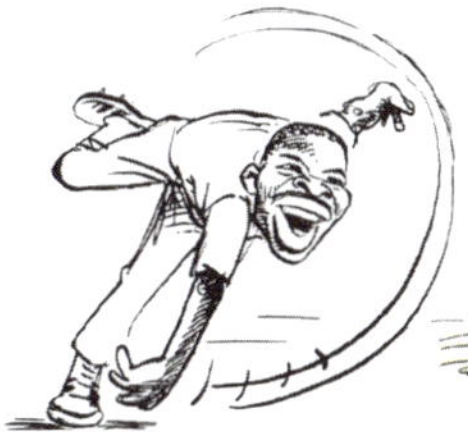

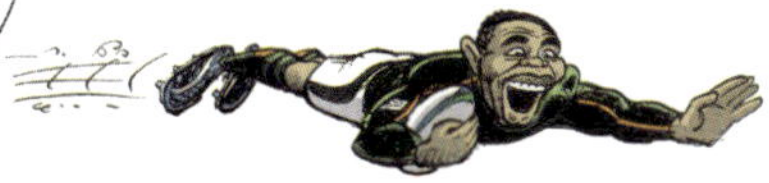

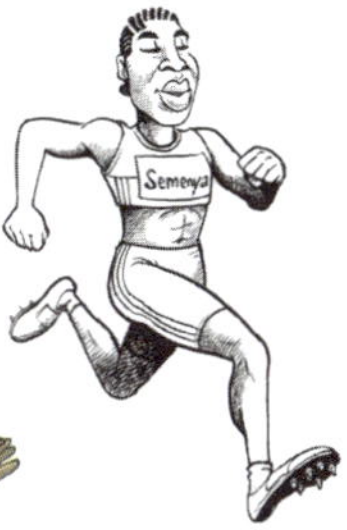

Semenya

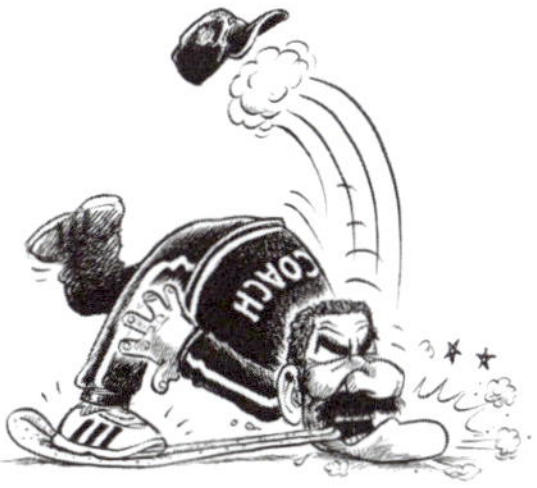

COACH

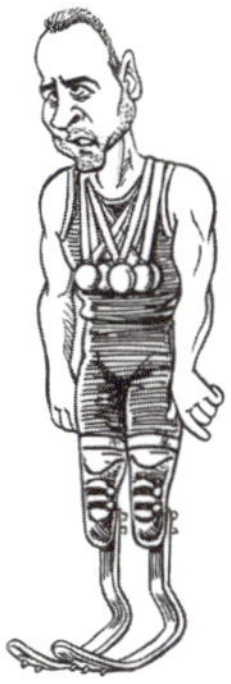

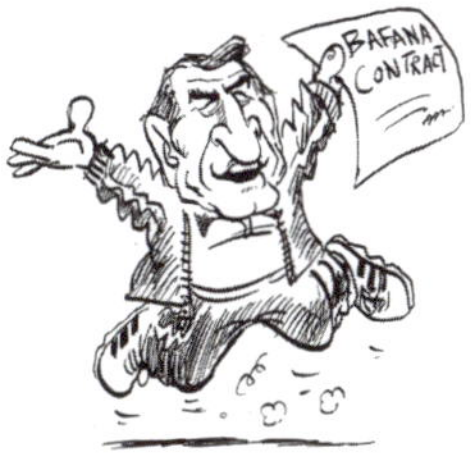

BAFANA
CONTRACT

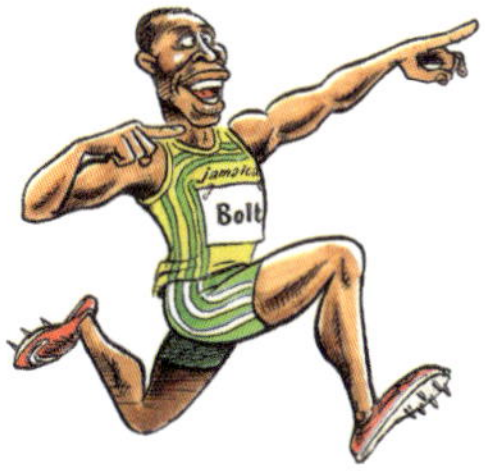

Jamaica
Bolt

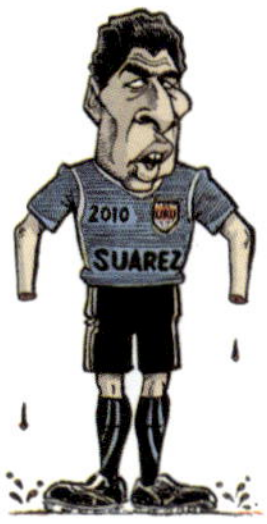

2010
SUÁREZ

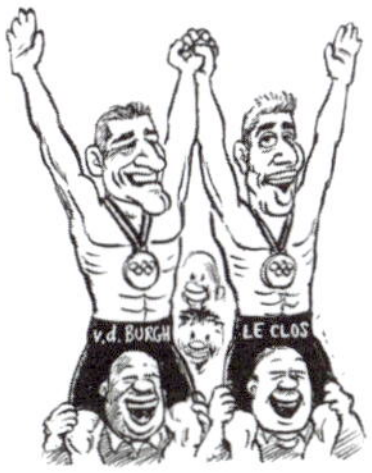

v.d. BURGH
LE CLOS

PREFACE

Most people think of me as an intensely political cartoonist and might be puzzled by a sports collection but, like so many South Africans, I love sport and, within its crazy emotions and curious actions, find constant inspiration for my work.

Somewhat to my bewilderment I was once voted CNN African Sports Journalist of the Year for a single cartoon after the FIFA hosting debacle in 2000.

At school I enjoyed sport, though I was pretty kak at the mainstream stuff like cricket, rugby and soccer. Table tennis was my thing.

I even went on a strange varsity ping pong tour of Taiwan, in our distant days as an outcast nation when that Far East island and Paraguay were our only options (and before my political activism led me to support the international boycott of SA sport).

My very first cartoons appeared in anti-apartheid publications and leaflets in the late 1980s, and, right from that starting point, sport was a recurring theme.

The Nats of old had the bare-faced cheek to complain that sport and politics should not be mixed even as they enforced the racial segregation of teams and stadium seating. Those horrendous laws might have changed but, in the new South Africa, race, politics and sport remain inextricably intertwined.

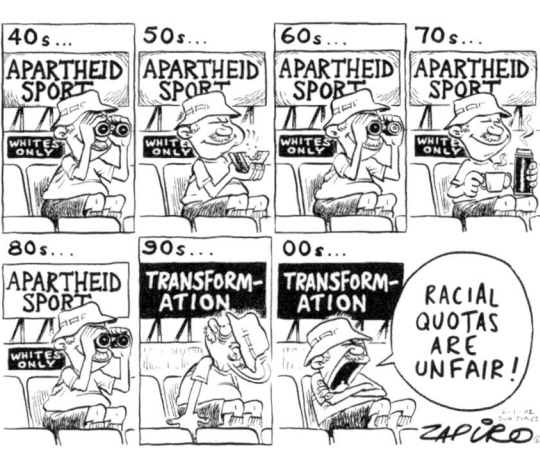

 When a deadline looms and our politicians unexpectedly let me down by behaving with dignity and honesty, I invariably find plenty to work with in the depressing incompetence and pettiness of so many of our sporting administrators.

And sport constantly provides me with a convenient, ready-made metaphor for commentary on our national politics and global events.

 But the ludicrously overblown schoolyard games we call sport also captivate me on a personal level. Along with most of the nation, I celebrate the glorious emotional highs ...

... and I despair at the embarrassing lows.

Of course we take our sport too seriously, yet that noisy passion defines us as this Vuvuzela Nation.

Sport is a key part of who we are, for better and for worse. It's also an endless well-spring of material for a cartoonist!

Looking back now, the mid-nineties in South Africa seem like a golden age. It was a time when, in our hazy and lazy memories, we only ever used words like miracle and rainbow, and wherever there were problems you simply had to add some Nelson and all would come right.

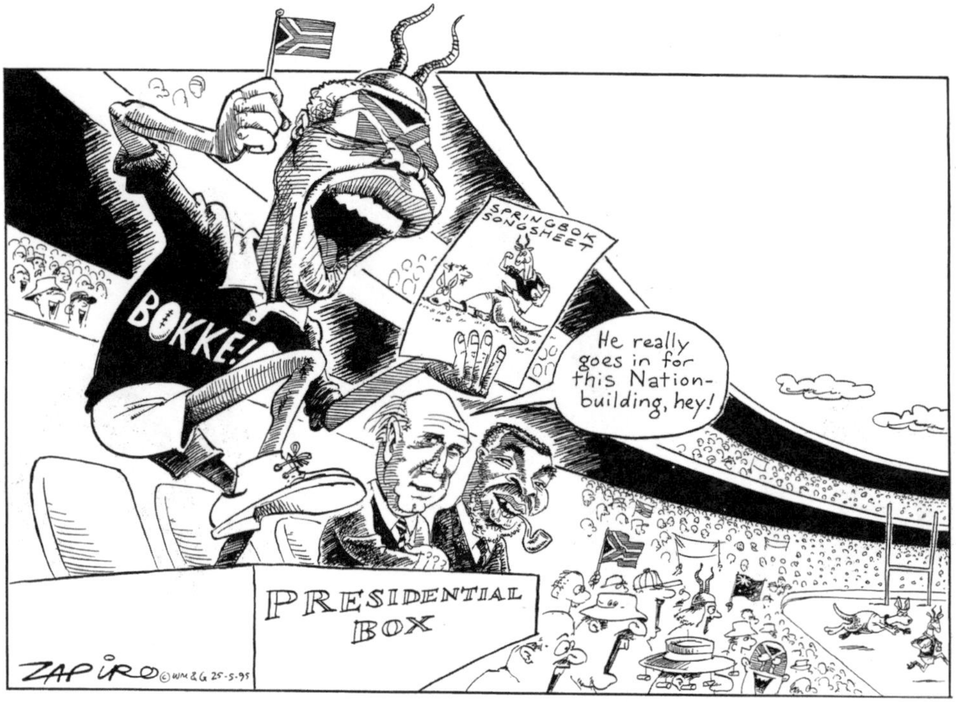
BOKKE!
SPRINGBOK SONGSHEET
He really goes in for this Nation-building, hey!
PRESIDENTIAL BOX
ZAPIRO ©WM&G 25-5-95

On the sports fields, international success arrived remarkably easily after readmission.

Mighty men in green thumped the defending champion Wallabies on the opening day of the 1995 rugby world cup and then went on to chop down the fearsome All Black wing Jonah Lomu in the final.

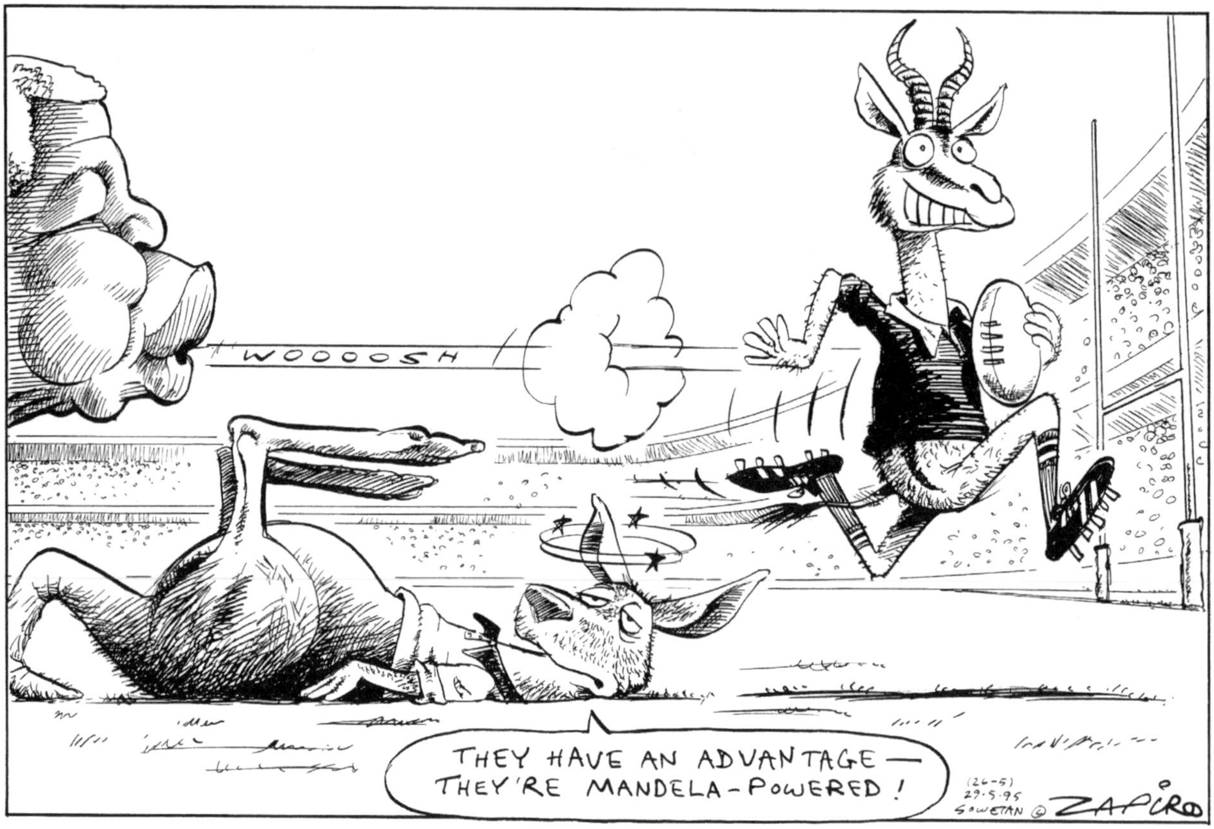
WOOOOOSH
THEY HAVE AN ADVANTAGE — THEY'RE MANDELA-POWERED!
(26-5) 29-5-95 SOWETAN © ZAPIRO

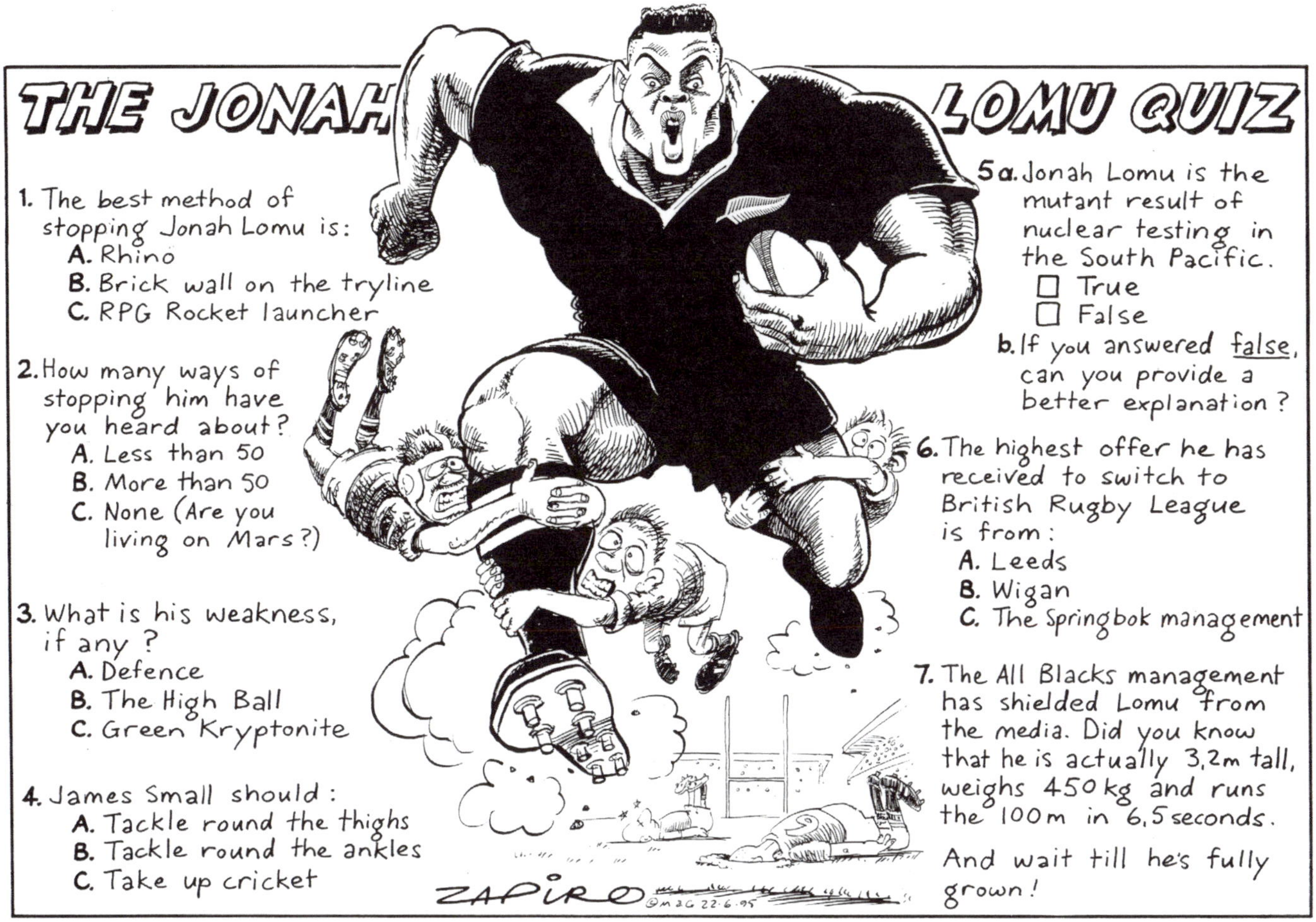
THE JONAH LOMU QUIZ
1. The best method of stopping Jonah Lomu is:
A. Rhino
B. Brick wall on the tryline
C. RPG Rocket launcher
2. How many ways of stopping him have you heard about?
A. Less than 50
B. More than 50
C. None (Are you living on Mars?)
3. What is his weakness, if any?
A. Defence
B. The High Ball
C. Green Kryptonite
4. James Small should:
A. Tackle round the thighs
B. Tackle round the ankles
C. Take up cricket
5 a. Jonah Lomu is the mutant result of nuclear testing in the South Pacific.
☐ True
☐ False
b. If you answered false, can you provide a better explanation?
6. The highest offer he has received to switch to British Rugby League is from:
A. Leeds
B. Wigan
C. The Springbok management
7. The All Blacks management has shielded Lomu from the media. Did you know that he is actually 3,2m tall, weighs 450kg and runs the 100m in 6,5 seconds.
And wait till he's fully grown!
ZAPIRO

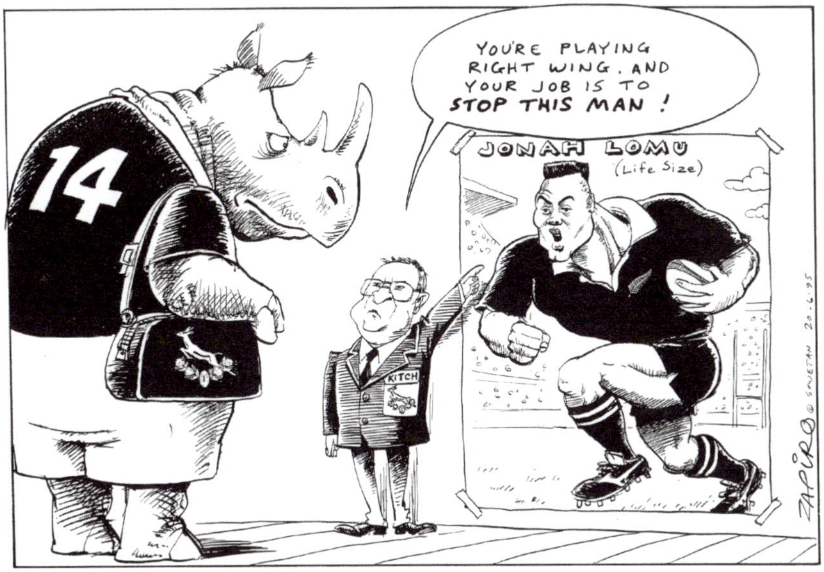
YOU'RE PLAYING RIGHT WING, AND YOUR JOB IS TO STOP THIS MAN!
JONAH LOMU
(Life Size)
14
KITCH
ZAPIRO

1995

A Madiba-inspiration legend was born so powerful that Clint Eastwood felt compelled to make a movie about it.

Bafana Bafana at this time was a team of legends – Neil "Codesa" Tovey, Mark "Feesh" Fish, John "Shoes" Mosheou, Lucas "Rhoo" Radebe – managed by Clive "The Dog" Barker.

They conquered Africa in AFCON 1995 beginning with a thumping of Cameroon.

In the semi-final they overcame a powerful Ghanaian side.

Victory in the final against Tunisia seemed almost predestined for the rainbow nation.

Olympic gold at Atlanta in 1996 for Penny Heyns and Josiah Thugwane was a cause for surprised national celebration without the petty SASCOC haggling which later was to become commonplace.

The plucky Proteas were in their pre-choking honeymoon led by a pre-Satanic Hansie Cronje and inspired by the youthful left-arm spinner Paul Adams who exploded on the international scene in 1996 and bewildered the touring English with an unconventional bowling action famously described as looking like "a frog in a blender".

But all that rosy glow conceals a grimmer truth. The scariest figure at the 1995 rugby world cup was not the gigantic Jonah Lomu but the late Louis Luyt, the former fertiliser king and swaggering braggart, who ruled rugby with iron in his fist and a foot in his mouth.

Even Max, the intimidating Johannesburg Zoo gorilla who had famously survived gunshots when an escaping criminal ended up in his enclosure, would be wary of such a beast.

The Springbok emblem was saved for SA rugby only after interventions by Nelson Mandela, other senior ANC figures and Archbishop Tutu. Luyt's gratitude for this gesture, characteristically, was expressed by his decision to haul the nation's iconic president through the courts in 1998.

Not everyone in the ANC was backing the Boks. Trevor Manuel famously declared his continuing support for the All Blacks because of the lack of transformation in the team, the administration and, often, in the stands.
In June 1996, the Springboks selected Henry Tromp as a hooker even though he had a conviction for manslaughter after the death of a farm labourer.

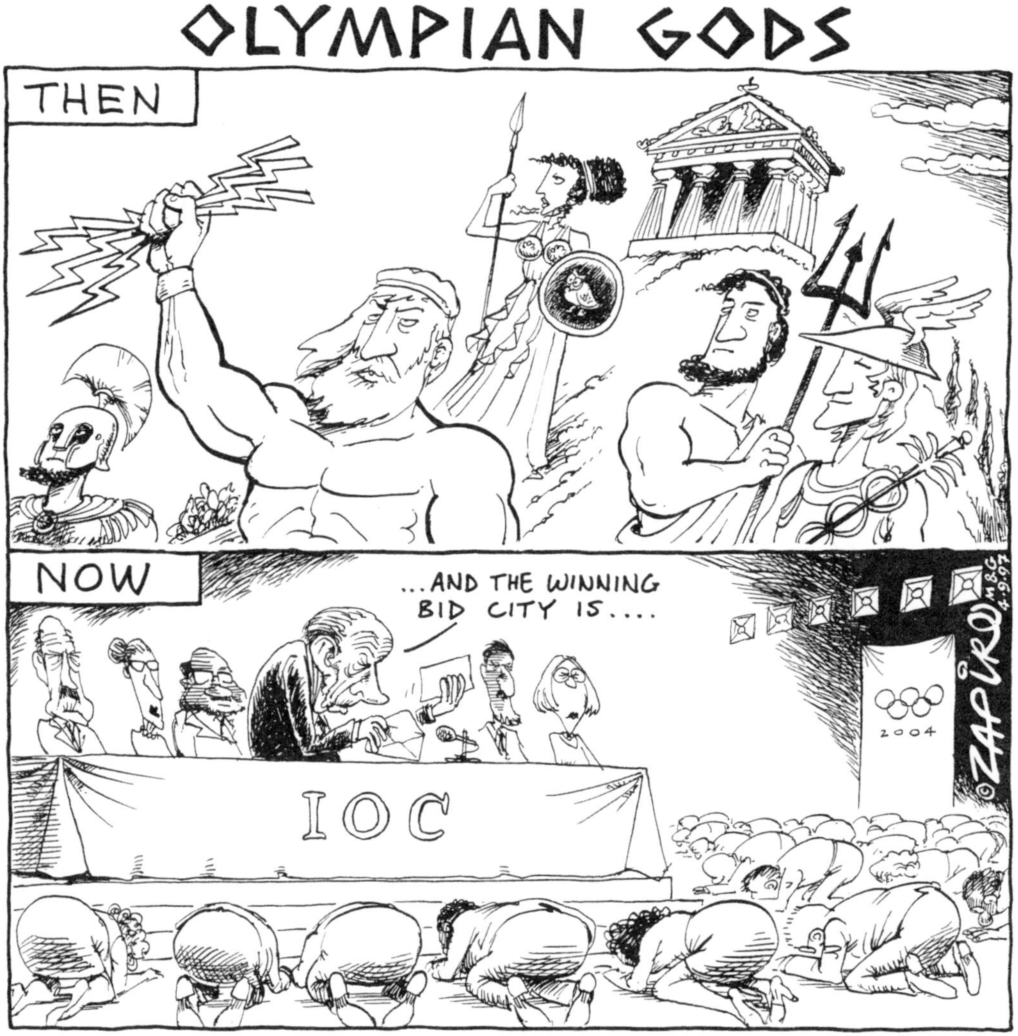
OLYMPIAN GODS
THEN
NOW
...AND THE WINNING BID CITY IS....
2004
IOC
ZAPIRO
M&G 4-9-97

Then there was Cape Town's bid to host the 2004 Olympic Games in which we assumed that the notoriously amoral IOC would vote in our favour simply in honour of our noble democratic transition.

The local bid team was riven by disagreement and petty squabbles but somehow got a passable act together.

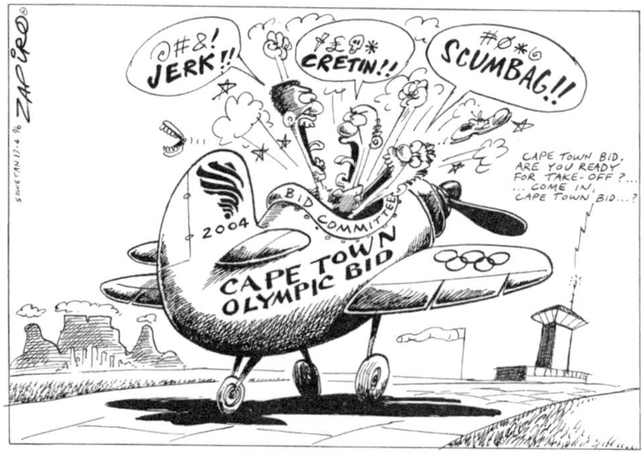
ZAPIRO
SOWETAN 17-4-96
JERK!!
CRETIN!!
SCUMBAG!!
CAPE TOWN BID, ARE YOU READY FOR TAKE-OFF?... ... COME IN, CAPE TOWN BID...?
2004
BID COMMITTEE
CAPE TOWN OLYMPIC BID

The 1996 games in Atlanta did nothing but damage to the image of that American city after a fatal bomb explosion and some serous logistical problems, which raised further doubts about Cape Town's ability to cope with the Olympian demands.

The Cape Town bid team, headed by former banker Chris Ball and burdened by negative headlines, pressed on into the final round of voting.

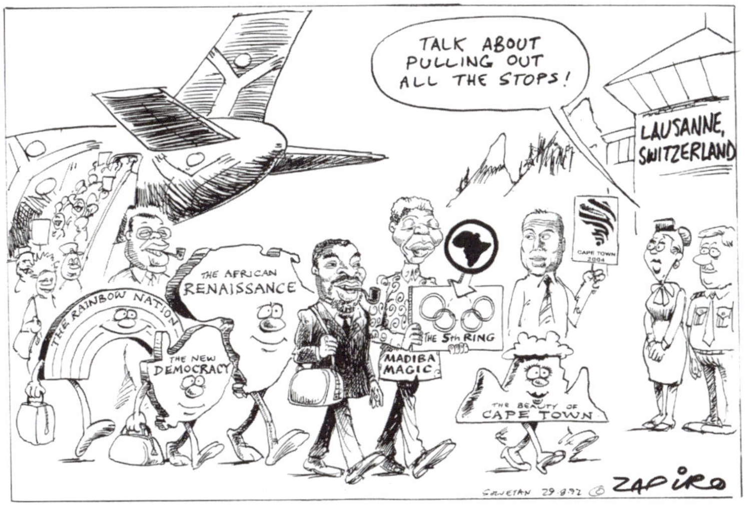
TALK ABOUT PULLING OUT ALL THE STOPS!
LAUSANNE, SWITZERLAND
THE AFRICAN RENAISSANCE
THE RAINBOW NATION
THE NEW DEMOCRACY
MADIBA MAGIC
THE 5th RING
THE BEAUTY OF CAPE TOWN
ZAPIRO

In the end it was the Greeks who won the dubious privilege of bankrupting themselves in seven years' time. The crowd on Cape Town's Grand Parade left the putative victory celebrations in deflated and disgruntled mood, prompting one of Zapiro's most famous drawings. President Mandela referred to this cartoon in a speech to the ANC caucus, saying it summed up his feelings, except he used the polite "se ma se moer" rather than the coarser Cape original.

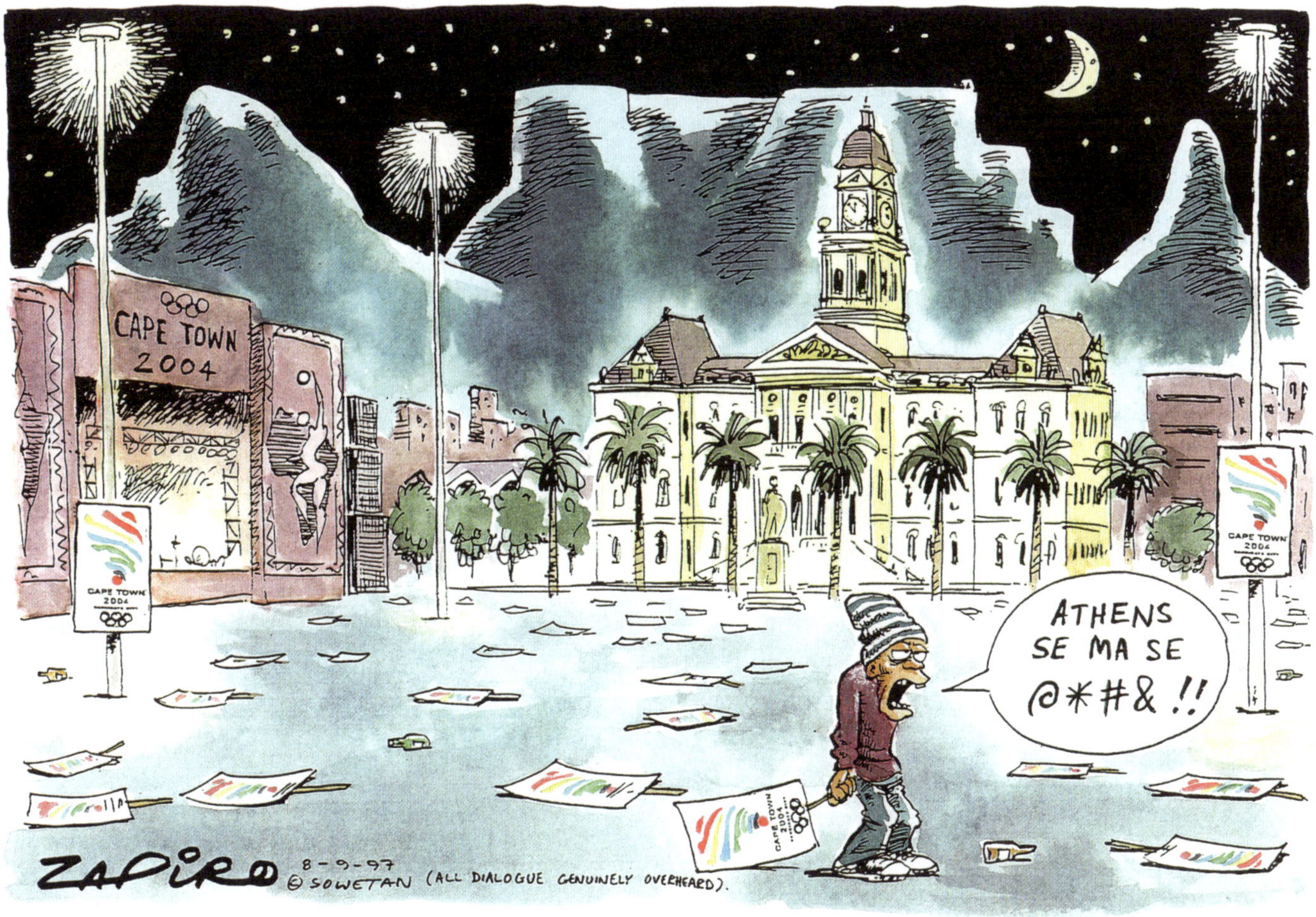
CAPE TOWN 2004
ATHENS SE MA SE @*#& !!
ZAPIRO 8-9-97 © SOWETAN (ALL DIALOGUE GENUINELY OVERHEARD).

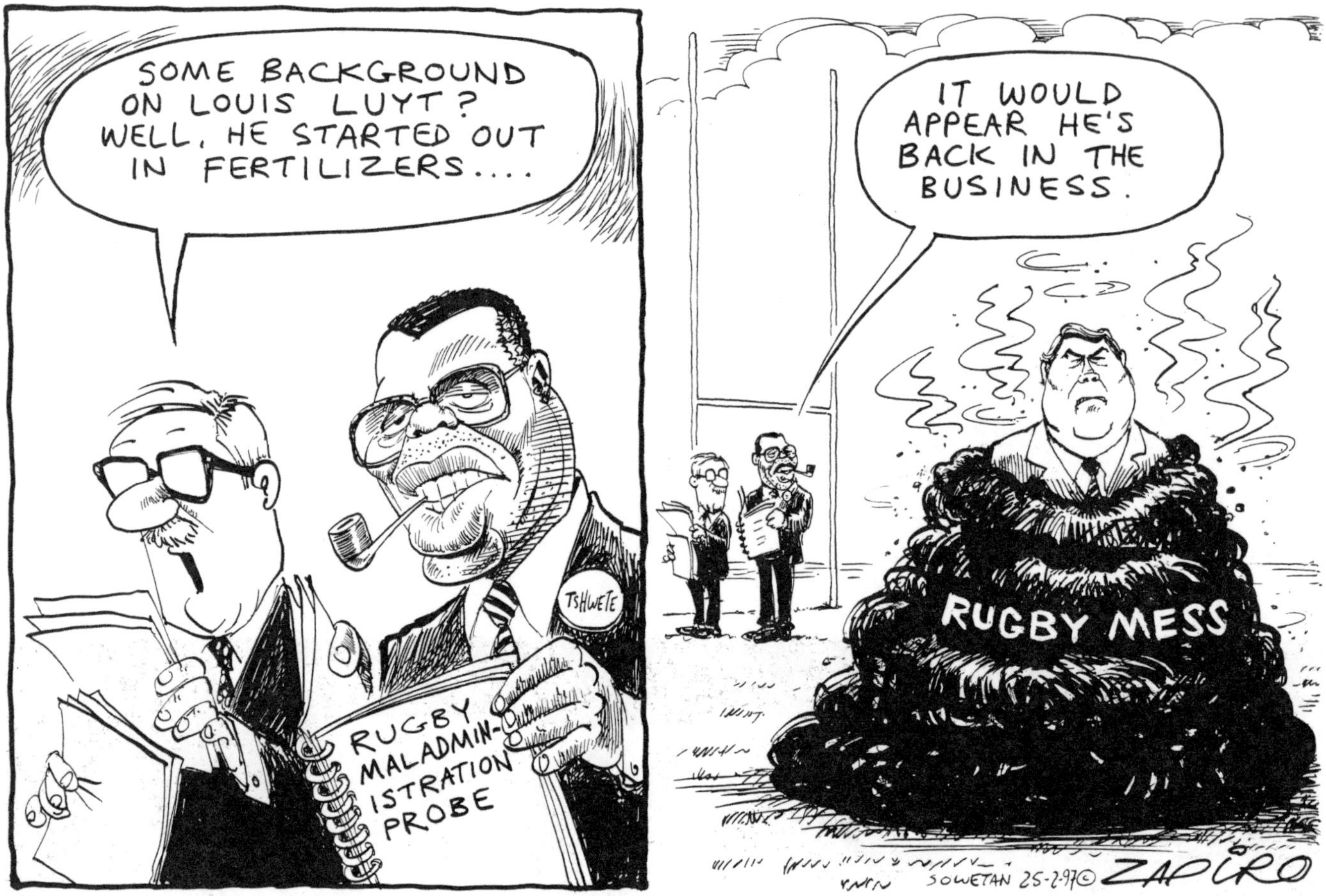
SOME BACKGROUND ON LOUIS LUYT? WELL, HE STARTED OUT IN FERTILIZERS....
IT WOULD APPEAR HE'S BACK IN THE BUSINESS.
TSHWETE
RUGBY MALADMIN-ISTRATION PROBE
RUGBY MESS
SOWETAN 25-2-97©
ZAPIRO

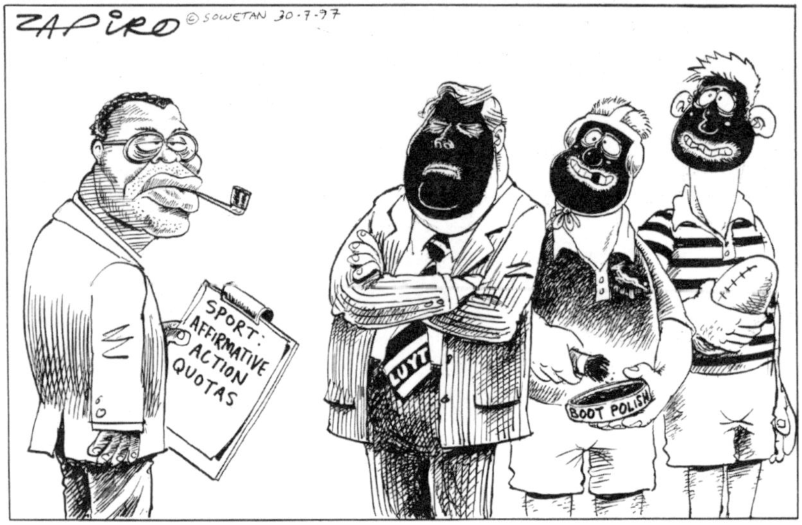
ZAPIRO
© SOWETAN 30-7-97
SPORT: AFFIRMATIVE ACTION QUOTAS
LUYT
BOOT POLISH

From 1994 to 1999 former Robben Islander Steve Tshwete was our first Minister for Sport & Recreation – a position with enviable access to free tickets but with unenviable and constant battles on governance and transformation.

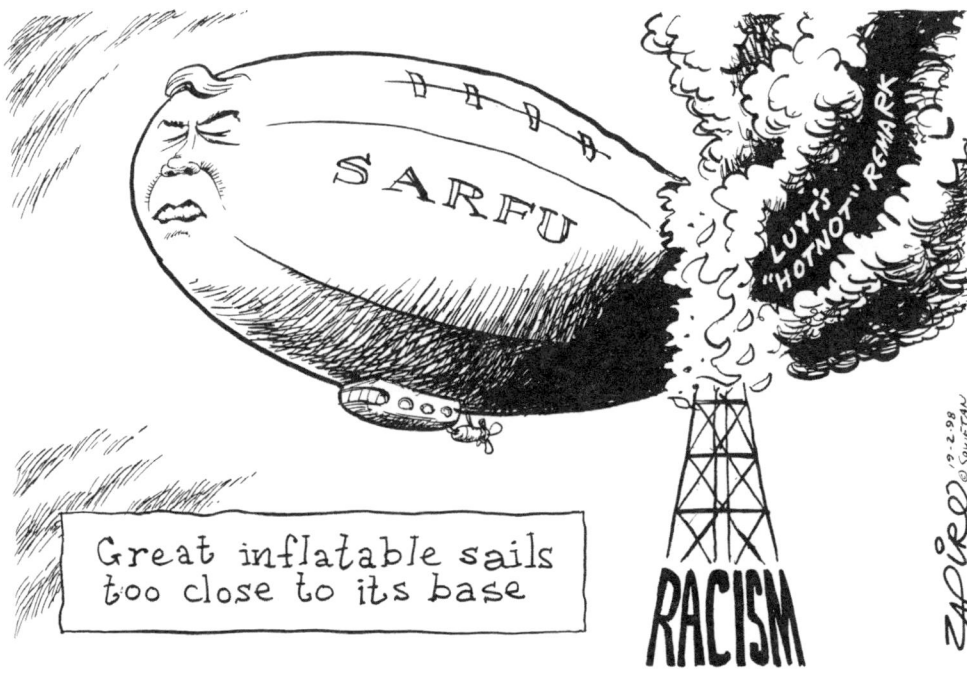

It was in a conversation with Tshwete that the ever-subtle Louis Luyt allegedly described his arch critic, and later successor as SARU President, Brian van Rooyen, as "a hotnot", adding "you cannot trust a hotnot".

Some of those under Luyt were no better. Bok coach André Markgraaff was caught on tape liberally, if that is the right word, using both the f-word and the k-word. He was fired but remained a powerful figure in the SA rugby landscape from his base in Kimberley.

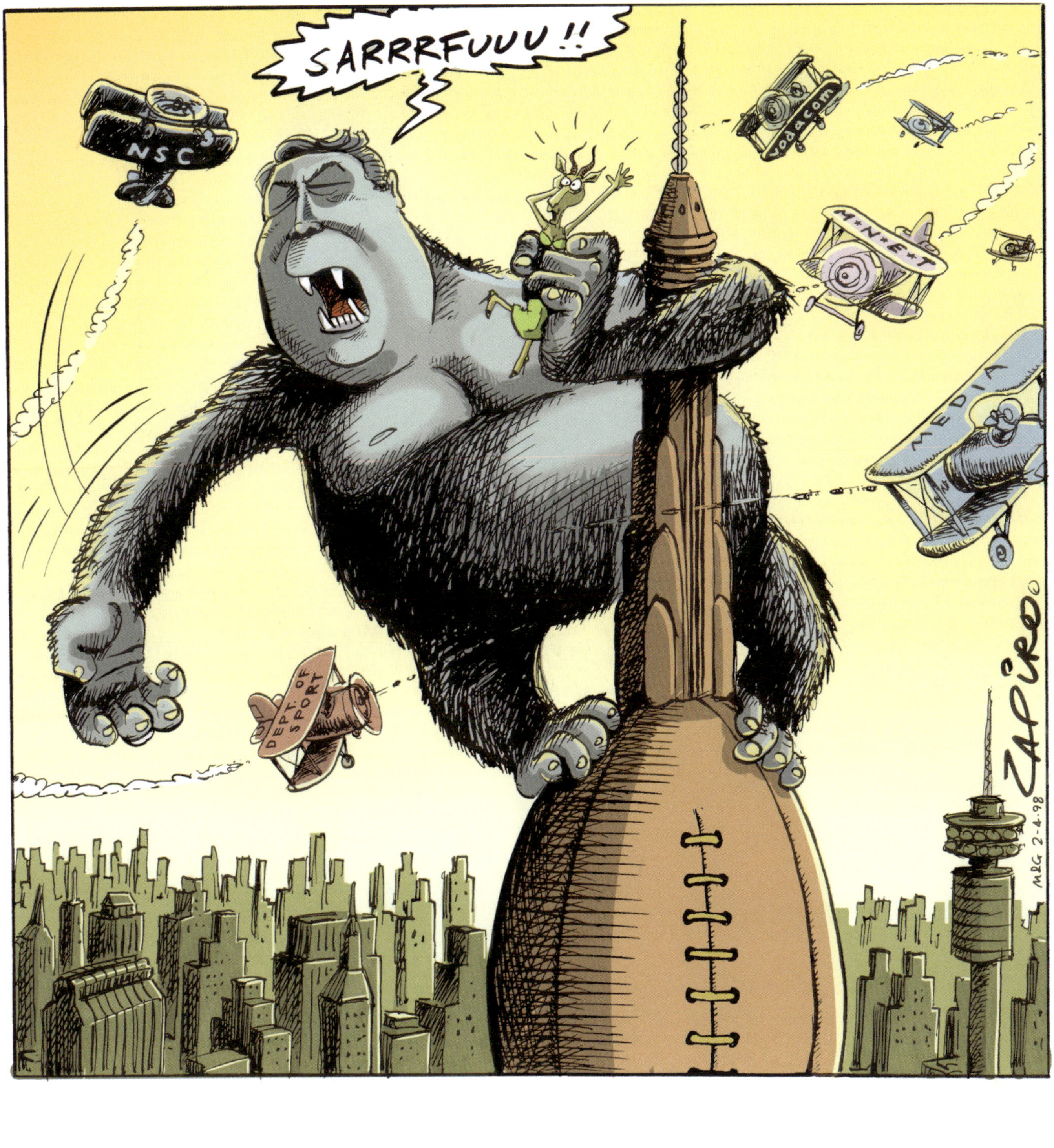
SARRRFUUU !!
NSC
vodacom
M*N*E*T
MEDIA
DEPT. OF SPORT
ZAPIRO
M&G 2-4-98

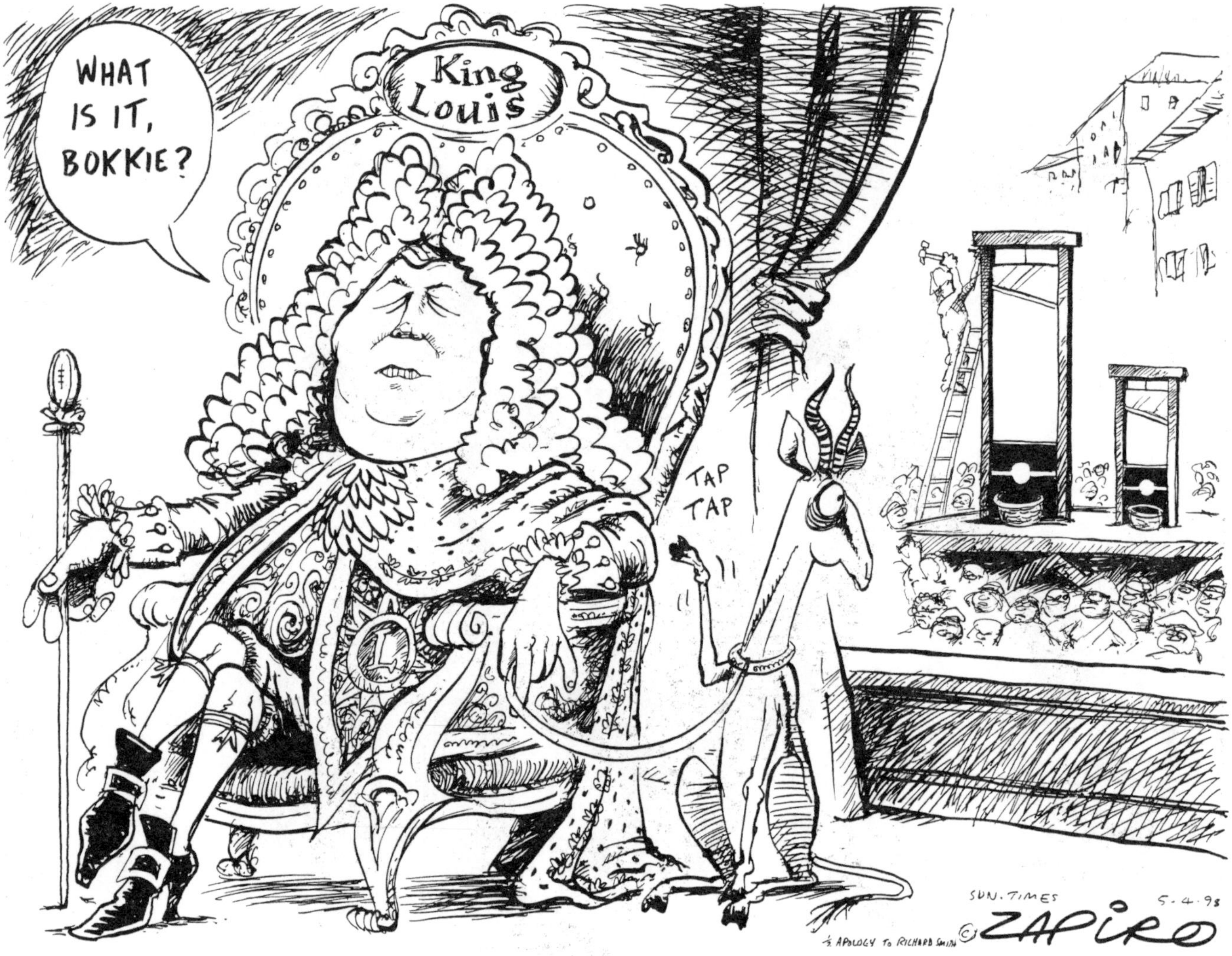
WHAT IS IT, BOKKIE?
King Louis
TAP TAP
SUN·TIMES
5·4·98
½ APOLOGY TO RICHARD SMITH
©ZAPIRO

Luyt believed he was indispensable to SA rugby but he had made too many enemies and they were lining up to get rid of him and, possibly, the Springbok emblem as well.

Finally in May 1998 rugby's answer to Eugene Terre'Blanche was evicted from power.

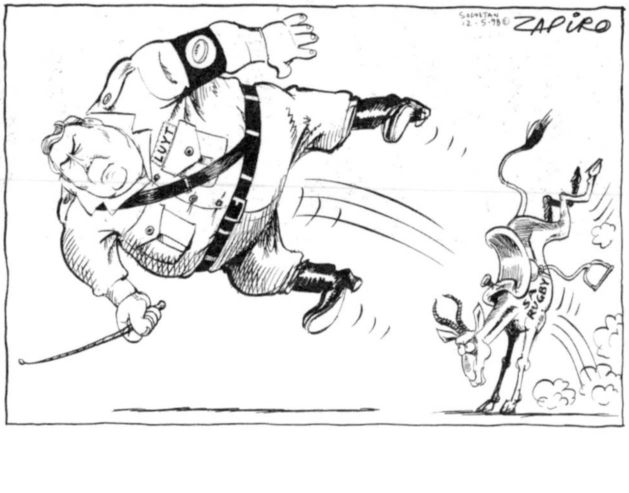
ZAPIRO
LUYT
SA RUGBY

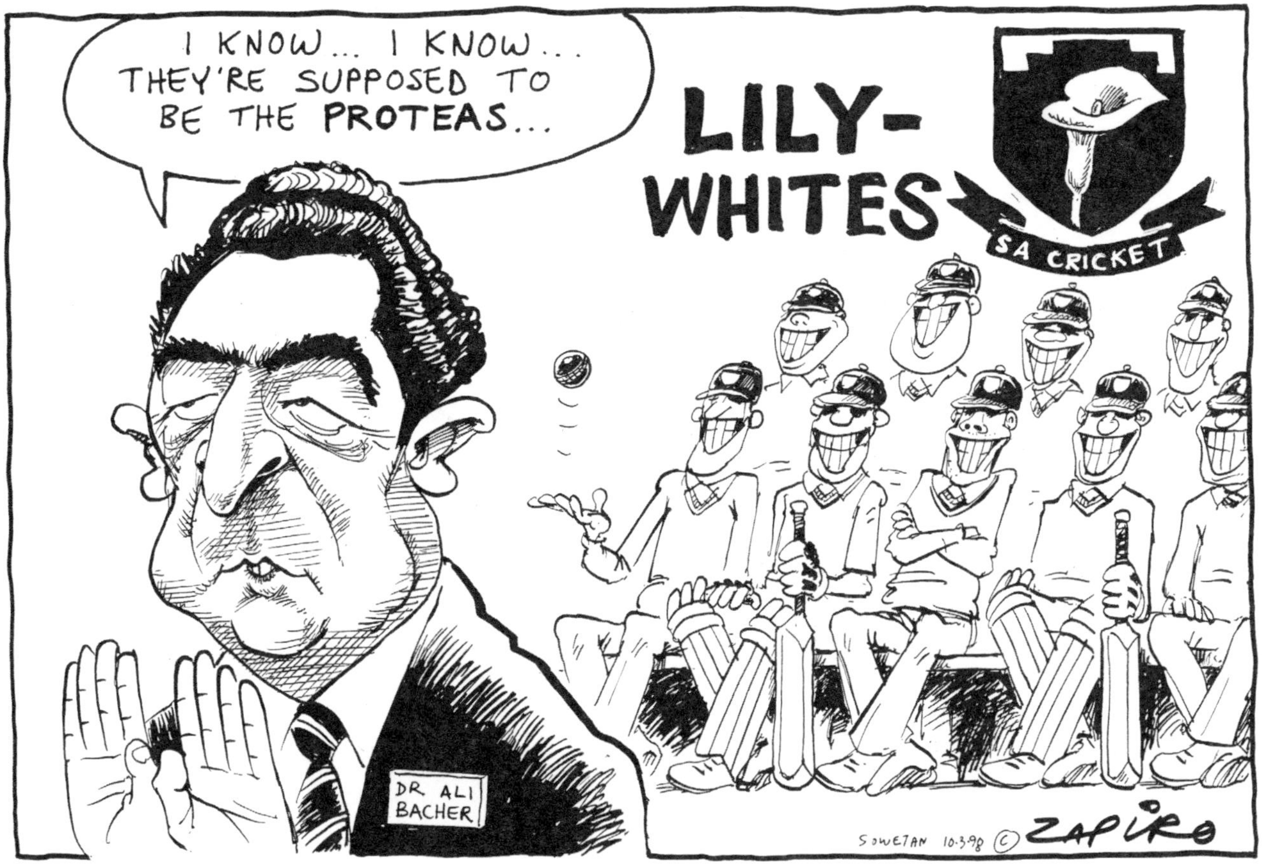
I KNOW... I KNOW...
THEY'RE SUPPOSED TO
BE THE PROTEAS...
LILY-
WHITES
SA CRICKET
DR ALI
BACHER
SOWETAN 10.3.98 © ZAPIRO

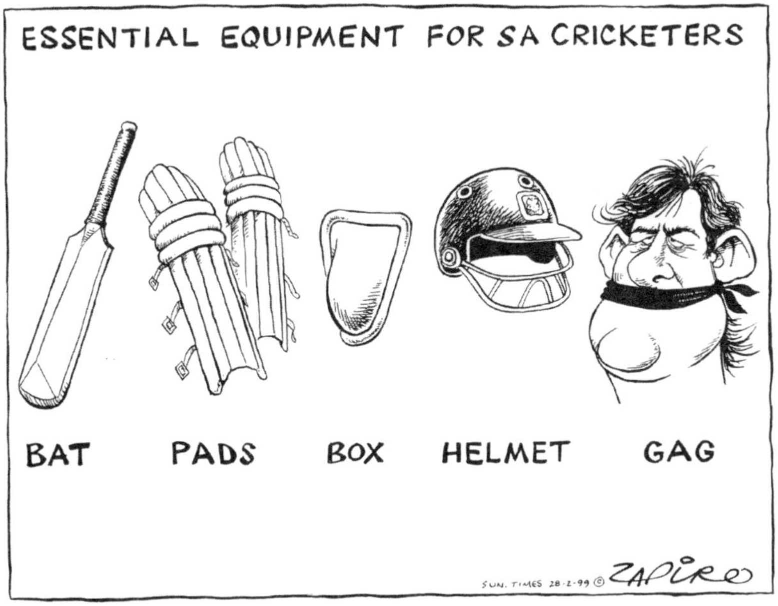
ESSENTIAL EQUIPMENT FOR SA CRICKETERS
BAT
PADS
BOX
HELMET
GAG
SUN. TIMES 28.2.99 © ZAPIRO

Cricket under Dr Ali Bacher also faced transformation pressures and also had a language problem. SA all-rounder Brian Macmillan had allegedly used the term coolie-creeper (a term offensive to Indians) to describe a ball which rolls along the ground.

On the cricket field things weren't much better in 1997 as the Proteas took a belting from the Australians at the Wanderers before losing the test series 2-1.

The rugby team's fortunes were also low until Carel du Plessis (the crown prince of wings but the clown prince of Bok coaches) was replaced, after a home series loss to the Lions, by the garrulous Nick Mallett.

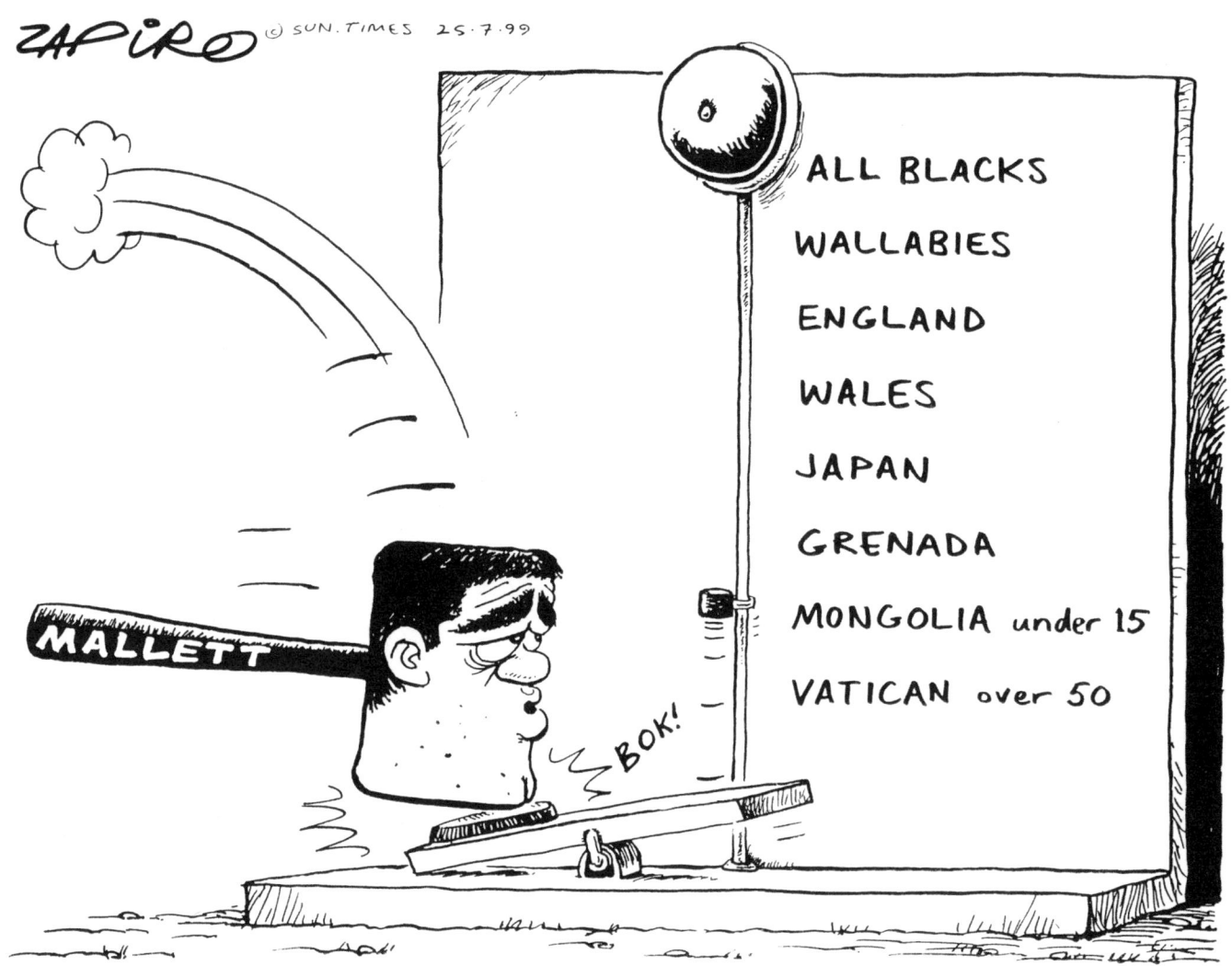

Mallett took the team on a world record-equalling 17 test wins in a row before the wheels came off and the media pack started hammering him.

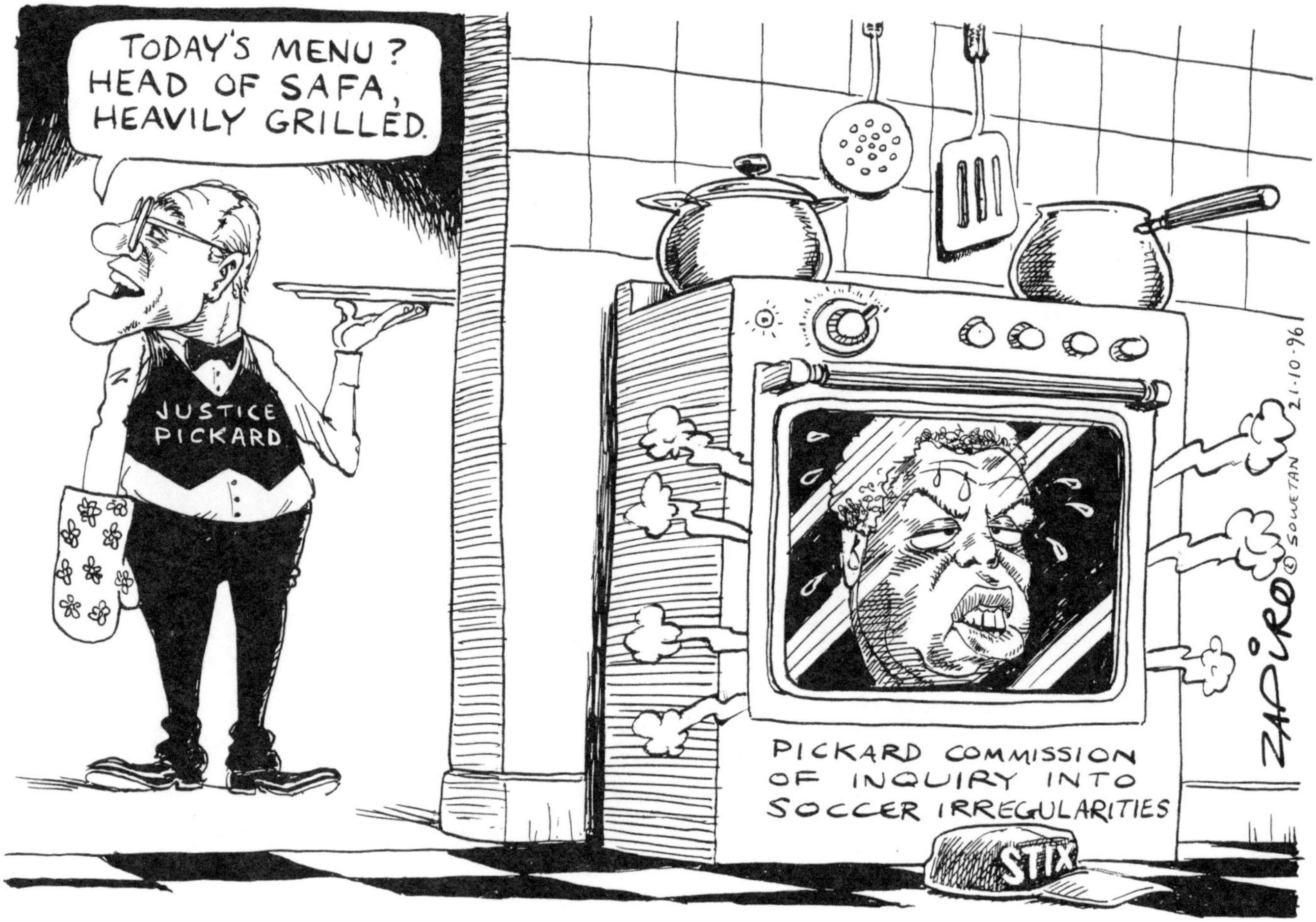
TODAY'S MENU? HEAD OF SAFA, HEAVILY GRILLED.
JUSTICE PICKARD
PICKARD COMMISSION OF INQUIRY INTO SOCCER IRREGULARITIES
STIX
ZAPIRO © SOWETAN 21-10-96

The sports minister was also trying to sort out the mess of SA soccer administration. The 'colourful' Abdul Bhamjee, from the apartheid era, went to jail for cooking the books and his successors had also indulged in some interesting accounting. Tshwete appointed Judge Benjamin Pickard to investigate allegations of corruption and mismanagement within SAFA and his findings damned president Solomon 'Stix' Morewa, Chiefs' owner Kaizer Motaung and Irish sports company boss Brian Mahon.

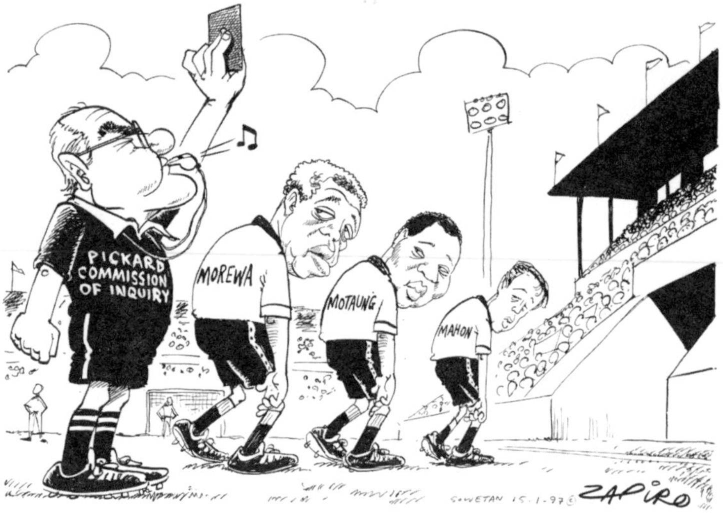
PICKARD COMMISSION OF INQUIRY
MOREWA
MOTAUNG
MAHON
SOWETAN 15-1-97 ©
ZAPIRO

Morewa tried to cling to power but even his eventual departure saw no improvement.

In spite of the administrative shambles, coach Clive Barker and his talented squad qualified comfortably for the 1998 FIFA world cup finals in France – South Africa's first-ever appearance on that exalted stage.

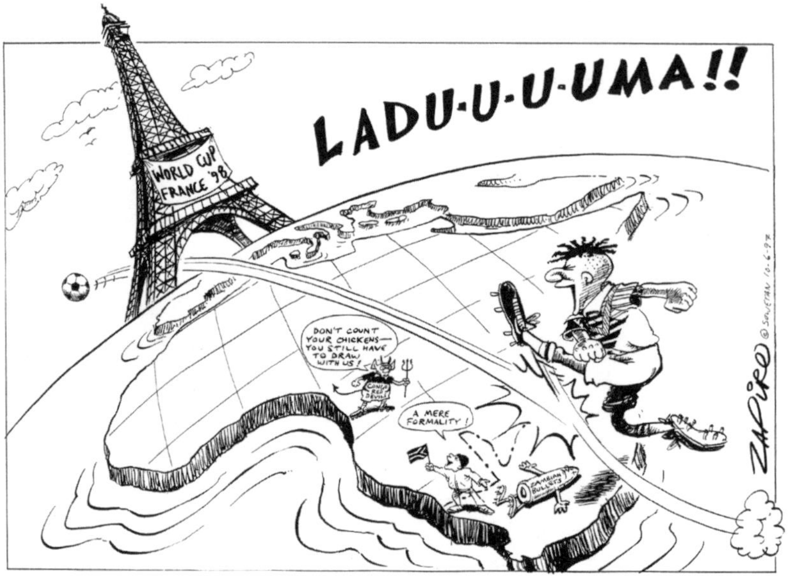

LADU-U-U-UMA!!
WORLD CUP FRANCE '98
DON'T COUNT YOUR CHICKENS— YOU STILL HAVE TO DRAW WITH US!
CONGO RED DEVILS
A MERE FORMALITY!
ZAMBIAN BULLETS
ZAPIRO © SOWETAN 10.6.97

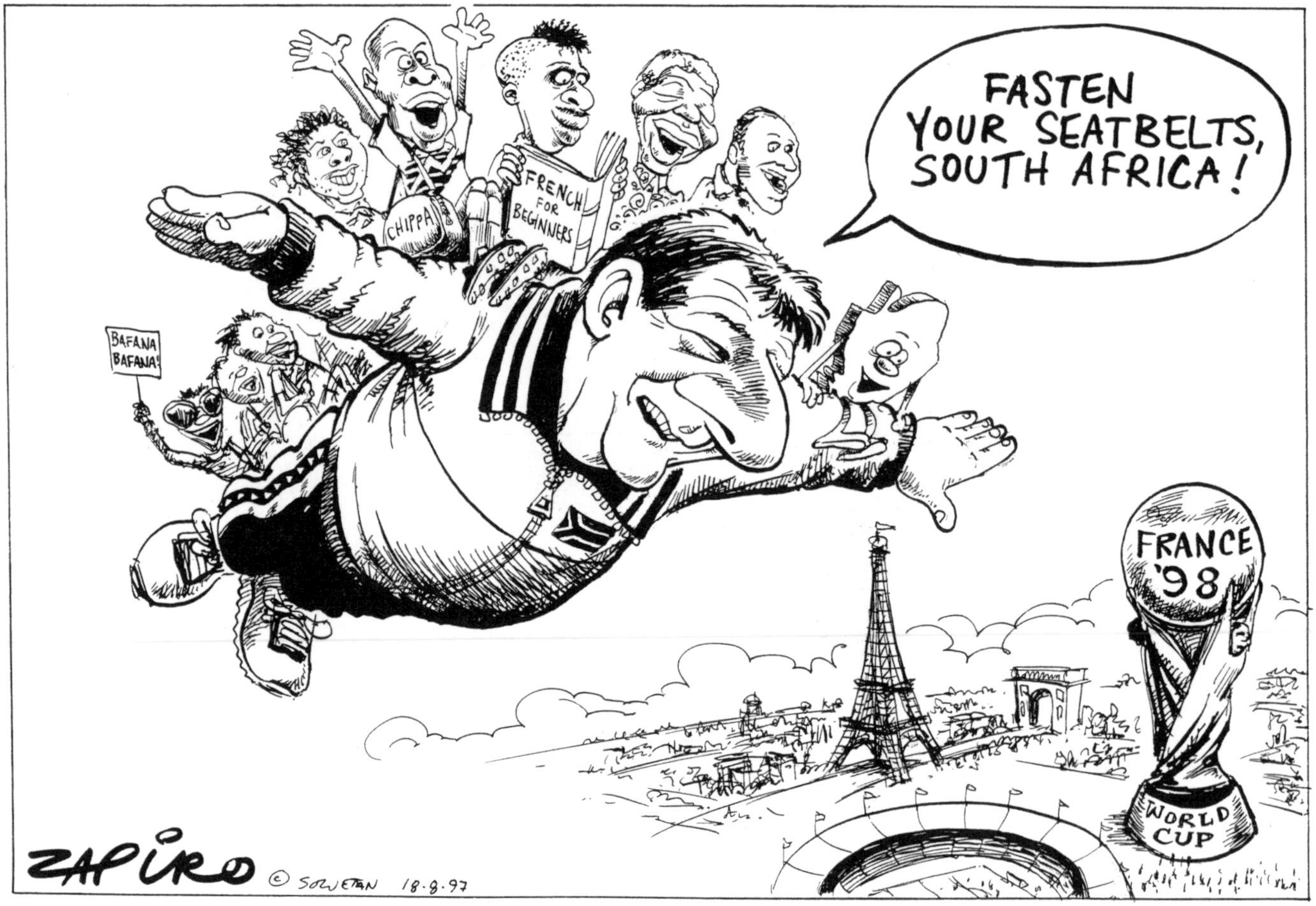

FASTEN YOUR SEATBELTS, SOUTH AFRICA!
CHIPPA
FRENCH FOR BEGINNERS
BAFANA BAFANA!
FRANCE '98
WORLD CUP
ZAPIRO © SOWETAN 18.8.97

But Barker and his famous aeroplane goal celebrations were never to be seen in France after his team's form faded amidst criticism that he kept faith for too long with senior players.

The Dog was sacked after a disappointing Confederations Cup tournament and the rotund maestro of yesteryear, Jomo "Troublemaker" Somo, stepped in as caretaker to guide Bafana through the bumpy 1998 AFCON campaign in Burkina Faso.

1998

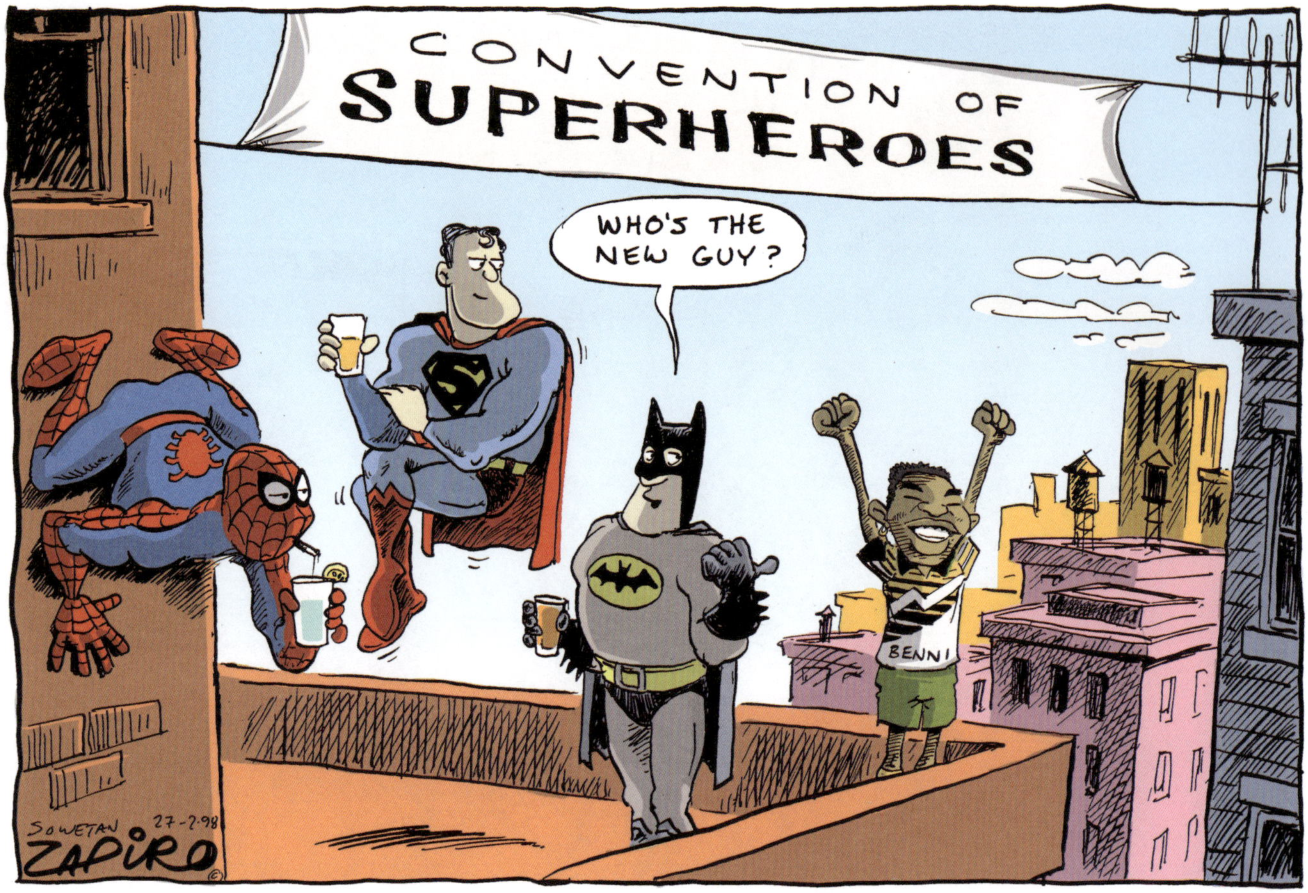
CONVENTION OF SUPERHEROES
WHO'S THE NEW GUY?
BENNI
SOWETAN 27-2-98
ZAPIRO

Somo's side – aided by a sensational burst of scoring from a youthful (and slim) Benni McCarthy – somehow reached the final where they were comfortably undone by an Egyptian team beginning an era of continental dominance.

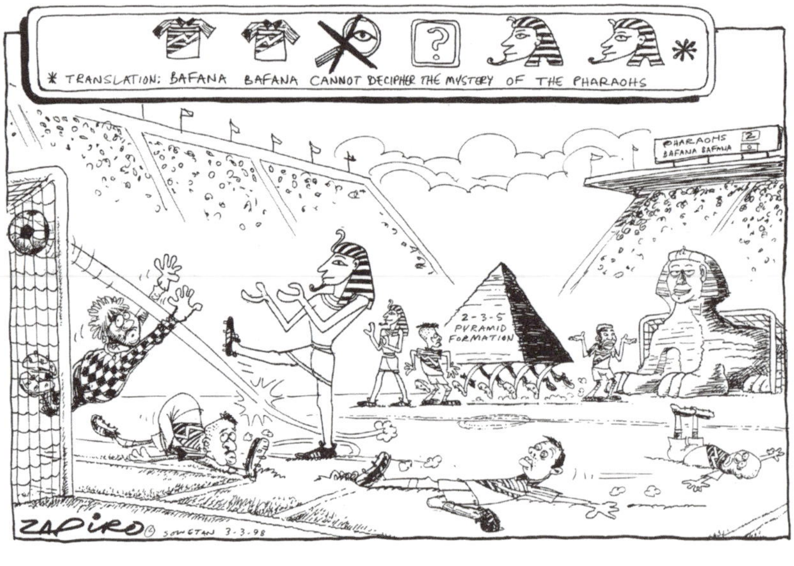
* TRANSLATION: BAFANA BAFANA CANNOT DECIPHER THE MYSTERY OF THE PHARAOHS
PHARAOHS 2
BAFANA BAFANA 0
2-3-5 PYRAMID FORMATION
ZAPIRO SOWETAN 3-3-98

For the in-demand McCarthy, the twelve-year soap opera was beginning – club v country, money v pride, playing v partying, burgers v lentils.

After AFCON, Sono stepped aside (fear not, he would be back several times) and Frenchman Philippe Troussier took control for the 1998 world cup. The White Witch Doctor was not known for his diplomacy with either media or players.

The finals campaign began with a 3-0 loss to hosts France, which included an infamous own goal from defender Pierre Issa.

Lucas Radebe then led the side to a creditable 1-1 draw with the almost great Danes.

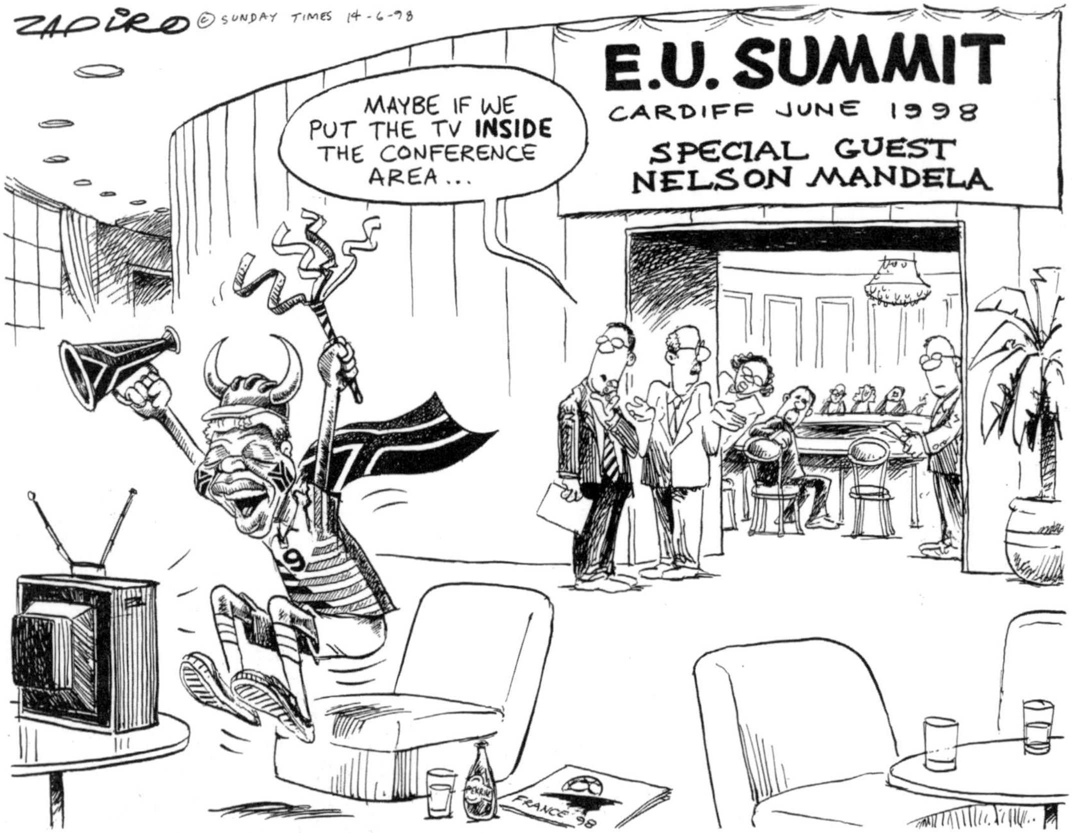
ZAPIRO © SUNDAY TIMES 14-6-98
E.U. SUMMIT
CARDIFF JUNE 1998
SPECIAL GUEST
NELSON MANDELA
MAYBE IF WE PUT THE TV INSIDE THE CONFERENCE AREA...
FRANCE 98

Like everyone else, Madiba was finding it hard to concentrate on work while a world cup was on.

The tempestuous Troussier sent home two players for indiscipline and a 2-2 draw with Saudi Arabia meant both teams were leaving the tournament early.

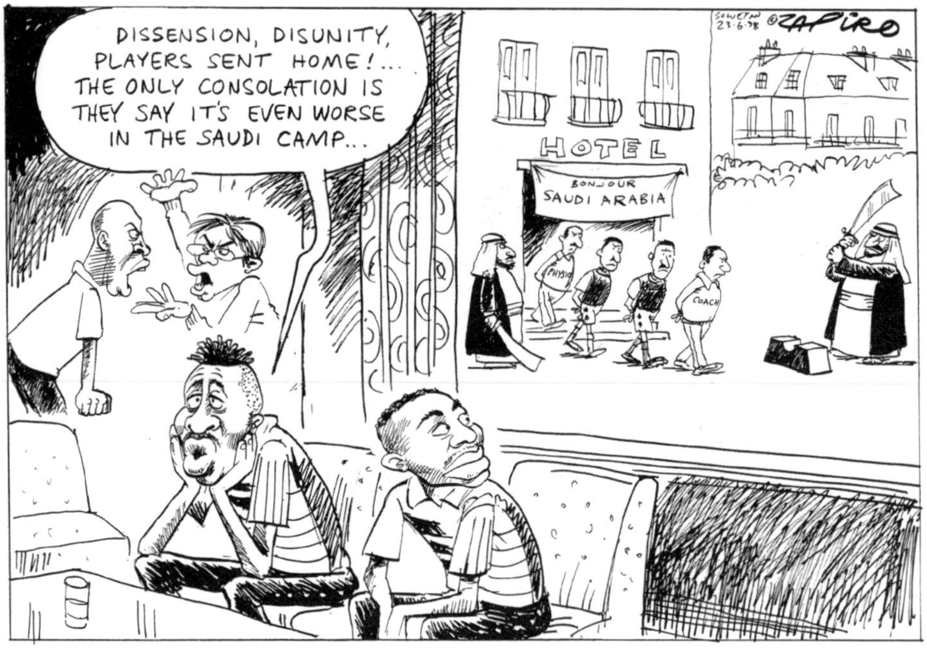
ZAPIRO
DISSENSION, DISUNITY, PLAYERS SENT HOME!... THE ONLY CONSOLATION IS THEY SAY IT'S EVEN WORSE IN THE SAUDI CAMP...
HOTEL
BONJOUR SAUDI ARABIA
PHYSIO
COACH

Cricket was suffering a Back To The Future moment. In the 1980s West Indian players had taken part in two controversial rebel tours to break apartheid sports' sanctions in return for huge payments. In 1998, key West Indians were refusing to tour the new SA because their board wasn't paying them enough to do so.

Eventually the Brian Lara-led team arrived and lost the five-test series 5-0 with the headline writers unable to decide whether it was a whitewash, a blackwash or a rainbow wash.

1998

In September 1999 Johannesburg hosted the 7th All-Africa Games ... but only just.

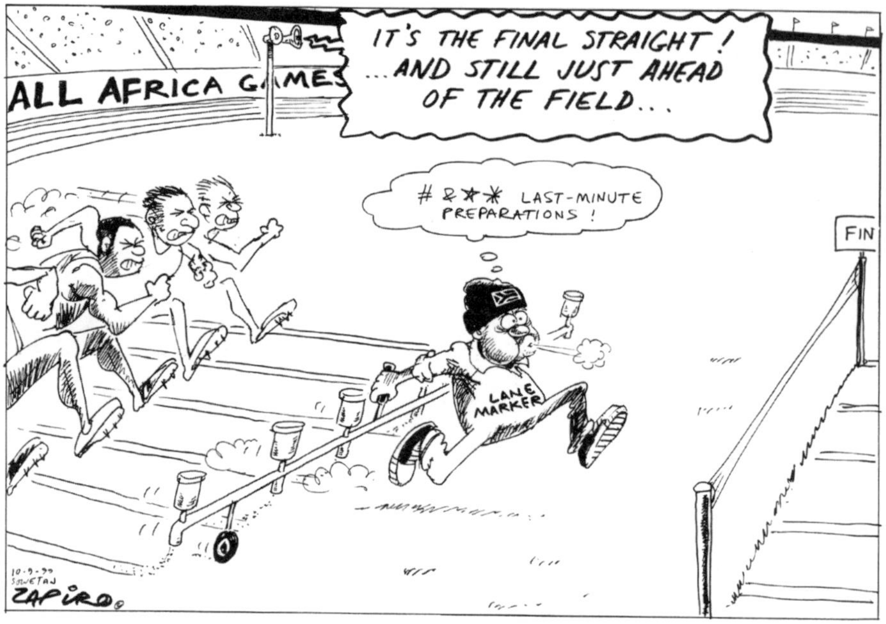
ALL AFRICA GAMES
IT'S THE FINAL STRAIGHT! ...AND STILL JUST AHEAD OF THE FIELD...
#&** LAST-MINUTE PREPARATIONS!
LANE MARKER
FIN
10-9-99 SOWETAN
ZAPIRO

The games were beset by logistical difficulties including striking workers, absent track stars and 600 children getting food poisoning after being fed boxed lunches at the practice session for the opening ceremony.

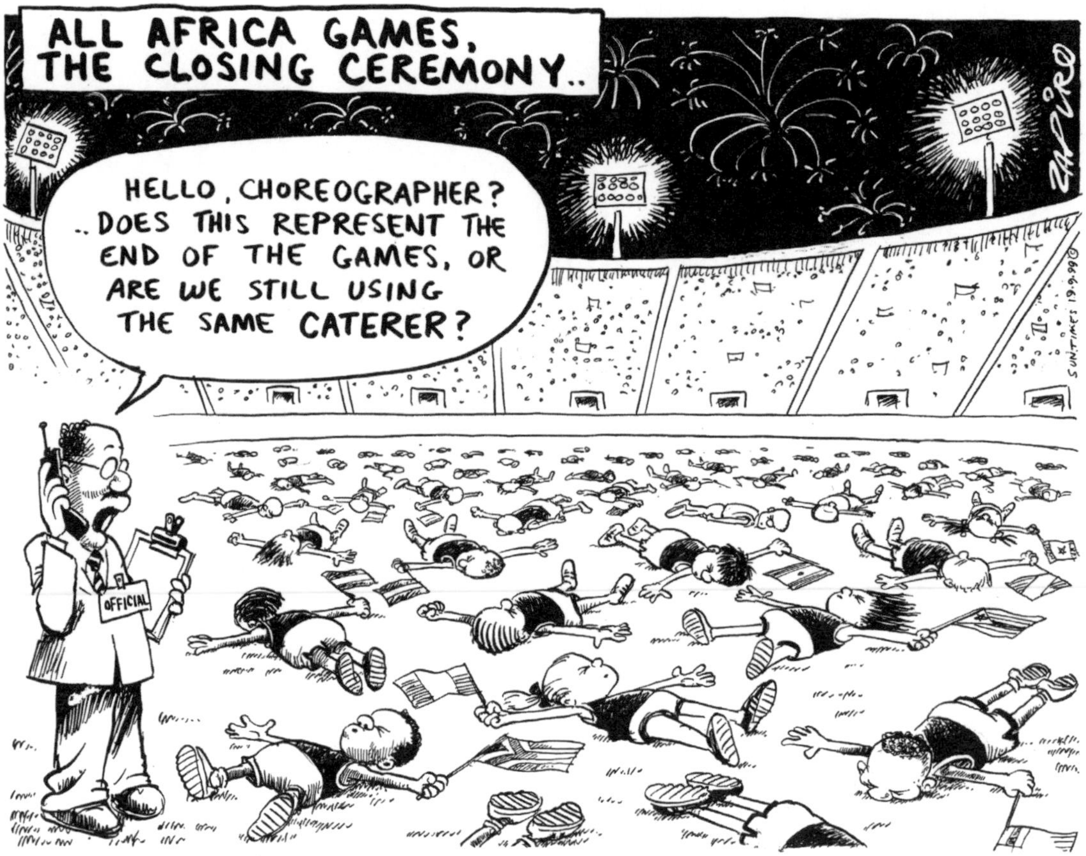
ALL AFRICA GAMES, THE CLOSING CEREMONY..
HELLO, CHOREOGRAPHER? ..DOES THIS REPRESENT THE END OF THE GAMES, OR ARE WE STILL USING THE SAME CATERER?
OFFICIAL
ZAPIRO
SUNTIMES 19-9-99

Trott Moloto took Troussier's Bafana job but a poor run of results saw him in similar trouble to Nick Mallett whose team was also under-performing.

The Boks were pounded 28-0 in Dunedin and then drubbed again, 34-18, at Loftus. Tjokkie (the late Bill Flynn) and Crispin (Paul Slabolepszy) took it all philosophically.

1999

Things did not look good for the defence of the rugby world cup in Britain and France.

The Boks reached the 1999 RWC semis on the back of five dropped goals against England from Jannie de Beer who attributed his success to divine inspiration. Unaccountably, God failed to deliver for the Boks in that semi-final as they lost narrowly to the Wallabies in extra-time.

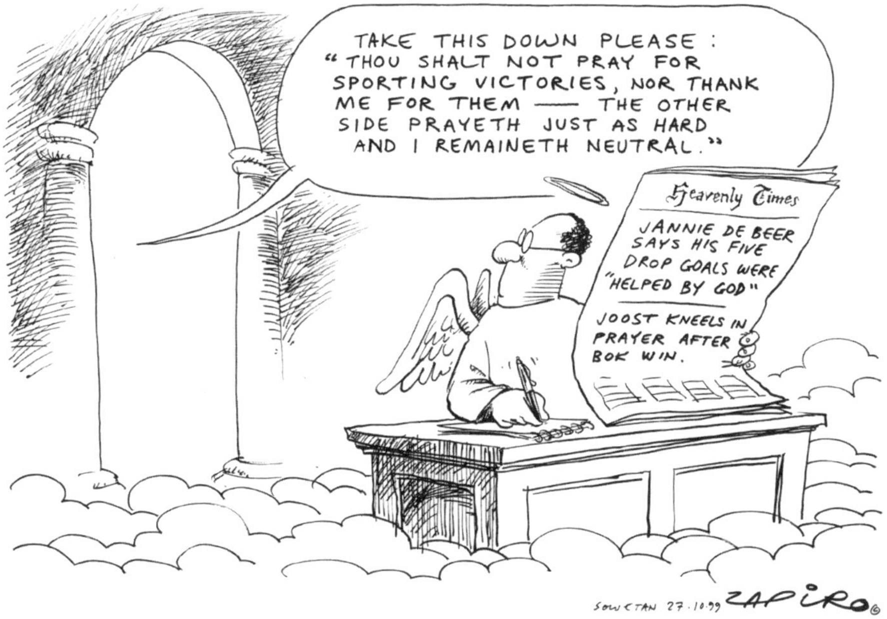
TAKE THIS DOWN PLEASE : "THOU SHALT NOT PRAY FOR SPORTING VICTORIES, NOR THANK ME FOR THEM — THE OTHER SIDE PRAYETH JUST AS HARD AND I REMAINETH NEUTRAL."
Heavenly Times
JANNIE DE BEER SAYS HIS FIVE DROP GOALS WERE "HELPED BY GOD"
JOOST KNEELS IN PRAYER AFTER BOK WIN.
SOWETAN 27.10.99 ZAPIRO

At home, Danny Jordaan was attempting to get some unity around the bid to host the FIFA world cup in 2006.

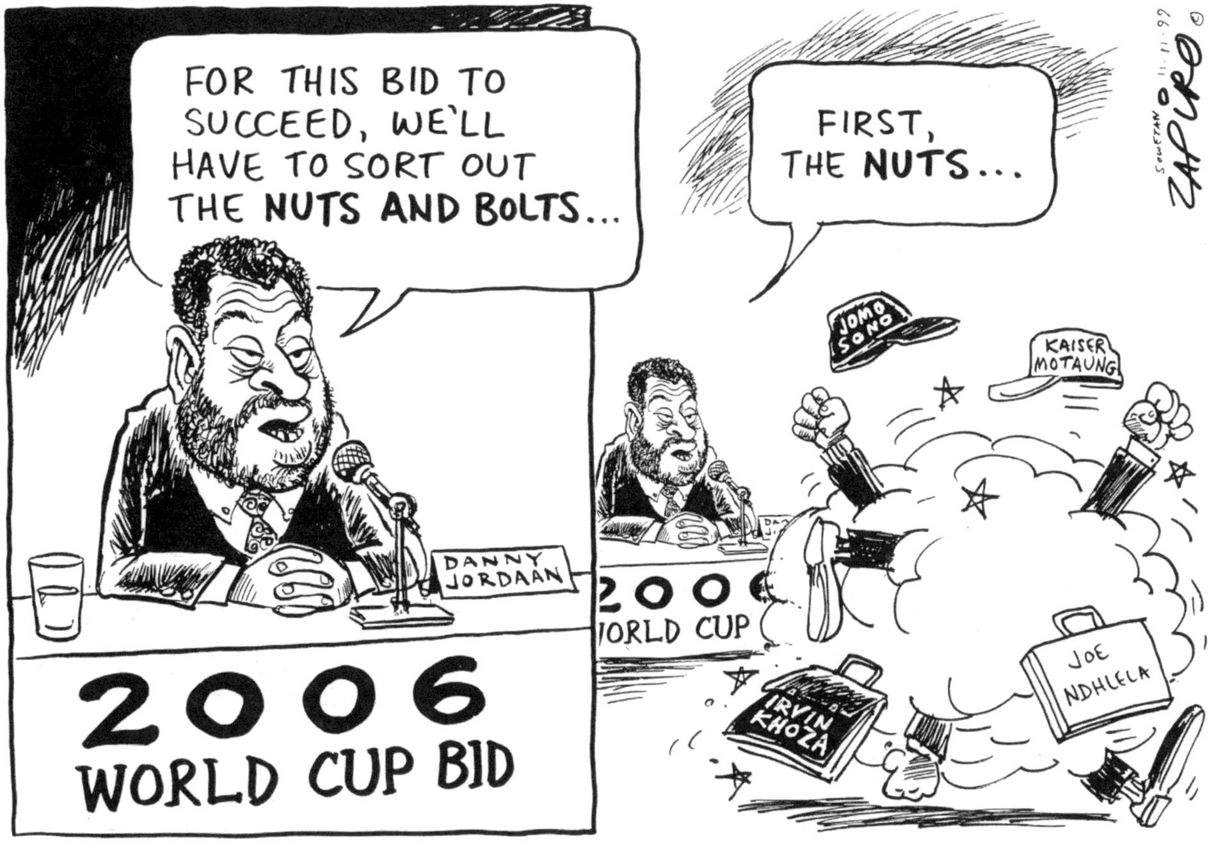
FOR THIS BID TO SUCCEED, WE'LL HAVE TO SORT OUT THE **NUTS AND BOLTS**...
DANNY JORDAAN
2006 WORLD CUP BID
FIRST, THE **NUTS**...
JOMO SONO
KAISER MOTAUNG
IRVIN KHOZA
JOE NDHLELA
2006 WORLD CUP
SOWETAN 11.11.99 ZAPIRO

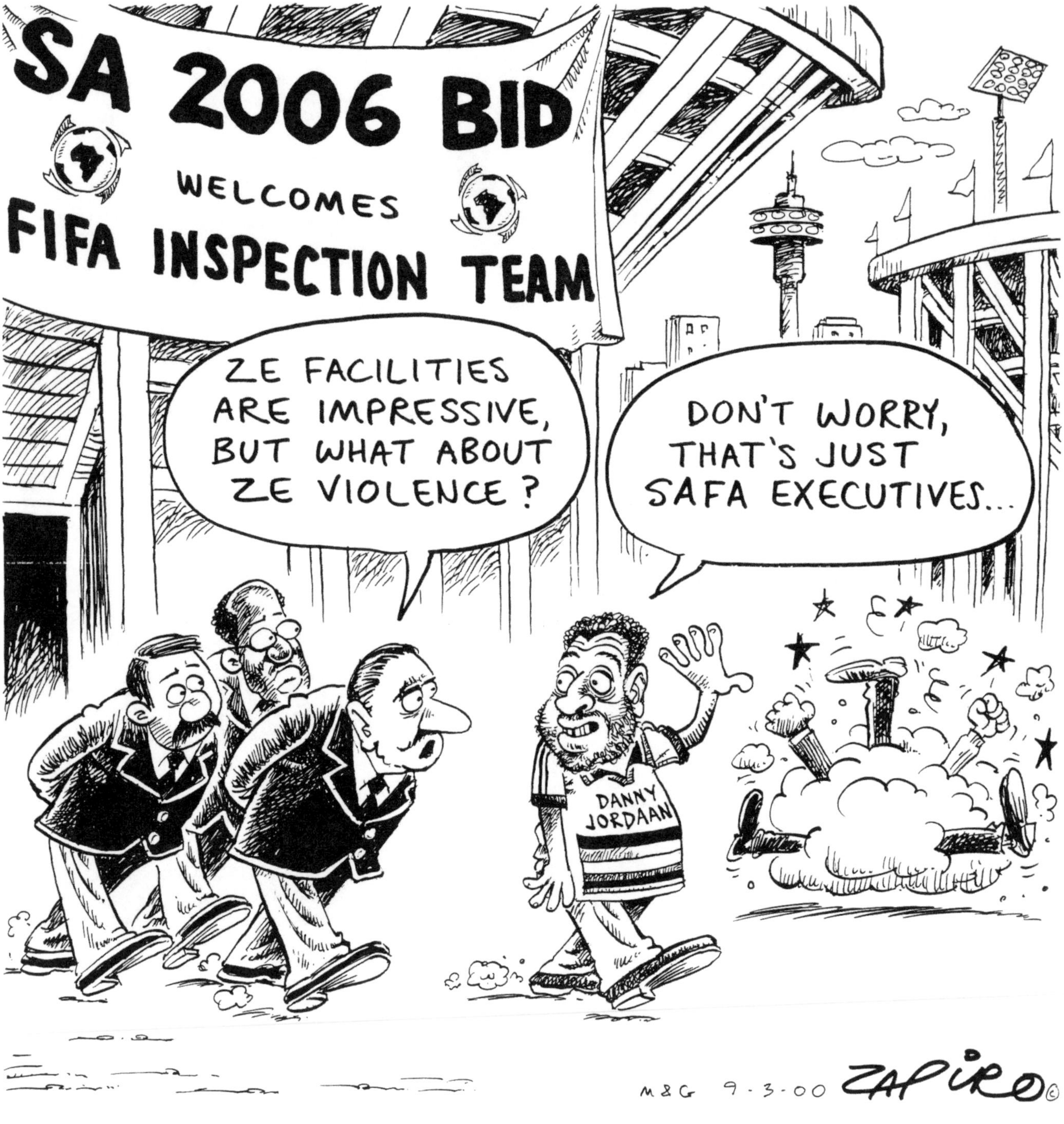
SA 2006 BID
WELCOMES
FIFA INSPECTION TEAM
ZE FACILITIES ARE IMPRESSIVE, BUT WHAT ABOUT ZE VIOLENCE?
DON'T WORRY, THAT'S JUST SAFA EXECUTIVES...
DANNY JORDAAN
M&G 9-3-00 ZAPIRO©

The SA cause was seriously set back when shots were allegedly fired at the home of Joe Ndhlela, CEO of the PSL, shortly after Moroka Swallows coach Walter da Silva had been kidnapped by club supporters in an attempt to force him to resign.

Such violent incidents were latched onto by rival bidders, England, to promote their own hosting cause until Arsenal fans went on the rampage before the UEFA cup final in Copenhagen.

Another AFCON loomed, this time in West Africa. Siyabonga Nomvethe, the man whose first name means "we give thanks" in Zulu, scored the winner for a grateful nation in the quarter-final against co-hosts Ghana.

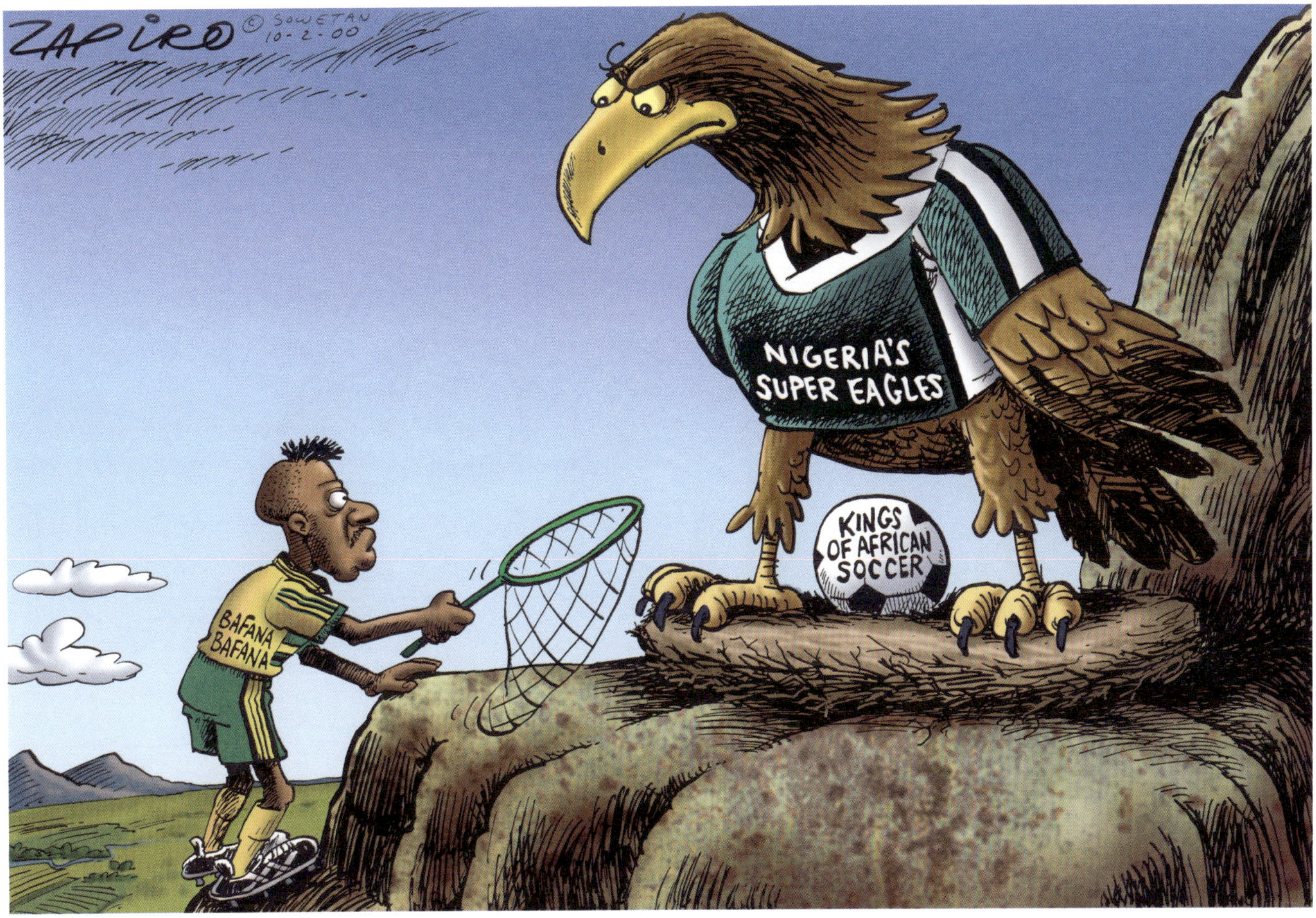
ZAPIRO © SOWETAN 10-2-00
NIGERIA'S SUPER EAGLES
KINGS OF AFRICAN SOCCER
BAFANA BAFANA

The other co-hosts, Nigeria's Super Eagles, were less accommodating, comfortably beating Bafana 2-0.

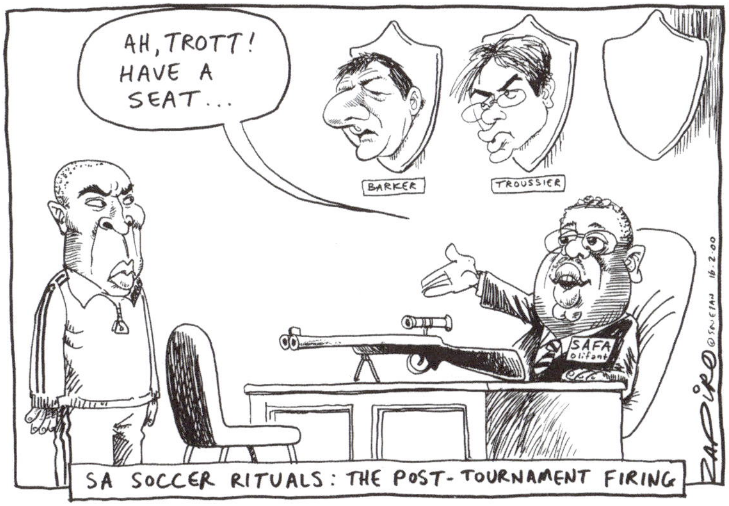
AH, TROTT! HAVE A SEAT...
BARKER
TROUSSIER
SAFA Olifant
ZAPIRO ©SOWETAN 16-2-00
SA SOCCER RITUALS: THE POST-TOURNAMENT FIRING

Coach Moloto met SAFA president Molefi Oliphant and knew the drill.

2000

Wessel Johannes Cronje had been a dominant captain of the South African cricket team for seven years. A meticulous, inspirational and generally successful leader, he was also overtly devout in his faith and had controversially employed Rhema churchman Ray McCauley as an official team pastor.

Hansie's world came crashing down on 7 April 2000 with an announcement from New Delhi police that they had recordings of conversations involving Cronje that implicated him in match-fixing.

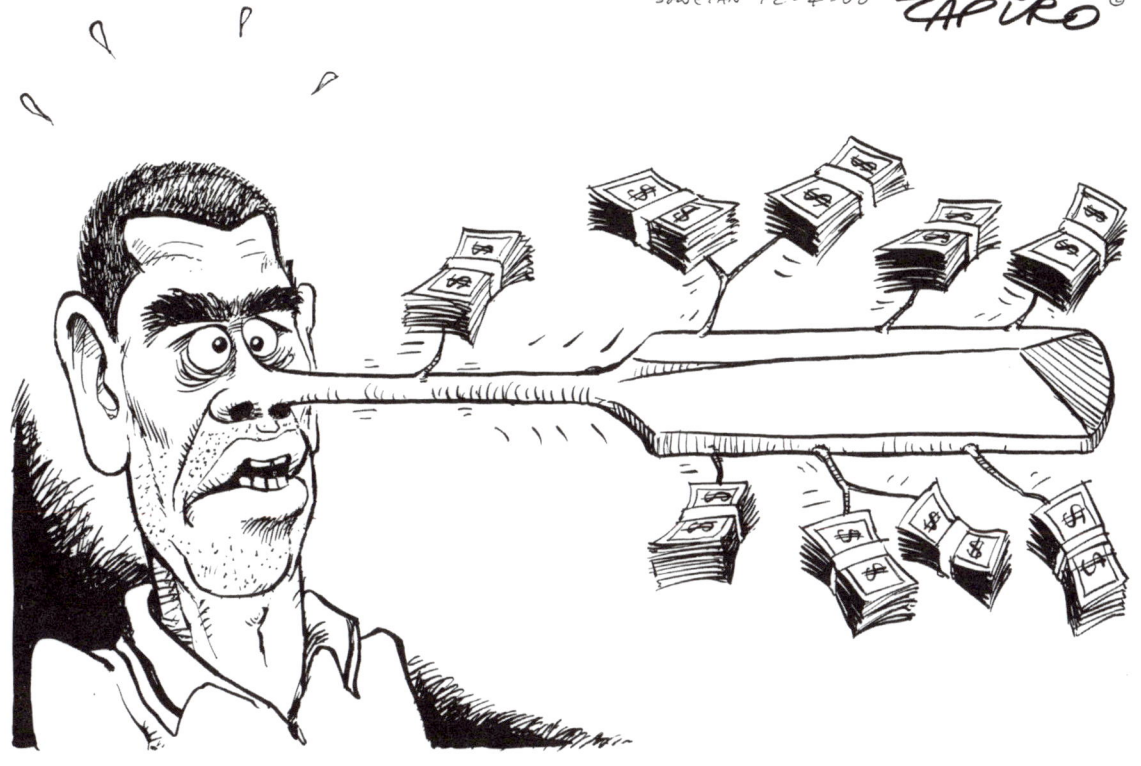

After initial denials, Cronje confessed to SA cricket boss Ali Bacher that "he had not been entirely honest".

Shaun Pollock took over the captaincy and, while Hansie-gate swirled and developed at a rapid rate, had to lead the Proteas against the visiting Australians.

The subsequent King Commission of Inquiry revealed a tawdry world of "Sanjay", Mukesh Gupta, Marlon Aronstam, leather jackets, cellphones, wads of cash and a jaded, money-obsessed Hansie Cronje, a world apart from his pristine public persona. The disgraced skipper gained further notoriety by suggesting that the devil was in some way responsible for his misdeeds.

Cronje's fate was the defining South African story of 2002 and earned Hansie the unwanted accolade of an appearance on the cover of Zapiro's annual collection alongside politicians Allan Boesak and Abe Williams and rapper Mzwakhe Mbuli, all of whom had gone to jail.

Herschelle Gibbs, Henry Williams, Nicky Boje and Pieter Strydom were also drawn into the morass but the curious official commission, headed by venerable judge Edwin King, ended inconclusively except for the lifetime ban from cricket for Cronje.

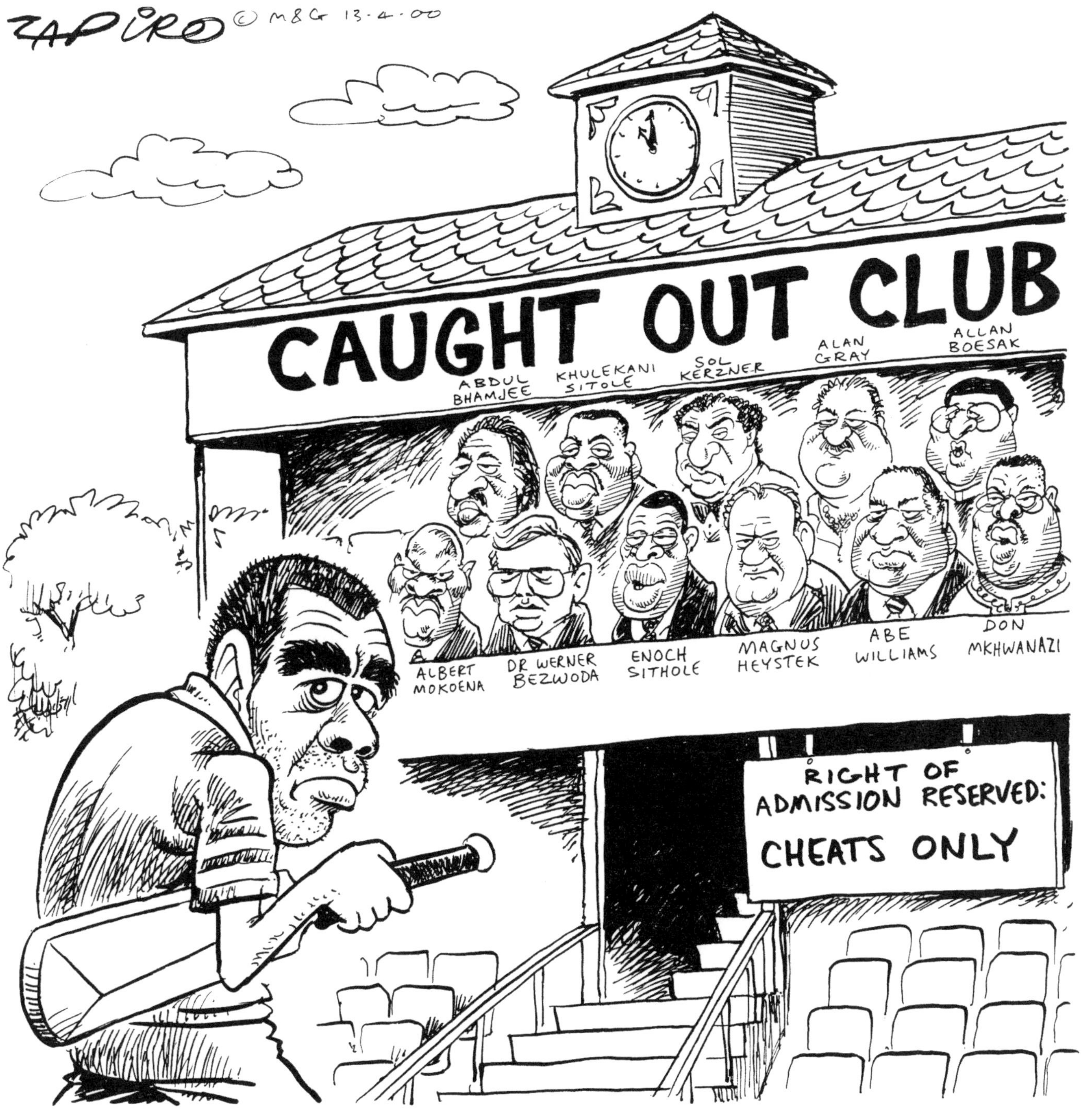
ZAPIRO © M&G 13-4-00
CAUGHT OUT CLUB
ABDUL BHAMJEE
KHULEKANI SITOLE
SOL KERZNER
ALAN GRAY
ALLAN BOESAK
ALBERT MOKOENA
DR WERNER BEZWODA
ENOCH SITHOLE
MAGNUS HEYSTEK
ABE WILLIAMS
DON MKHWANAZI
RIGHT OF ADMISSION RESERVED:
CHEATS ONLY

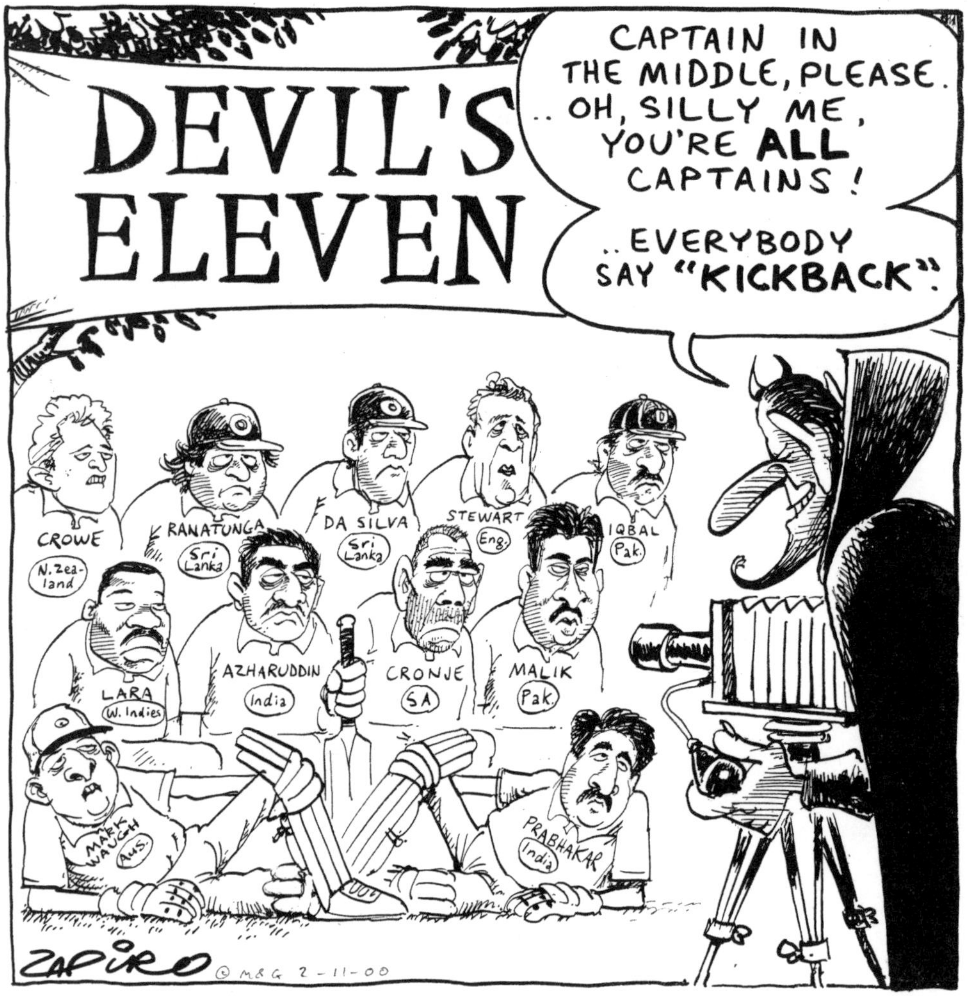
DEVIL'S ELEVEN
CAPTAIN IN THE MIDDLE, PLEASE. .. OH, SILLY ME, YOU'RE ALL CAPTAINS!
.. EVERYBODY SAY "KICKBACK".
CROWE
N. Zealand
RANATUNGA
Sri Lanka
DA SILVA
Sri Lanka
STEWART
Eng.
IQBAL
Pak.
LARA
W. Indies
AZHARUDDIN
India
CRONJE
SA
MALIK
Pak.
MARK WAUGH
Aus.
PRABHAKAR
India
ZAPIRO © M&G 2-11-00

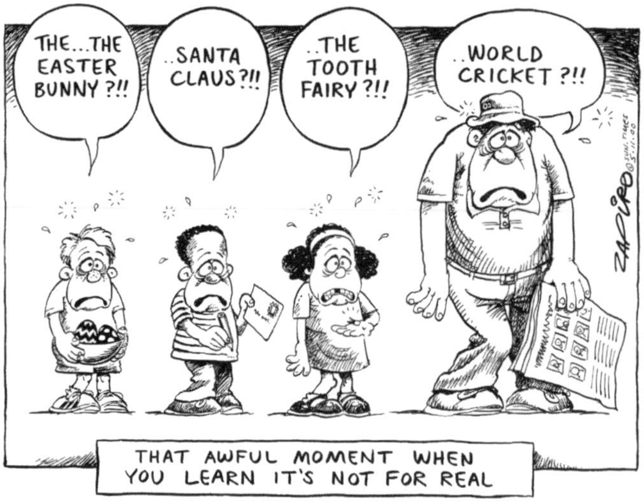
THE...THE EASTER BUNNY?!!
..SANTA CLAUS?!!
..THE TOOTH FAIRY?!!
..WORLD CRICKET?!!
ZAPIRO
THAT AWFUL MOMENT WHEN YOU LEARN IT'S NOT FOR REAL

On 6 July 2000 South Africa anticipated better news and final affirmation of its post-apartheid place on the world stage. The nation held its breath as FIFA secretary-general Sepp Blatter opened the envelope to reveal the host of the 2006 soccer world cup.

In a moment of deep anti-climax, Germany was revealed as hosts for 2006 – the tenth time the tournament would be held in Europe while Africa still awaited its first chance.

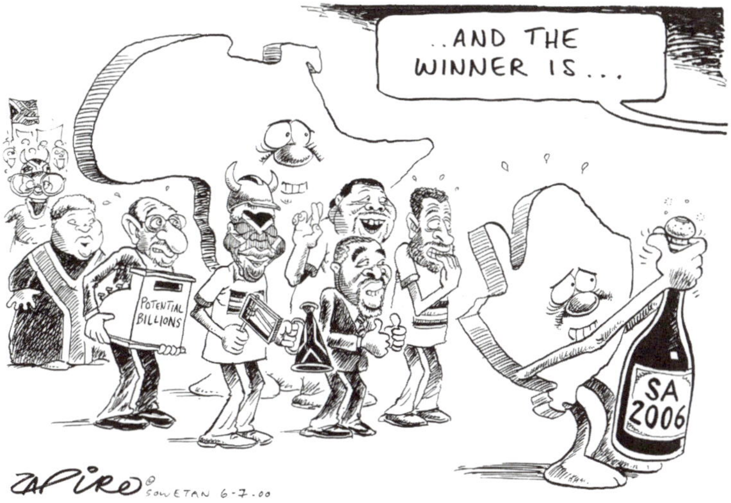
..AND THE WINNER IS...
POTENTIAL BILLIONS
SA 2006
ZAPIRO © SOWETAN 6-7-00

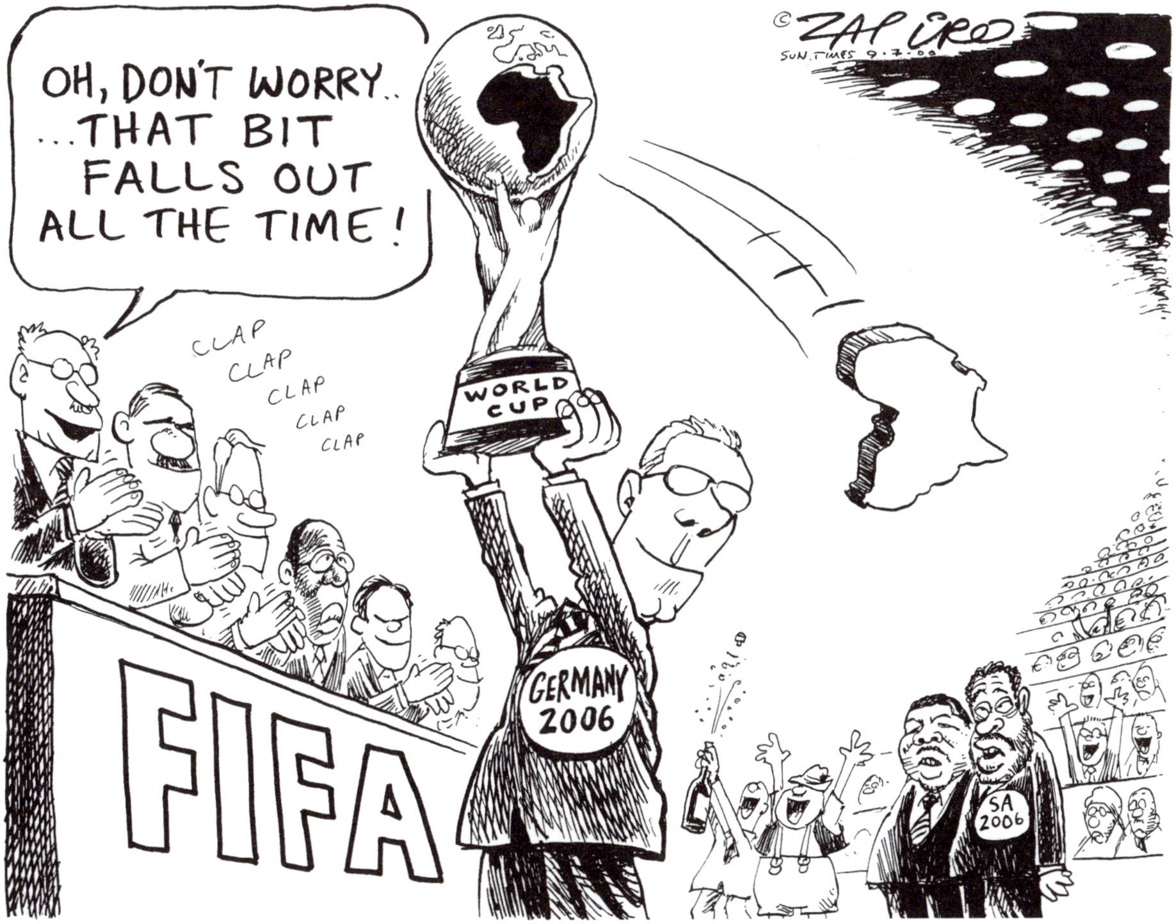
© ZAPIRO SUN.TIMES 9-7-00
OH, DON'T WORRY.. ...THAT BIT FALLS OUT ALL THE TIME!
CLAP CLAP CLAP CLAP CLAP
WORLD CUP
GERMANY 2006
FIFA
SA 2006

2000

The deciding ballot was that of 79-year-old Glasgow-born New Zealander Charles Dempsey, who had been mandated by his Oceania Confederation to vote for SA but instead mysteriously abstained at the last minute, and immediately entered the local pantheon of sporting hate figures.

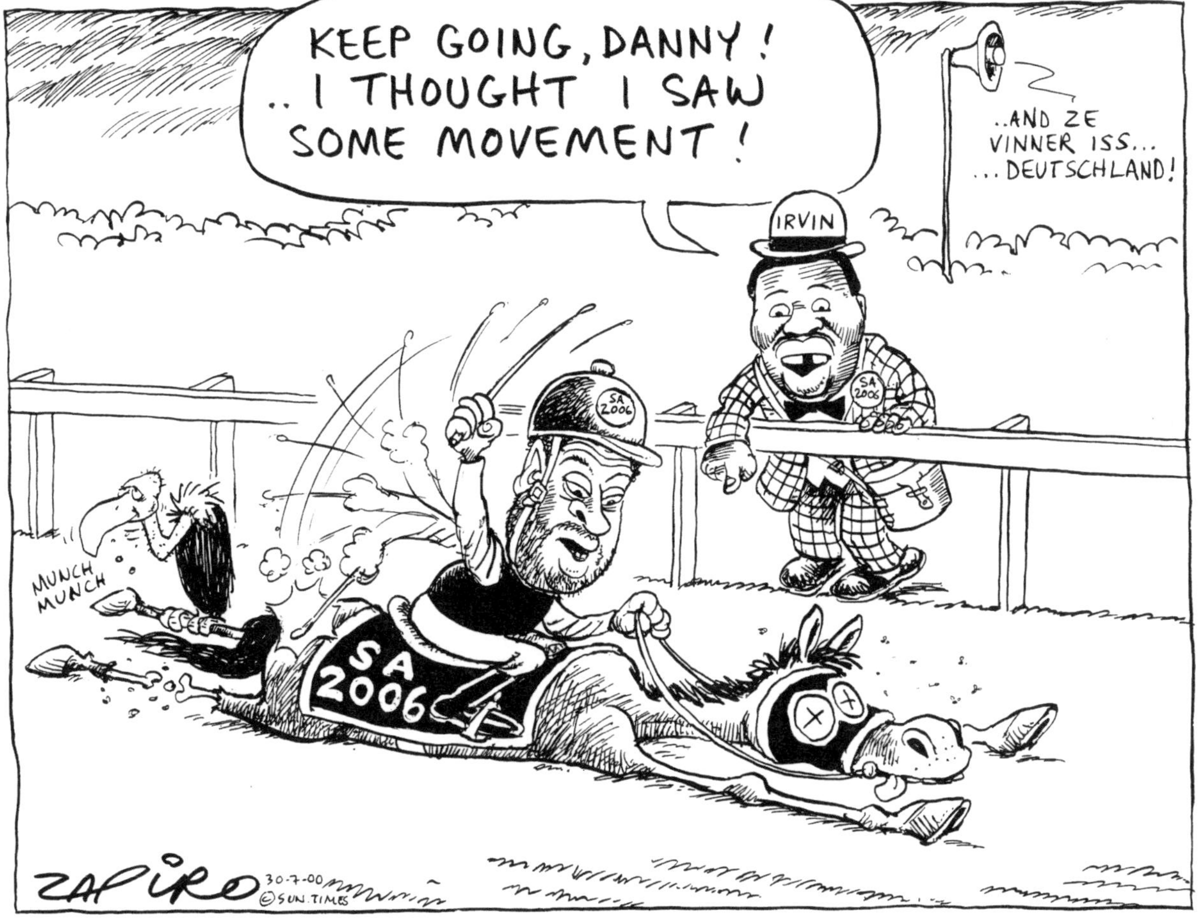
KEEP GOING, DANNY! .. I THOUGHT I SAW SOME MOVEMENT!
..AND ZE VINNER ISS... ...DEUTSCHLAND!
IRVIN
SA 2006
MUNCH MUNCH
ZAPIRO 30-7-00 ©SUN.TIMES

A desperate Danny Jordaan and bid chair Irwin Khoza attempted to overturn the vote but FIFA and the world had moved on.

A deflated Jordaan finally picked himself up and set off in pursuit of the 2010 hosting rights while Bafana Bafana installed yet another coach – this time it was the Portuguese Carlos Queiroz (known to some locals as Carlos The Queer Ou) who would later manage Real Madrid, which is a trifling task compared to handling SAFA politics.

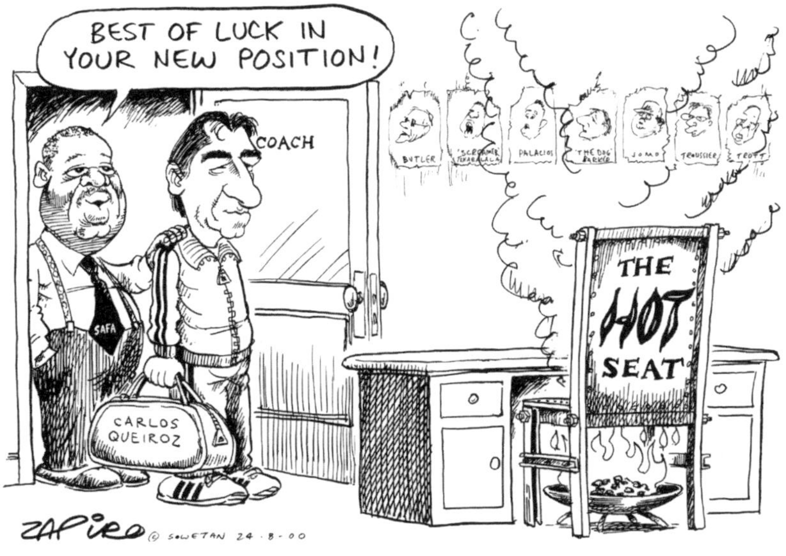
BEST OF LUCK IN YOUR NEW POSITION!
COACH
BUTLER
PALACIOS
'THE DOG' BARKER
JOMO
TROUSSIER
TROTT
SAFA
CARLOS QUEIROZ
THE HOT SEAT
ZAPIRO © SOWETAN 24-8-00

The 2000 Olympic Games in Sydney were a disappointment with no golds for SA. There was a fleeting moment of glory when our under-23 soccer team beat mighty Brazil 3-1 but coach Shakes Mashaba unaccountably left out the most obvious candidate for one of the over-age places permitted in the squad.

2000

Our able-bodied Olympians might have under-performed but our Paralympians were beginning to stake their place among the world's best.

After the games, the pressure piled on SA Olympics boss Sam Ramsamy to improve both governance and results.

Steve Tshwete had given up the sports ministry for the far more peaceful task of running the police force and Ngconde Balfour was now the man trying to make Ramsamy and the National Olympic Committee accountable.

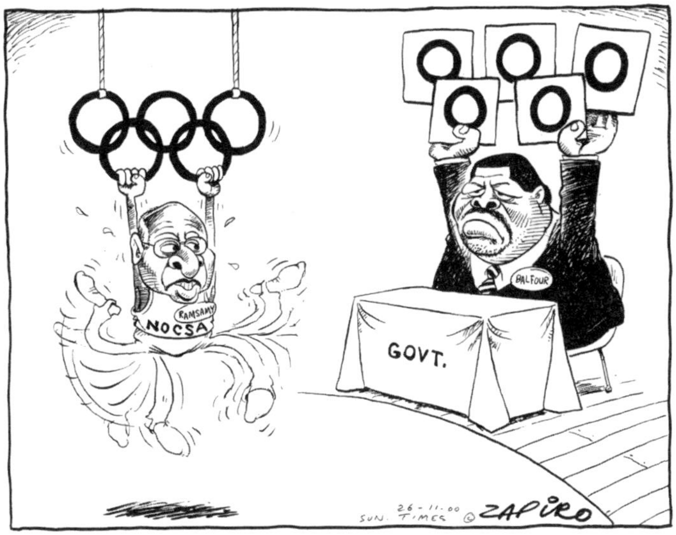

RAMSAMY
NOCSA
BALFOUR
GOVT.
26-11-00 SUN. TIMES © ZAPIRO

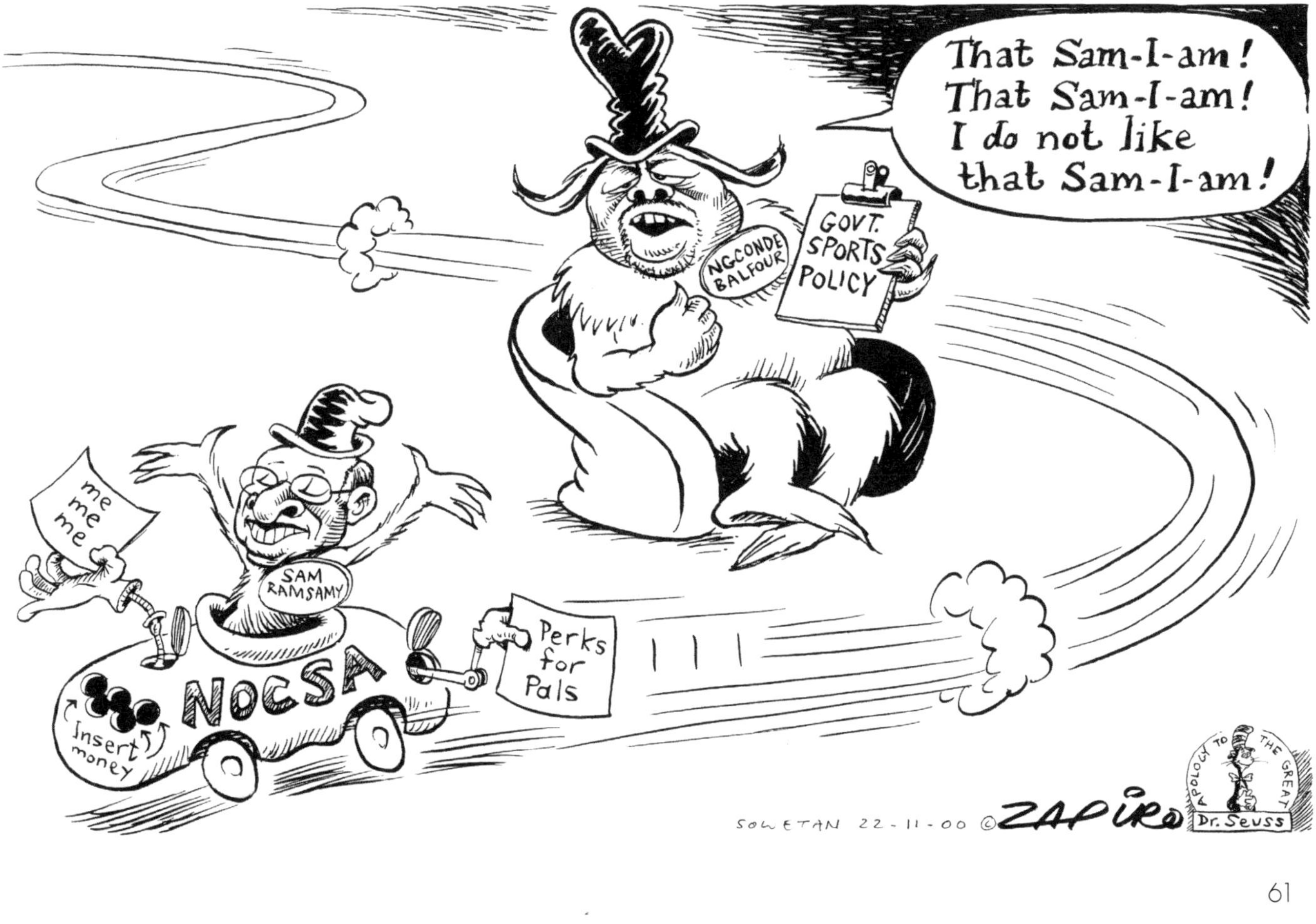

That Sam-I-am! That Sam-I-am! I do not like that Sam-I-am!
NGCONDE BALFOUR
GOVT. SPORTS POLICY
me me me
SAM RAMSAMY
NOCSA
Insert money
Perks for Pals
APOLOGY TO THE GREAT Dr. Seuss
SOWETAN 22-11-00 © ZAPIRO

Balfour also had his hands full with local soccer as a series of corruption allegations once again rocked the sport.

Even the compromise FIFA announcement of football's player of the millennium was not without controversy.

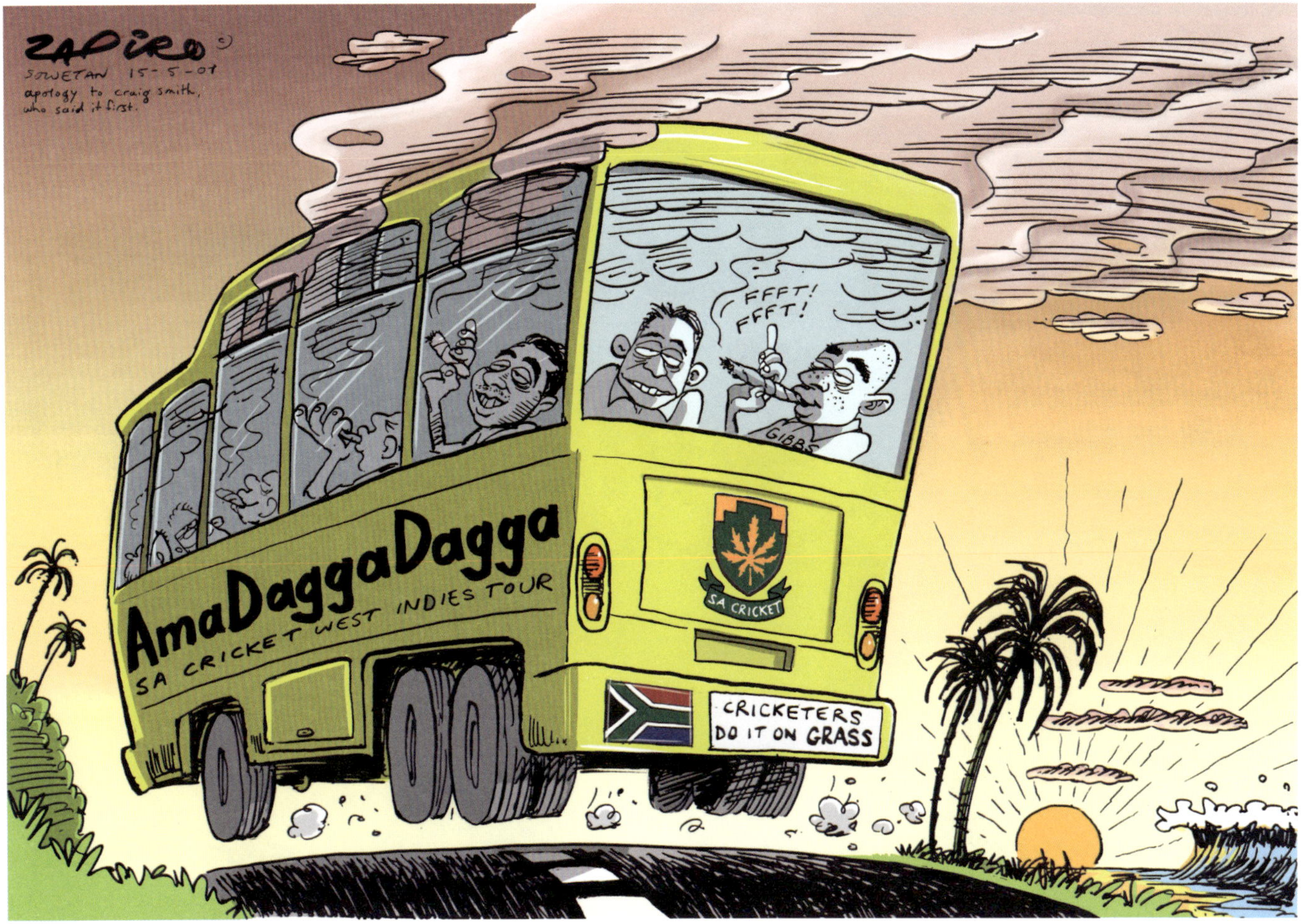
ZAPIRO ©
SOWETAN 15-5-01
apology to craig smith, who said it first.
FFFT! FFFT!
GIBBS
AmaDaggaDagga
SA CRICKET WEST INDIES TOUR
SA CRICKET
CRICKETERS DO IT ON GRASS

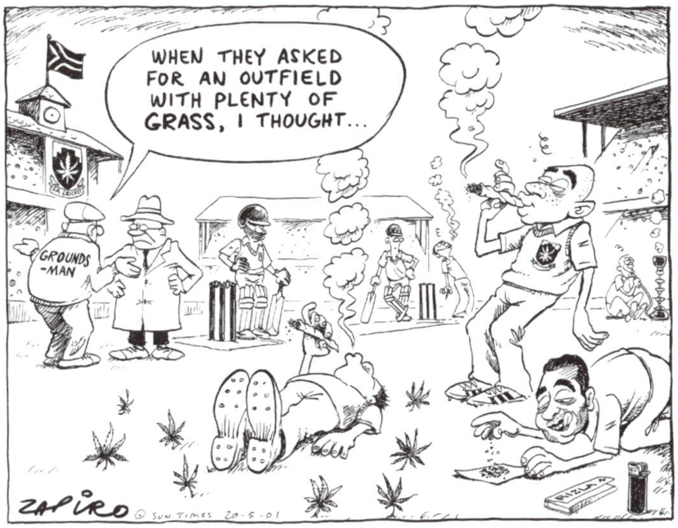
WHEN THEY ASKED FOR AN OUTFIELD WITH PLENTY OF GRASS, I THOUGHT...
GROUNDS -MAN
ZAPIRO © SUN-TIMES 20-5-01

In early 2001, Shaun Pollock led the Proteas on a highly successful tour of the West Indies, which was remembered less for the success and more for how high some of the players got off the pitch.

2001

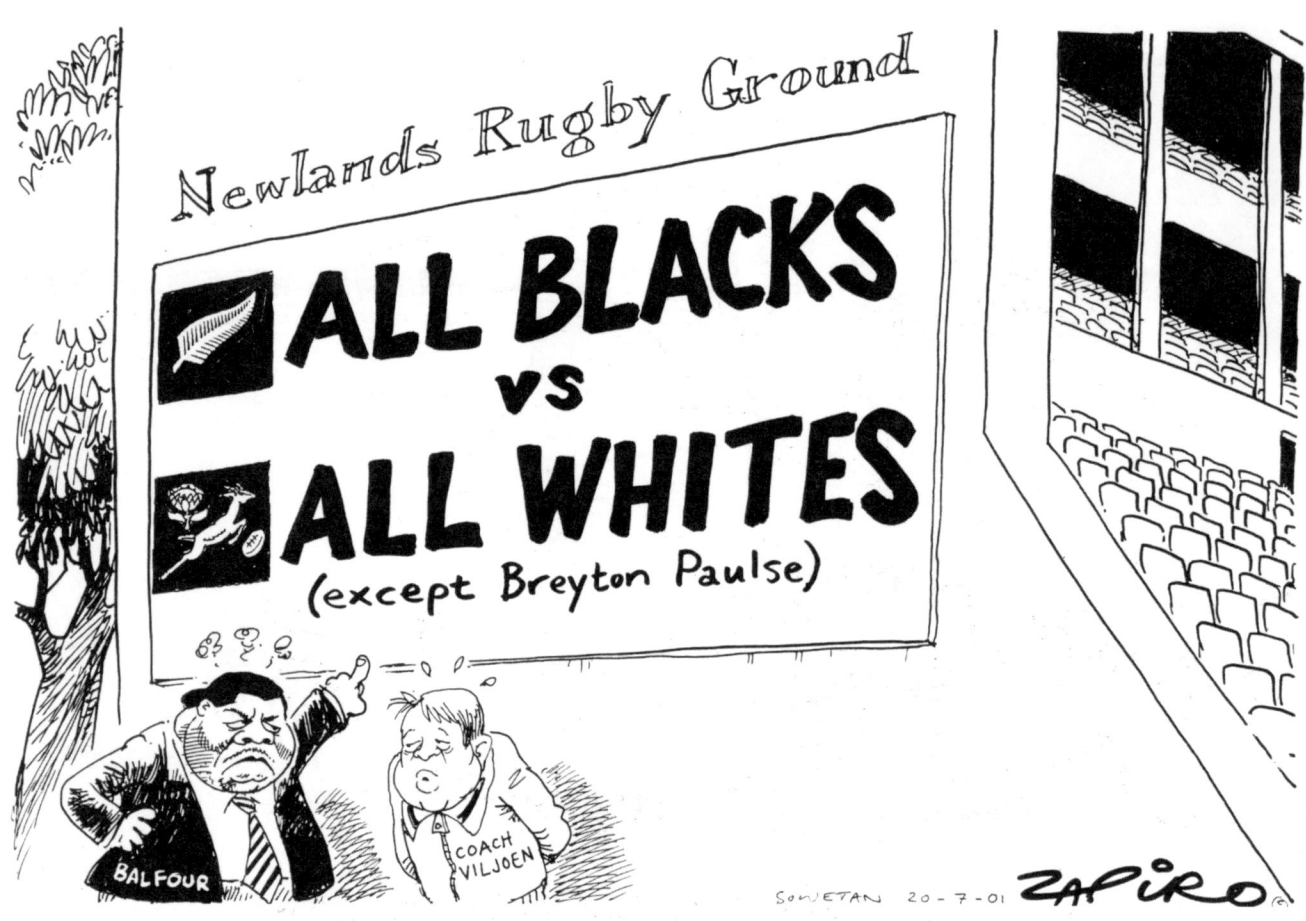

To Ngconde Balfour's manifest frustration, the Springboks during 2001 were still only prepared to wing it on transformation with Breyton Paulse the sole black player in new coach Harry Viljoen's XV. In July the almost-monochrome Boks lost 12-3 to NZ to start a record sequence of eight consecutive losses to the All Blacks.

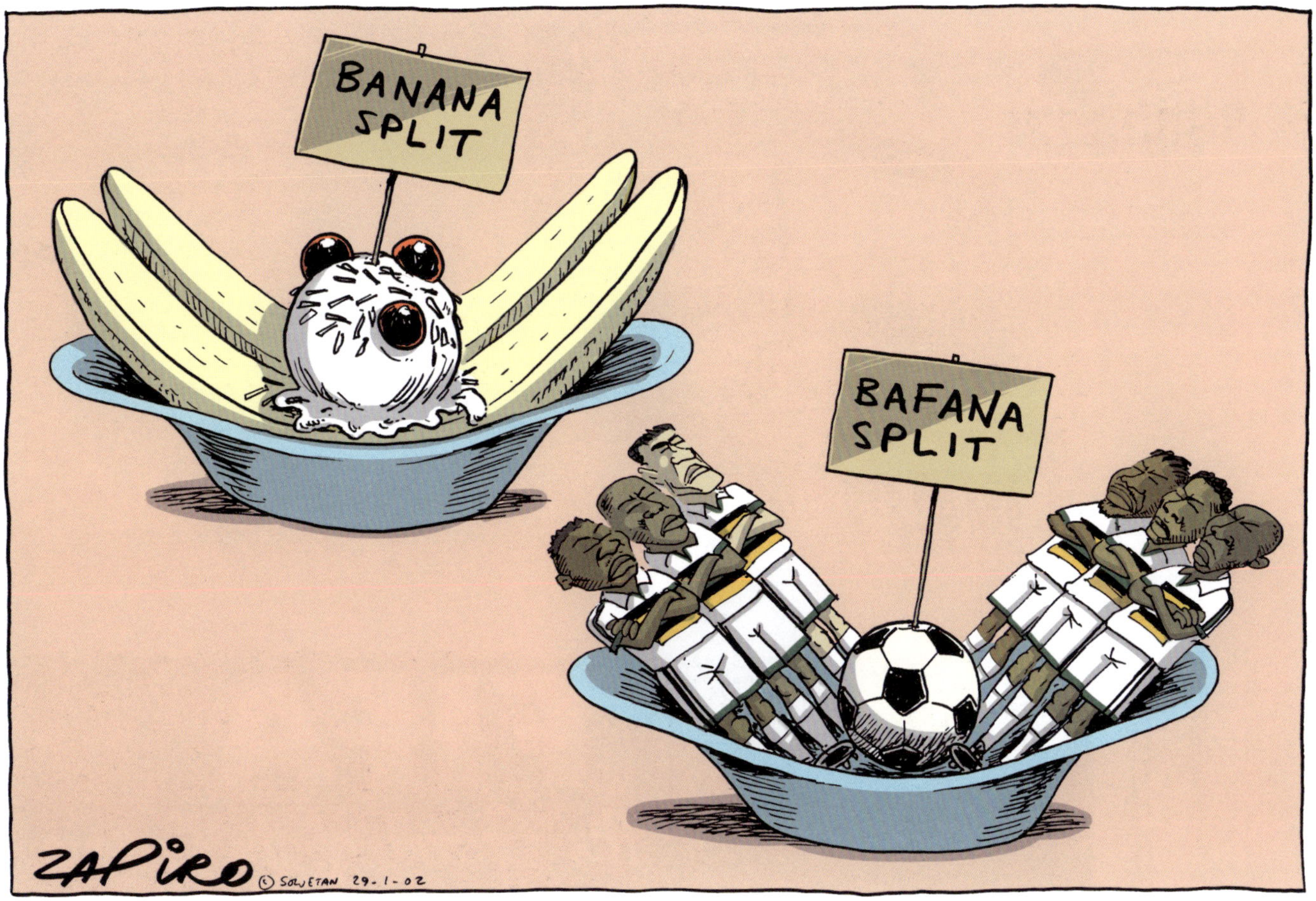
BANANA SPLIT
BAFANA SPLIT
ZAPIRO © SOWETAN 29-1-02

Early in 2002 Carlos Queiroz's preparations for AFCON were not going well. He was struggling to inspan foreign-based players and there were rumours of big divisions in the camp.

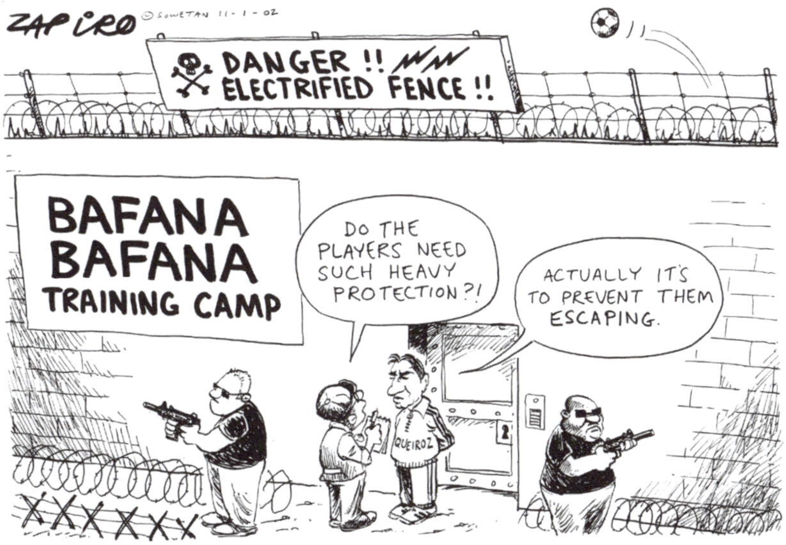
ZAPIRO © SOWETAN 11-1-02
DANGER !! ELECTRIFIED FENCE !!
BAFANA BAFANA TRAINING CAMP
DO THE PLAYERS NEED SUCH HEAVY PROTECTION ?!
ACTUALLY IT'S TO PREVENT THEM ESCAPING.
QUEIROZ

2002

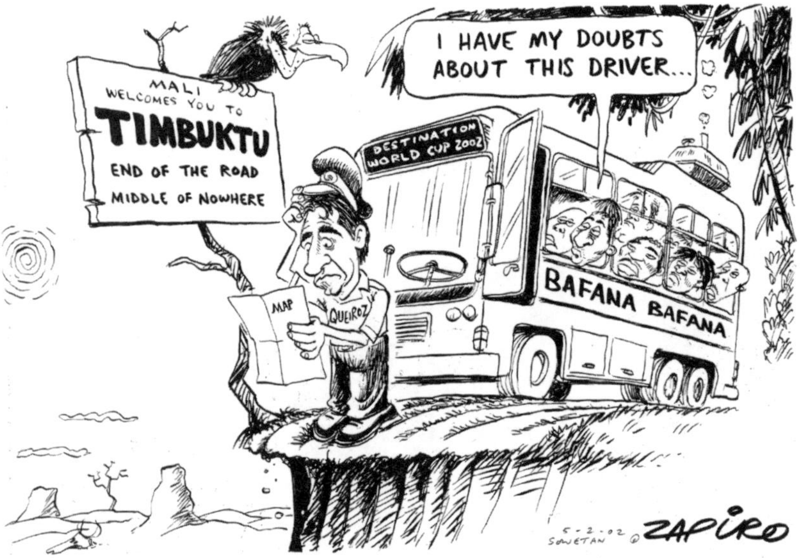
MALI WELCOMES YOU TO
TIMBUKTU
END OF THE ROAD
MIDDLE OF NOWHERE
I HAVE MY DOUBTS ABOUT THIS DRIVER...
DESTINATION WORLD CUP 2002
BAFANA BAFANA
MAP
QUEIROZ
5-2-02 SOWETAN © ZAPIRO

At the tournament in Mali, Bafana exited tamely in the quarter-finals, having failed to score in three of their four matches.

In stark contrast to Bafana Bafana, the FIFA elite were demonstrating their remarkable ability to score all the time ... with backhanders and perks.

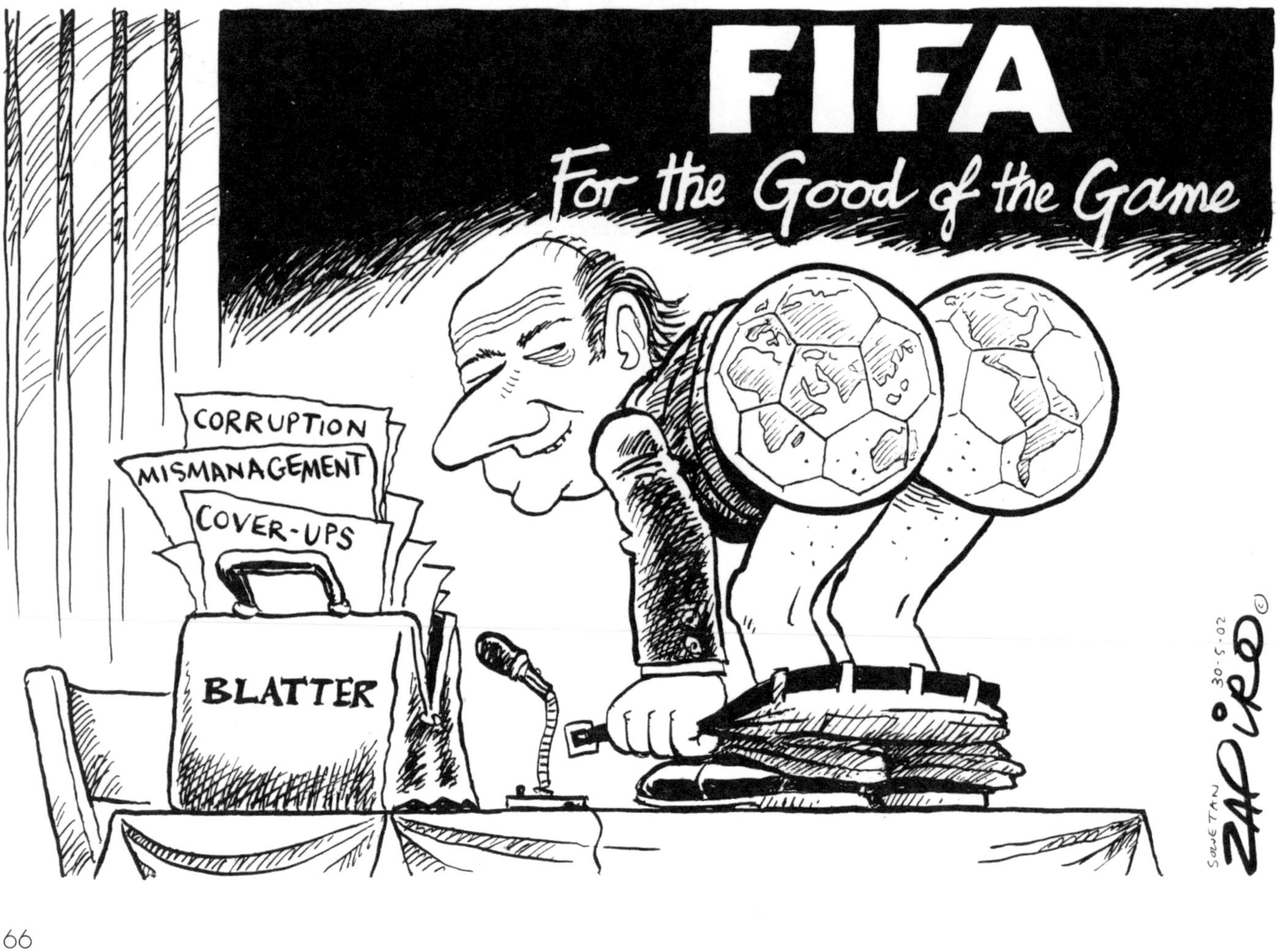
FIFA
For the Good of the Game
CORRUPTION
MISMANAGEMENT
COVER-UPS
BLATTER
SOWETAN 30-5-02 ZAPIRO ©

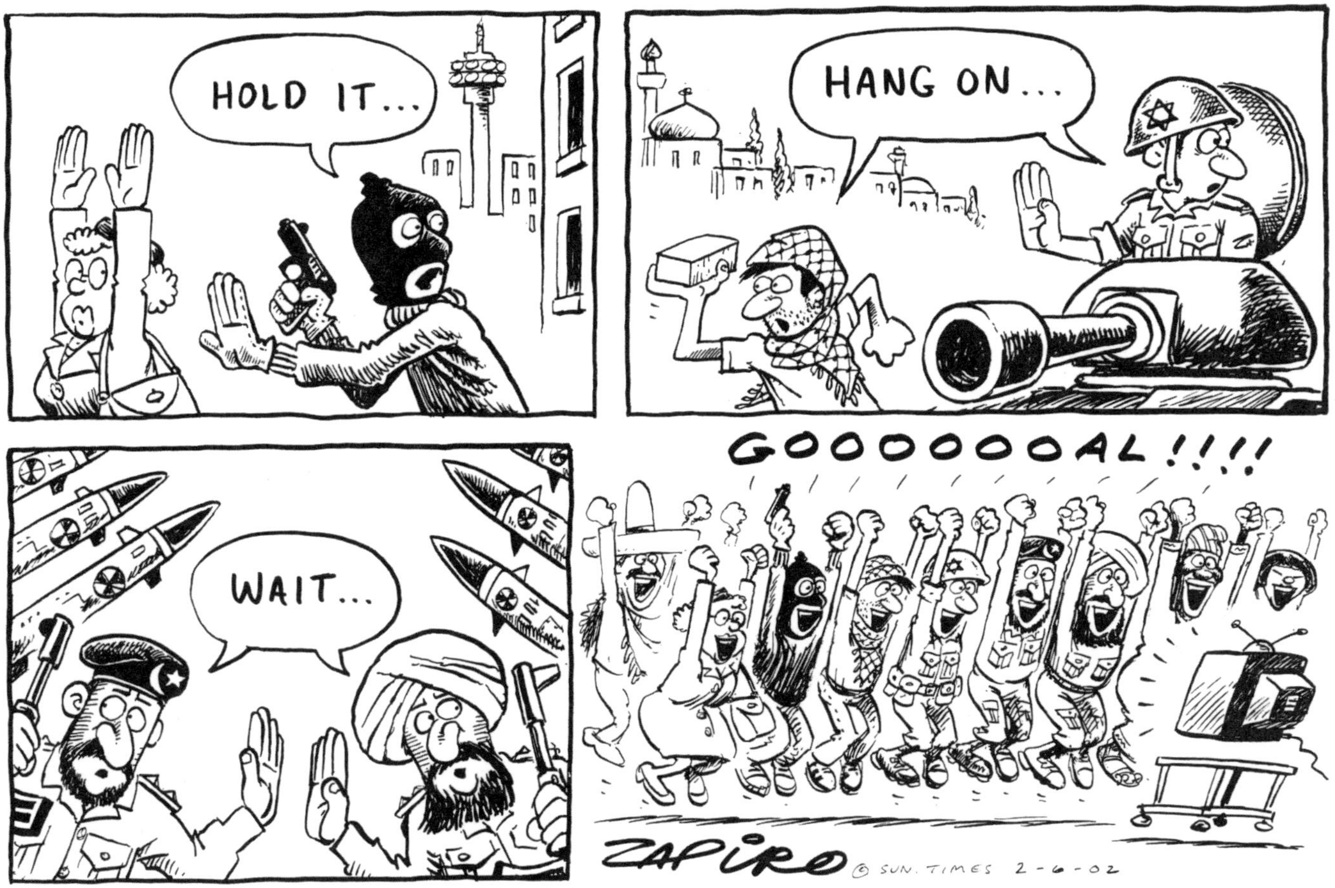
HOLD IT...
HANG ON...
WAIT...
GOOOOOOAL!!!!
ZAPIRO © SUN. TIMES 2-6-02

In spite of the scandals surrounding the global administration of the game, South Africa and the world, as usual, were transfixed by the world cup finals.

Bafana Bafana, once again under the caretaker coaching of Jomo Sono and the captaincy of Lucas Radebe, started with a draw against Paraguay and then beat Slovenia, but Spain lay in wait.

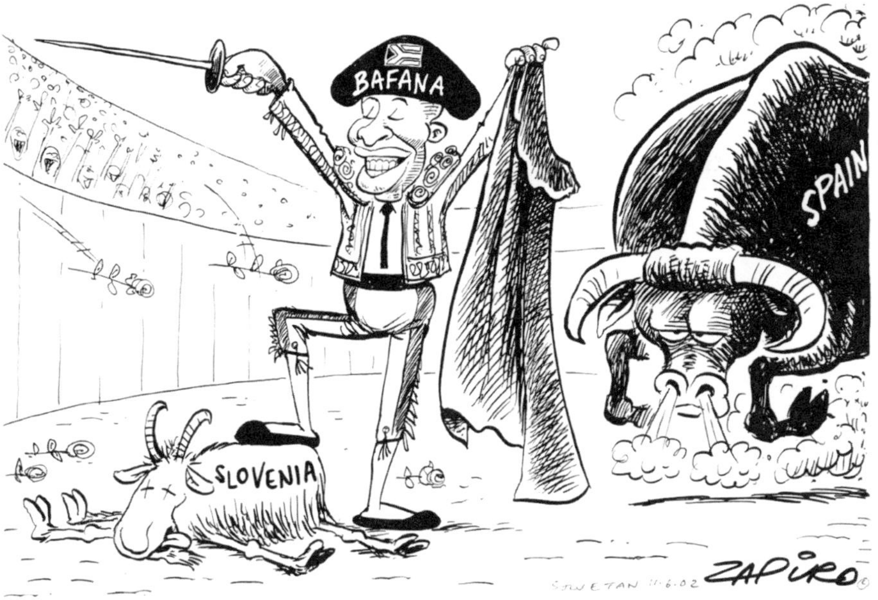
BAFANA
SPAIN
SLOVENIA
ZAPIRO

After defeat by Spain, Bafana departed early, in the company of pre-tournament favourites Argentina and holders France, but the portly Sono's exuberant sideline chicken dance had certainly left an impression.

Immediately after the world cup, Sono vacated the Bafana Bafana job (fear not, he would be back again very soon) and the successful Olympic coach Shakes Mashaba took over.

The shortest world boxing champion ever at 1.47m, Jacob 'Baby Jake' Matlala, finally hung up his gloves in 2002 after winning a fourth title. Nelson Mandela and Will Smith turned up at the ringside in the middle of that last bout, causing pandemonium in the crowd and spurring Matlala to a famous victory.

In July 2002, Ernie Els slew Tiger Woods and some of his own golfing demons to win the British Open at Muirfield after a four-way playoff.

Little did we know that it would be a decade before Els would win another major and even littler did we know what would befall Tiger off the course in 2009.

South Africa's sporting image suffered a setback in August 2003 when Irish rugby ref David McHugh was assaulted and injured during a Tri-Nations test in Durban by a drunk fan, Pieter van Zyl, who, unaccountably, became something of a folk figure and the face of at least one advertising campaign.

Viljoen had resigned as Bok coach and Rudi Straeuli was now in charge. He led the team on a disastrous European tour which began with the Massacre of Marseilles, a 30-10 walloping by the French, followed by a 21-6 loss to lowly Scotland. The powerful English were next in line to feast off the Springbok carcass.

The score (or, more accurately, scar) at Twickenham was 52-3, a record defeat for the Springboks.

Meanwhile Danny Jordaan was quietly and calmly gaining traction for the 2010 world cup bid until noisy and riotous Kaizer Chiefs fans threatened to wreck the whole thing.

One world cup which definitely was going to be held in SA was the 2003 cricket event. ICC world cups had provided nothing but woe and trauma for Protea supporters since readmission in 1991 but there was considerable optimism that, on home soil, things would improve, provided the event's organiser Dr Ali Bacher could hold the tournament together in the face of political objections to one co-host, Zimbabwe, and security concerns about another, Kenya.

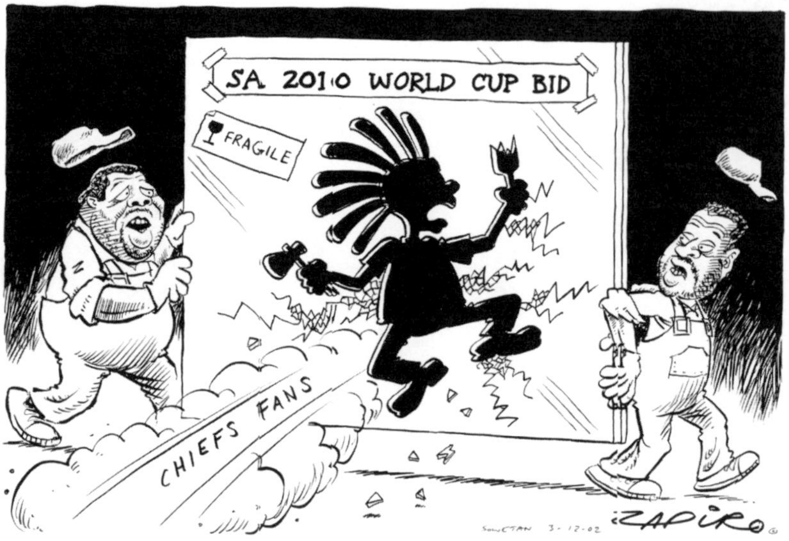
SA 2010 WORLD CUP BID
FRAGILE
CHIEFS FANS
SOWETAN 3-12-02
ZAPIRO

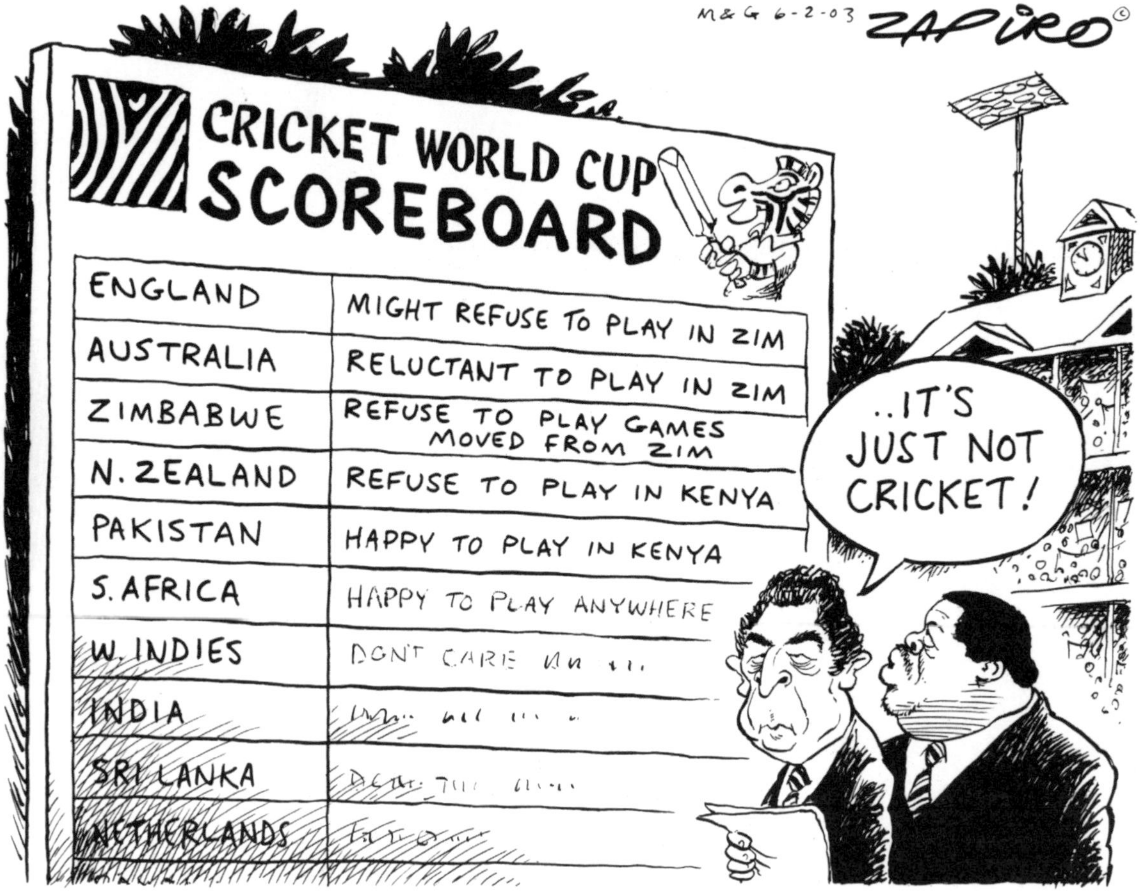
M&G 6-2-03 ZAPIRO
CRICKET WORLD CUP SCOREBOARD
ENGLAND
MIGHT REFUSE TO PLAY IN ZIM
AUSTRALIA
RELUCTANT TO PLAY IN ZIM
ZIMBABWE
REFUSE TO PLAY GAMES MOVED FROM ZIM
N. ZEALAND
REFUSE TO PLAY IN KENYA
PAKISTAN
HAPPY TO PLAY IN KENYA
S. AFRICA
HAPPY TO PLAY ANYWHERE
W. INDIES
INDIA
SRI LANKA
NETHERLANDS
..IT'S JUST NOT CRICKET!

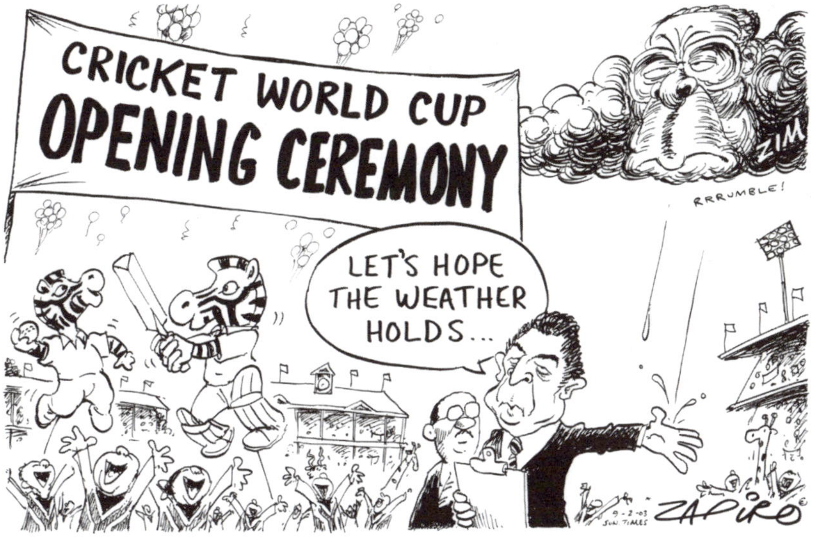
CRICKET WORLD CUP
OPENING CEREMONY
LET'S HOPE THE WEATHER HOLDS...
ZIM
RRRUMBLE!
9-2-03
SUN TIMES
ZAPIRO

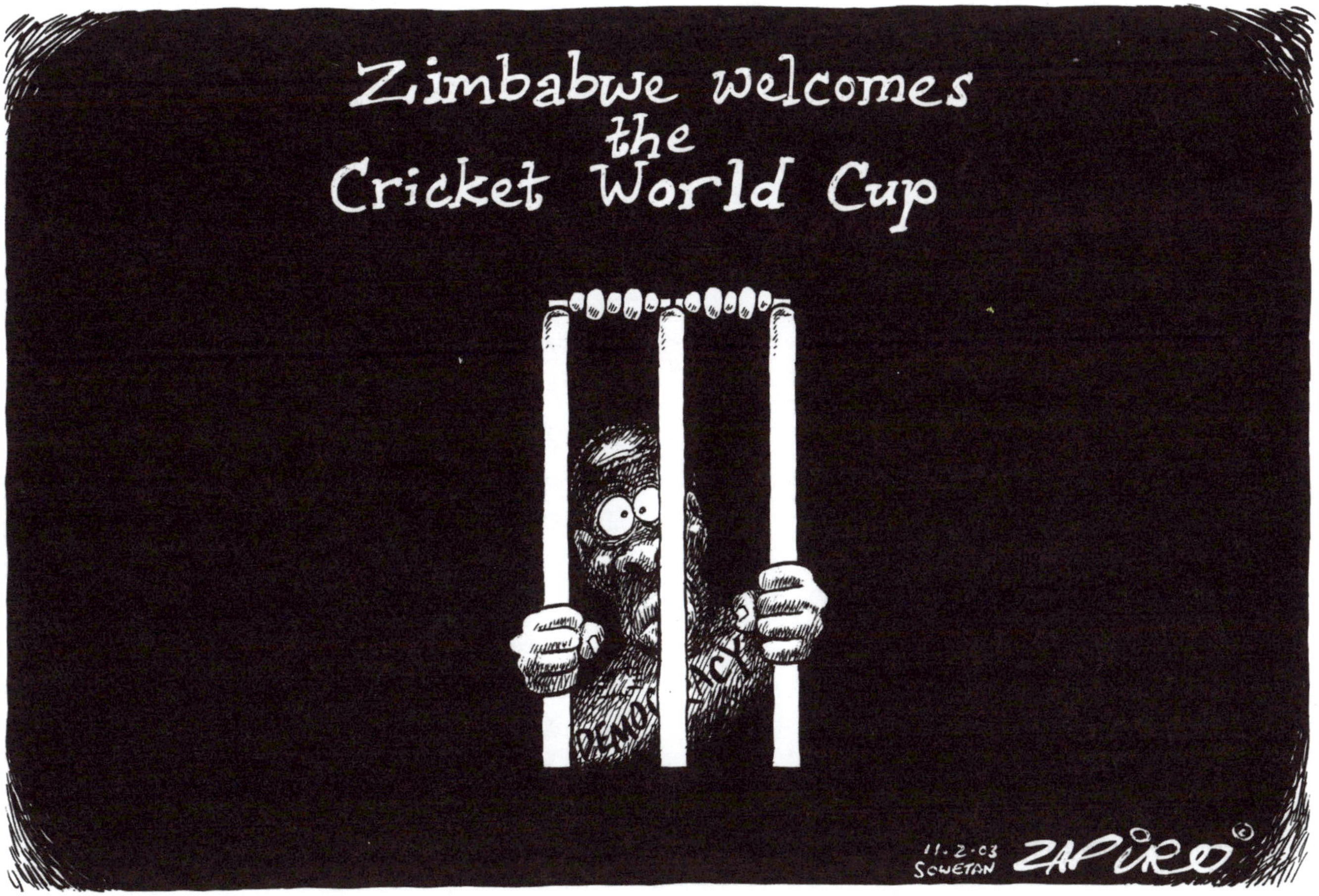
Zimbabwe welcomes the Cricket World Cup
11-2-03
SOWETAN
ZAPIRO

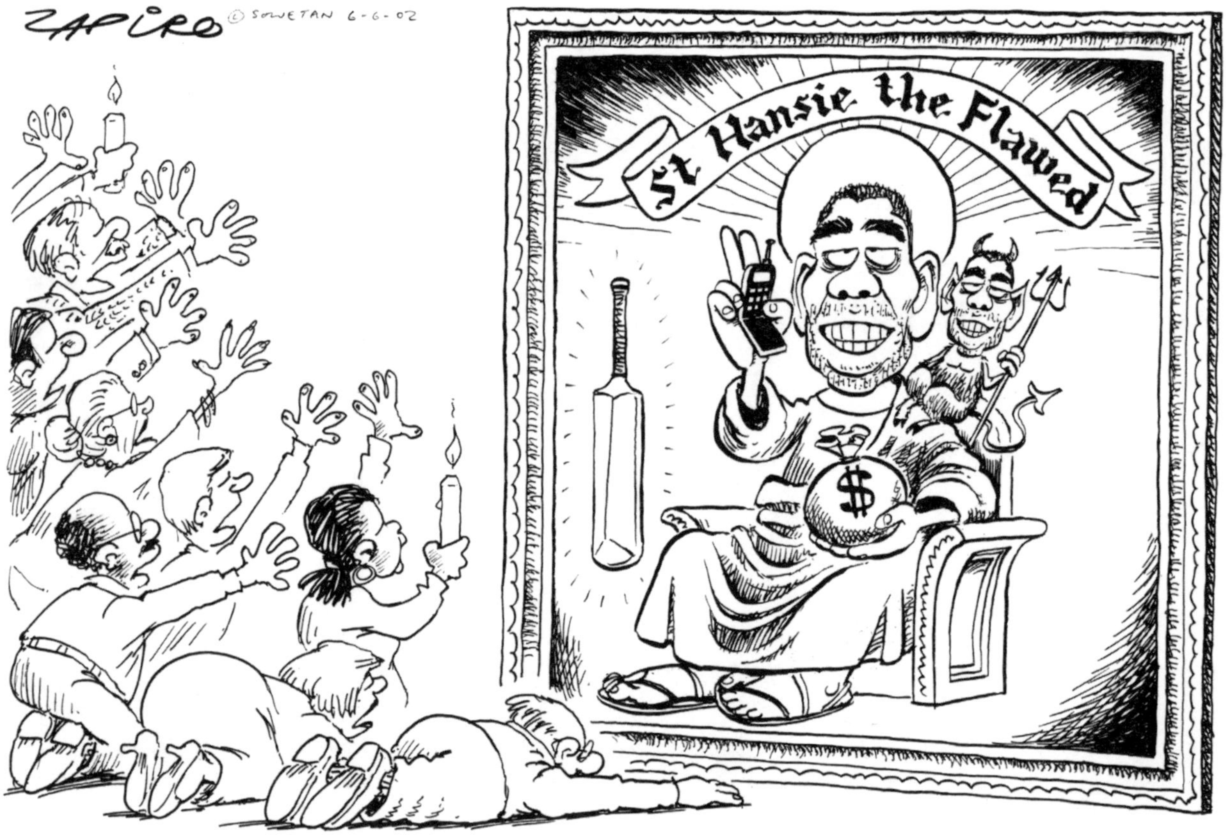
ZAPIRO © SOWETAN 6-6-02
St Hansie the Flawed
$

South African cricket had conspicuously failed to move on from the Hansie saga. Large sections of the population still idolised him and believed he had been unfairly treated, and that number seemed to include many in the Proteas' team.

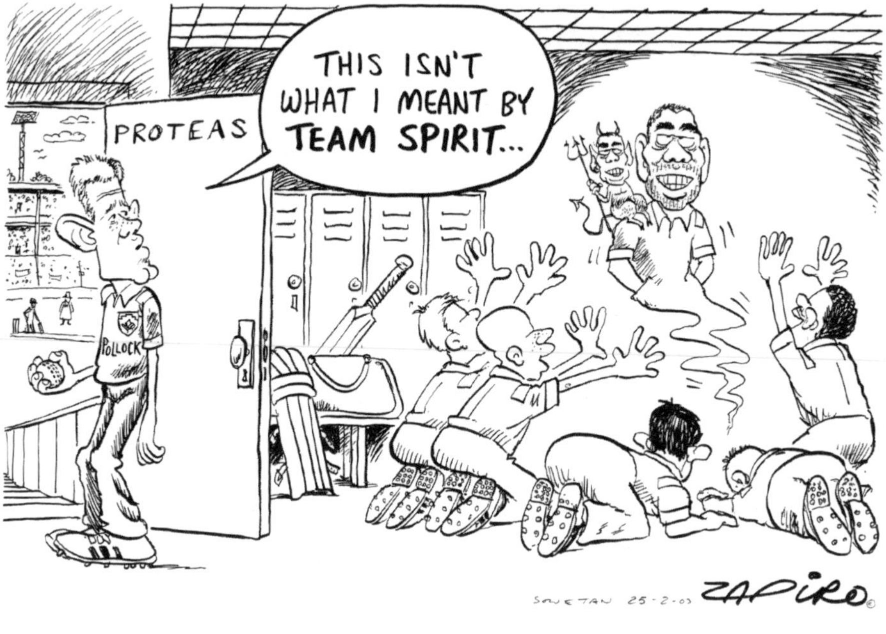
PROTEAS
THIS ISN'T WHAT I MEANT BY TEAM SPIRIT...
POLLOCK
SOWETAN 25-2-03 ZAPIRO ©

Shane Warne provided the early world cup headlines with a drug scandal. The vain Shane spun the story that he had inadvertently taken the banned substances in a slimming diuretic which was "given to me by my mum".

Even without their superstar, the Aussies rampaged to another world cup while the Proteas found another crazy way to exit a major tournament – misreading the Duckworth-Lewis scorecard against Sri Lanka as the rain tumbled down at Kingsmead.

It was hard to imagine a more embarrassing moment for South African sport in 2003 but we could always rely on Springbok rugby to find several that were far worse before that grim year was out.

In September, Bakkies Botha was suspended for eight weeks following charges of biting, eye-gouging and spitting at Wallaby hooker Brendan Cannon.

Another Blue Bulls lock, and Groot Trek throwback, Geo Cronje, then sparked a major controversy by reportedly refusing to room with coloured team-mate Quentin Davids.

SARFU sorted the problem out with characteristic decisiveness.

The Boks went to the 2003 world cup in Australia in disarray on and off the field.

2003

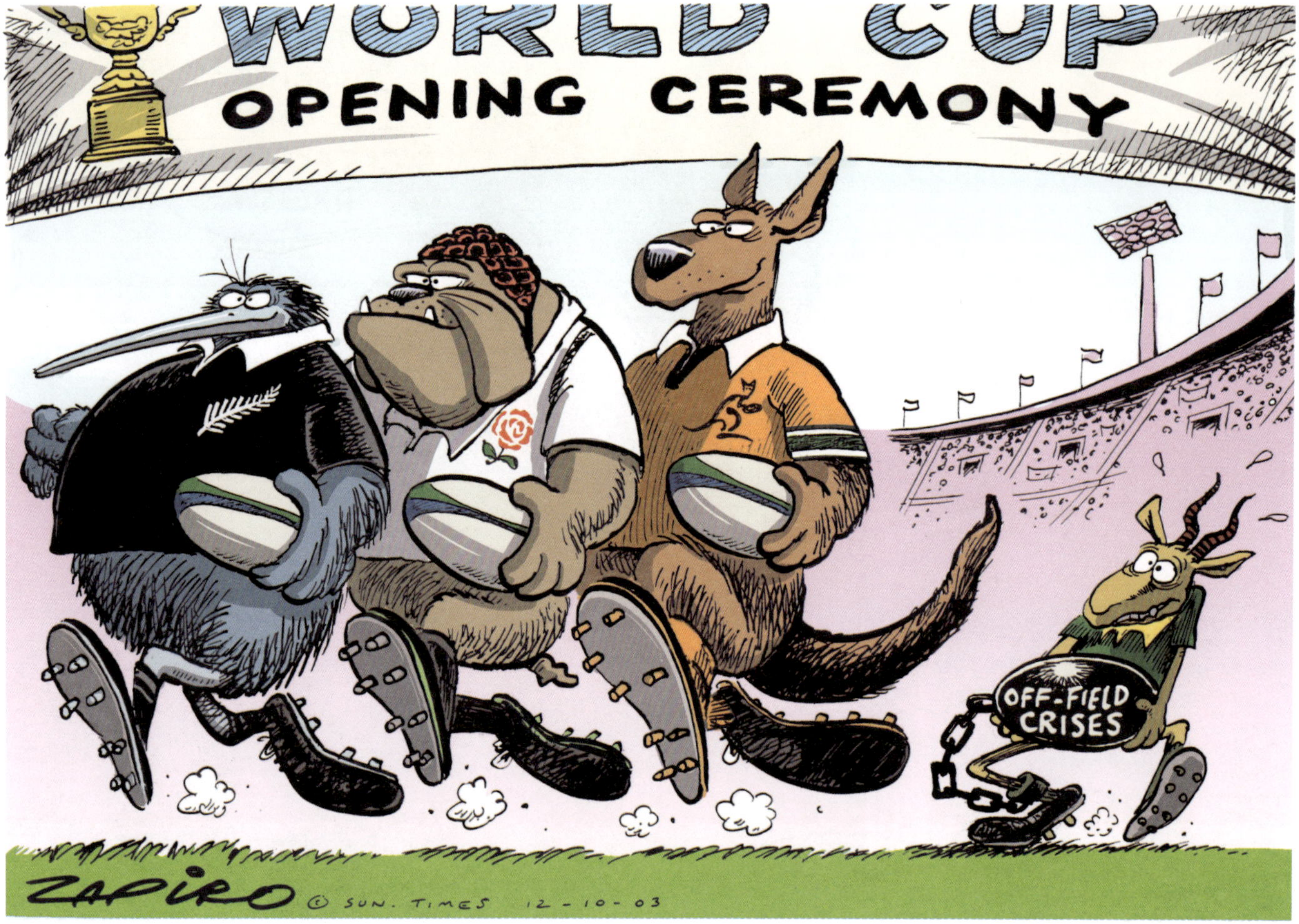
WORLD CUP
OPENING CEREMONY
OFF-FIELD CRISES
ZAPIRO © SUN. TIMES 12-10-03

The Boks, captained by Corné Krige, came up well short, dismissed with contemptuous ease by the All Blacks in the quarter-finals.

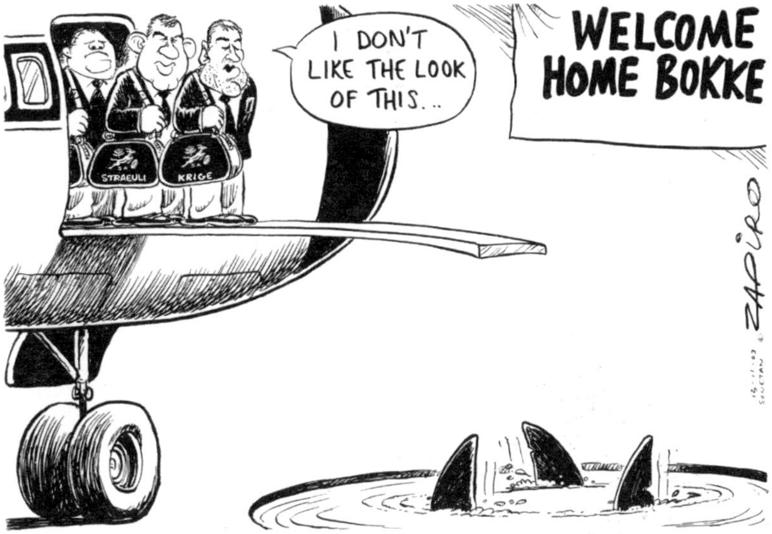
I DON'T LIKE THE LOOK OF THIS...
WELCOME HOME BOKKE
STRAEULI
KRIGE
ZAPIRO

Things got worse all round when humiliating pictures and reports were leaked of the brutal pre-world cup training exercise at Kamp Staaldraad.

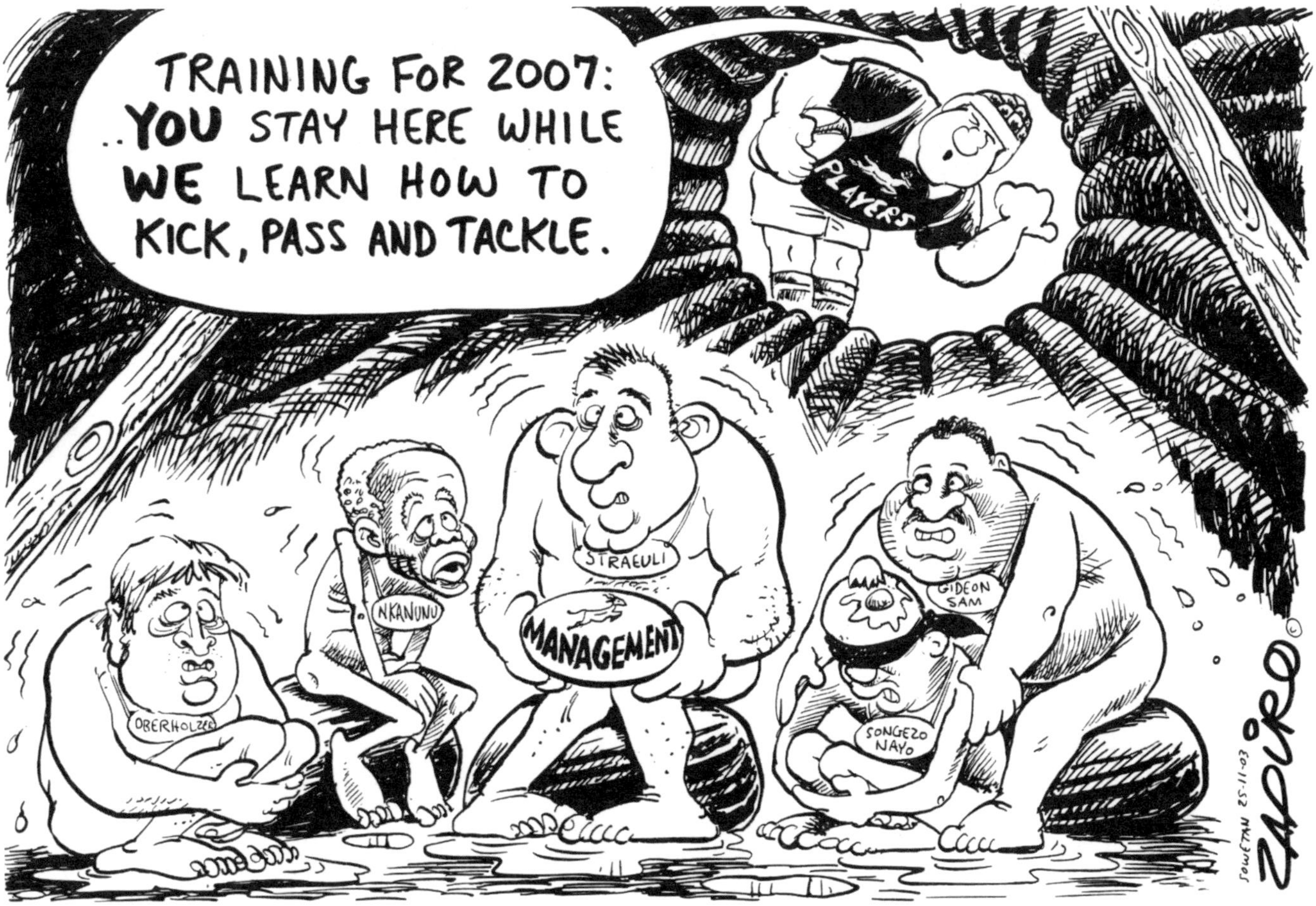
TRAINING FOR 2007: ..YOU STAY HERE WHILE WE LEARN HOW TO KICK, PASS AND TACKLE.
PLAYERS
STRAEULI
MANAGEMENT
NKANUNU
OBERHOLZER
GIDEON SAM
SONGEZO NAYO
SOWETAN 25-11-03
ZAPIRO

Coach Straeuli was summoned to face a SARFU committee.

By the end of the year, the two men primarily responsible for the debacle, SARFU CEO Riaan Oberholzer and Straeuli, had left their jobs with massive payouts.

HI HONEY, HOW'D THE HEARING GO?

HOW TO WIN A FEW MILLION

THE LOTTO? NOT LIKELY.

THE HORSES? FAT CHANCE.

THE CASINO? YEAH, SURE.

THERE IS AN EASIER WAY...

SIMPLY SCREW UP SA RUGBY.

Bafana coach Mashaba doggedly favoured home-based players over the reportedly troublesome foreign legion but when he excluded the likes of Leeds United's Lucas Radebe and Manchester United's Quinton Fortune from a showpiece fixture in Durban against David Beckham's England he was temporarily removed from office and replaced by ... Jomo Sono ... who ultimately couldn't select Fortune either because the player's cellphone was switched off.

Mashaba was then restored to his position after he announced a "voluntary" change in his selection policy.

2003

The world cup bid rumbled on. FIFA had ruled that the 2010 world cup must take place on the African continent so our only hosting rivals were Morocco and Egypt – characteristic cockiness had taken hold.

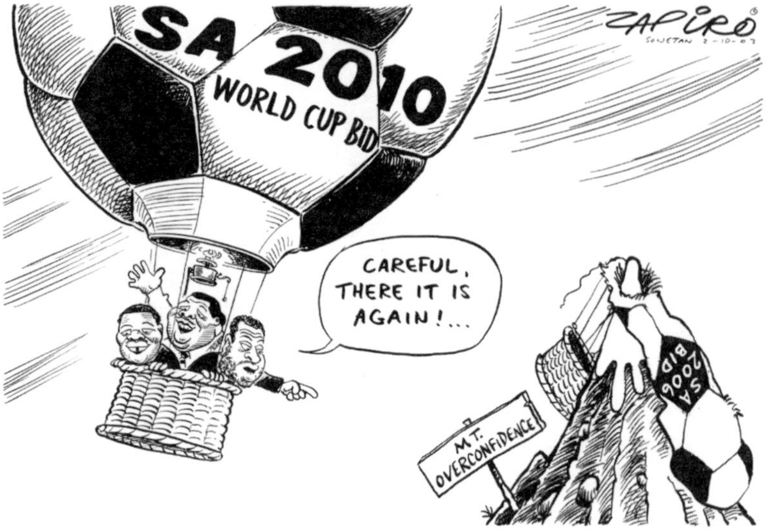
SA 2010
WORLD CUP BID
CAREFUL, THERE IT IS AGAIN!...
SA 2006 BID
MT. OVERCONFIDENCE
ZAPIRO
SOWETAN 2-10-03

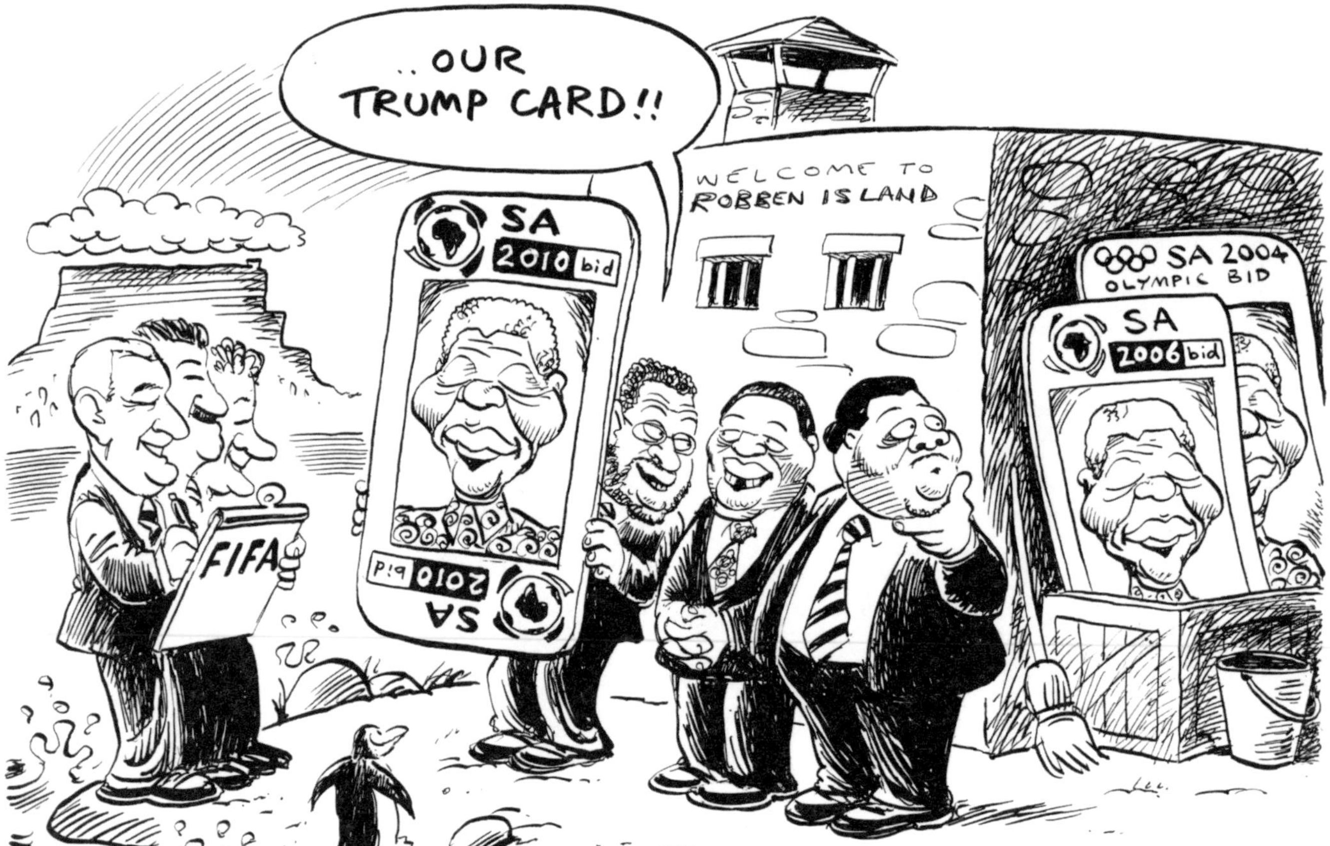
.. OUR TRUMP CARD!!
WELCOME TO ROBBEN ISLAND
SA 2010 bid
SA 2010 bid
FIFA
SA 2004 OLYMPIC BID
SA 2006 bid
SOWETAN 6-11-03 ZAPIRO

In the local game, the standard of refereeing was causing major concerns.

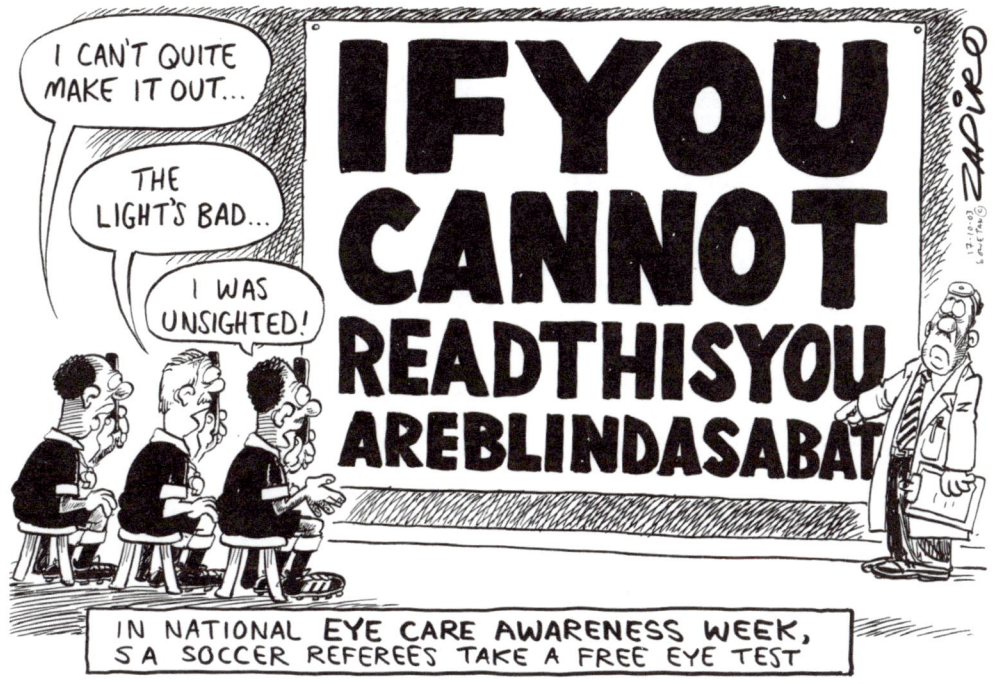

At the start of 2004 Shakes Mashaba was sacked and both the major winter codes were looking for the next Messiah.

2004

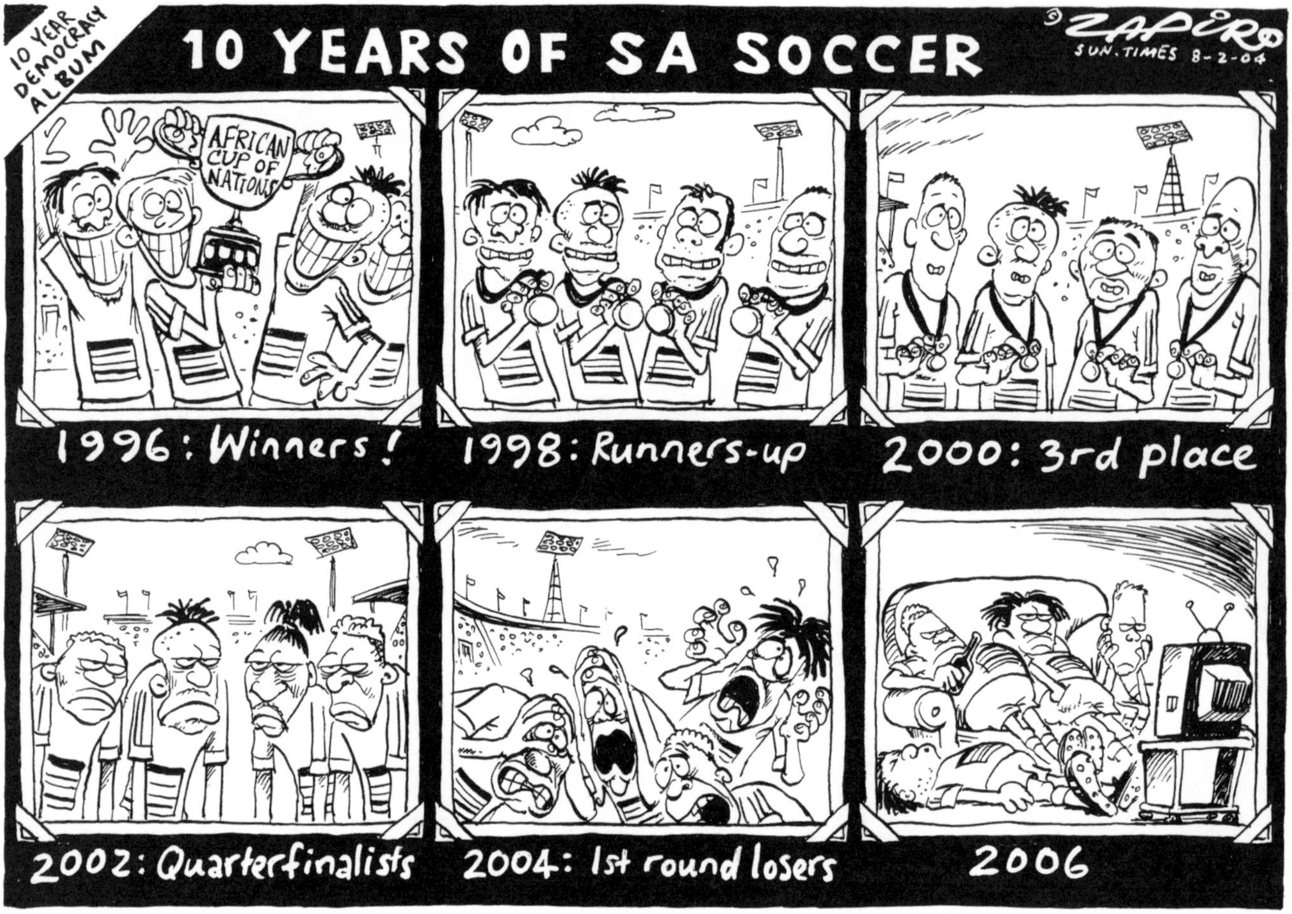
10 YEAR DEMOCRACY ALBUM
10 YEARS OF SA SOCCER
©ZAPIRO
SUN.TIMES 8-2-04
AFRICAN CUP OF NATIONS
1996: Winners!
1998: Runners-up
2000: 3rd place
2002: Quarterfinalists
2004: 1st round losers
2006

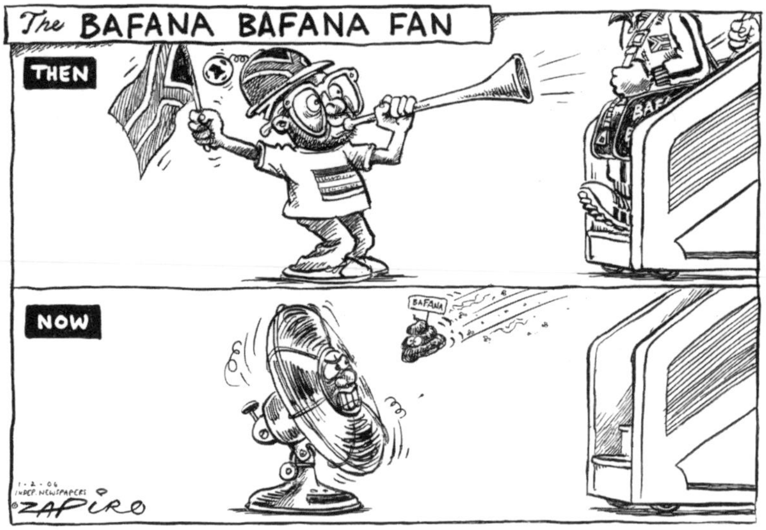
The BAFANA BAFANA FAN
THEN
NOW
BAFANA
1-2-04
INDEP. NEWSPAPERS
©ZAPIRO

The late Styles Phumo took the Bafana reins as a caretaker for AFCON 2004. The team were eliminated in the group stages. The 2–0 win over Benin during that tournament was to be the last South African victory in any AFCON finals game until the defeat of Angola in Durban in 2013.

Bafana Bafana and the Boks were both now the pits.

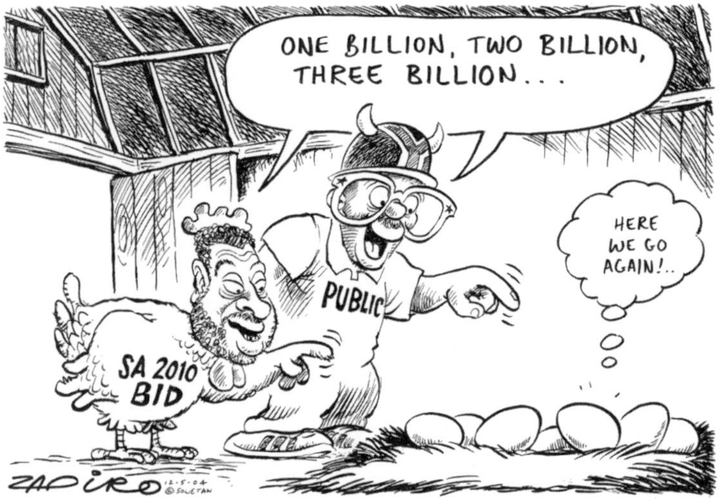
ONE BILLION, TWO BILLION, THREE BILLION...
HERE WE GO AGAIN!..
PUBLIC
SA 2010 BID
ZAPIRO

Off the field, the nation was fixated on the hosting rights for the 2010 world cup.

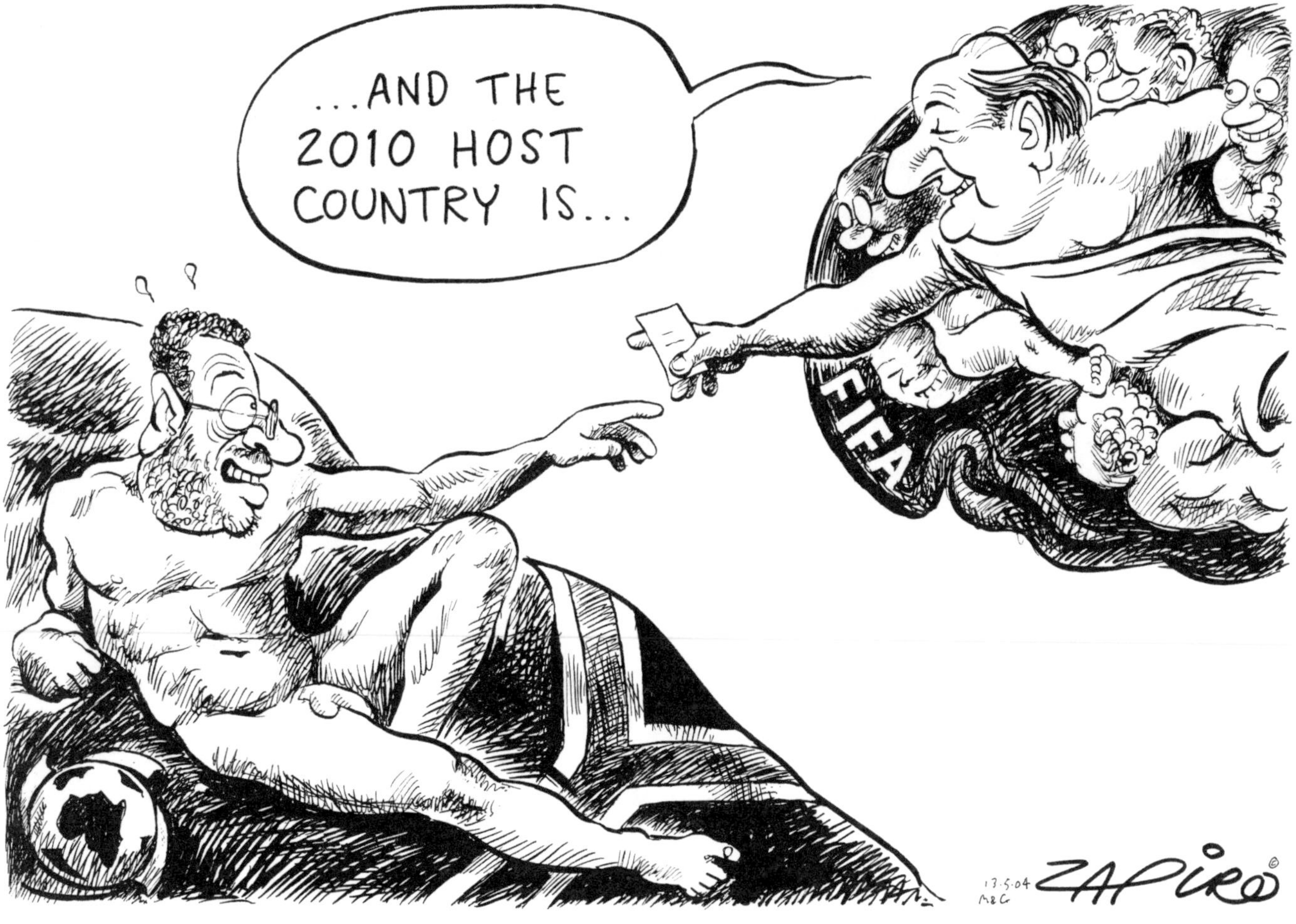
...AND THE 2010 HOST COUNTRY IS...
FIFA
ZAPIRO

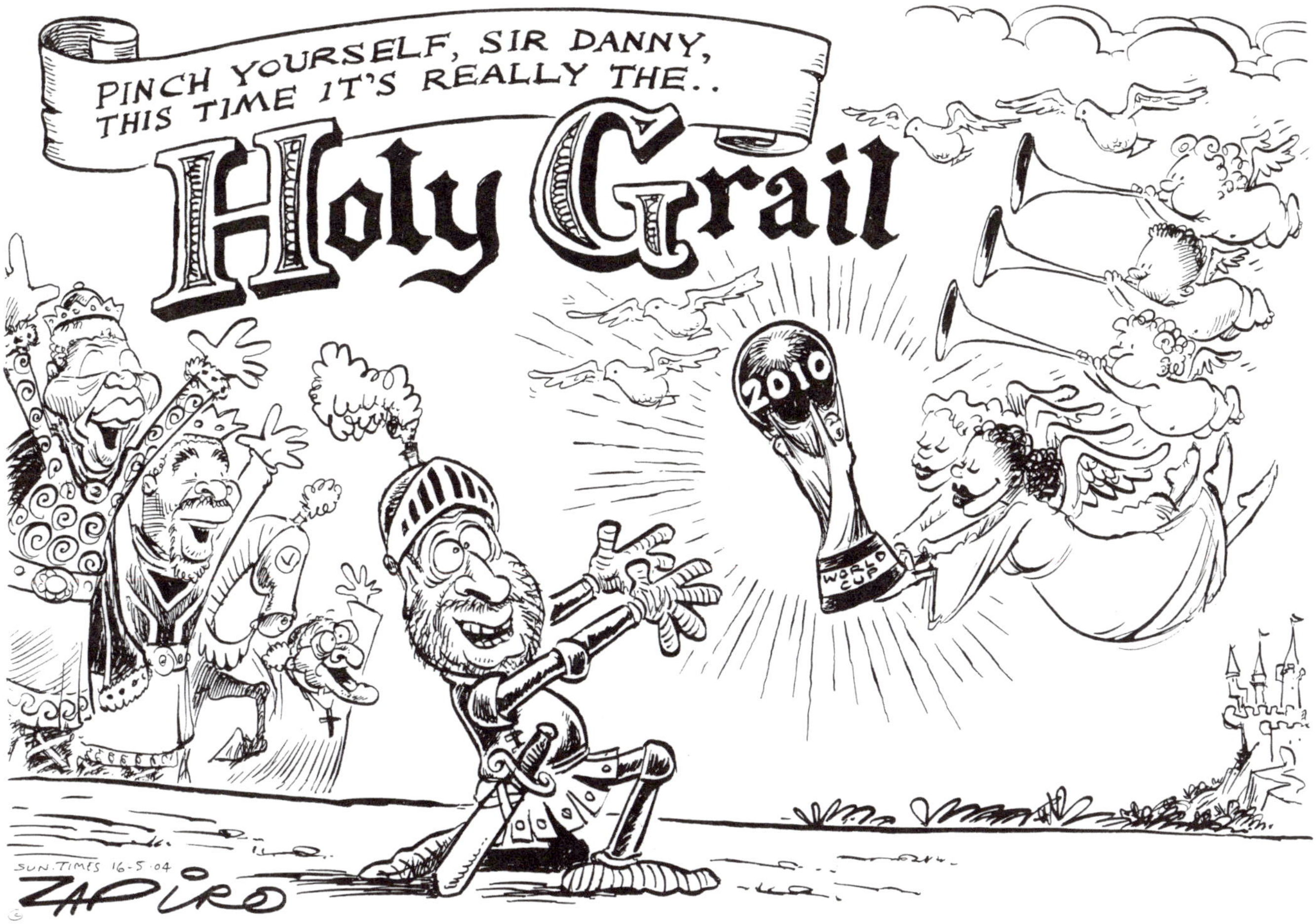
PINCH YOURSELF, SIR DANNY, THIS TIME IT'S REALLY THE..
Holy Grail
2010
WORLD CUP
SUN.TIMES 16-5-04
ZAPIRO

2004

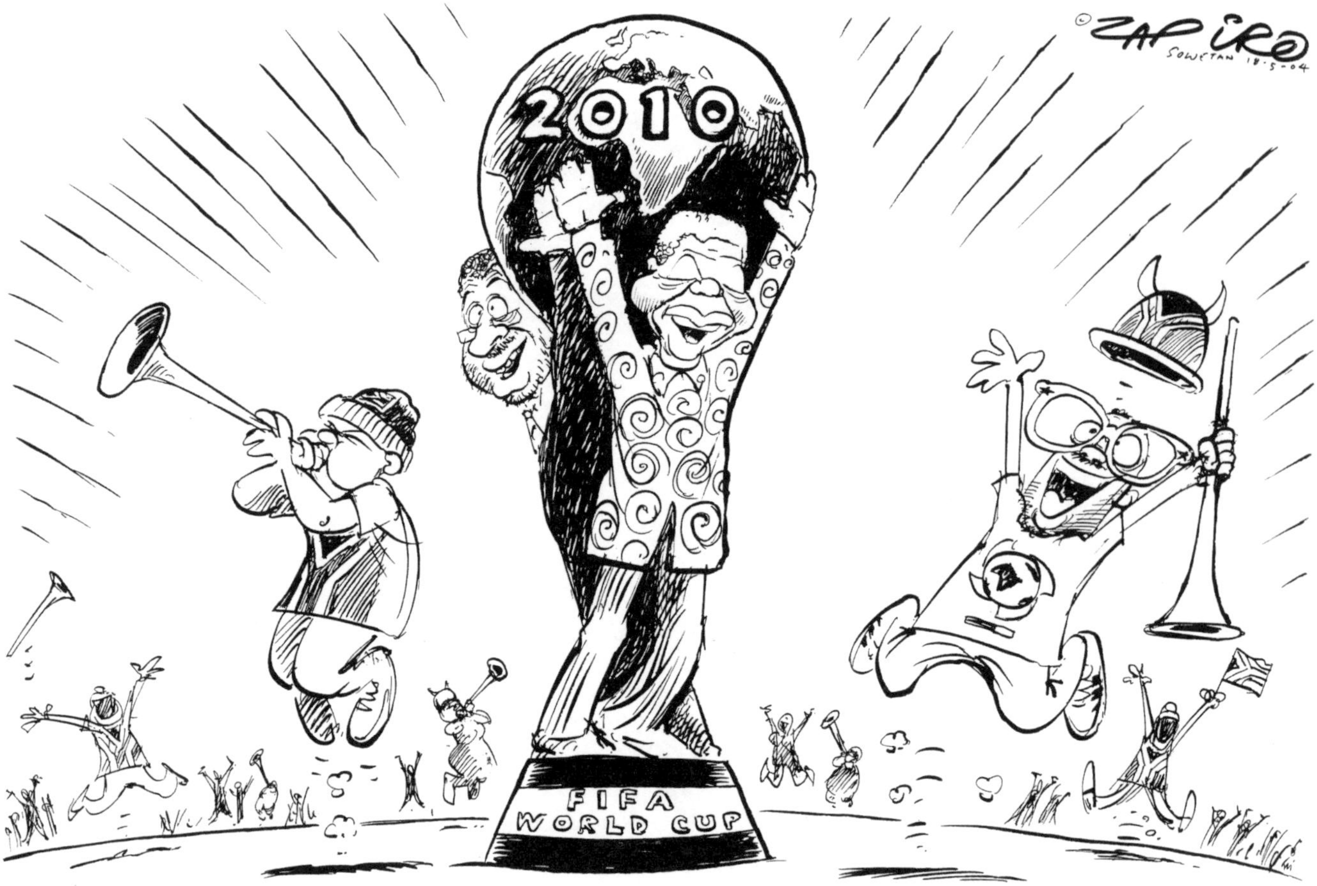
2010
FIFA
WORLD CUP
©ZAPIRO
SOWETAN 18-5-04

This time round, our vuvuzela moment had finally arrived.

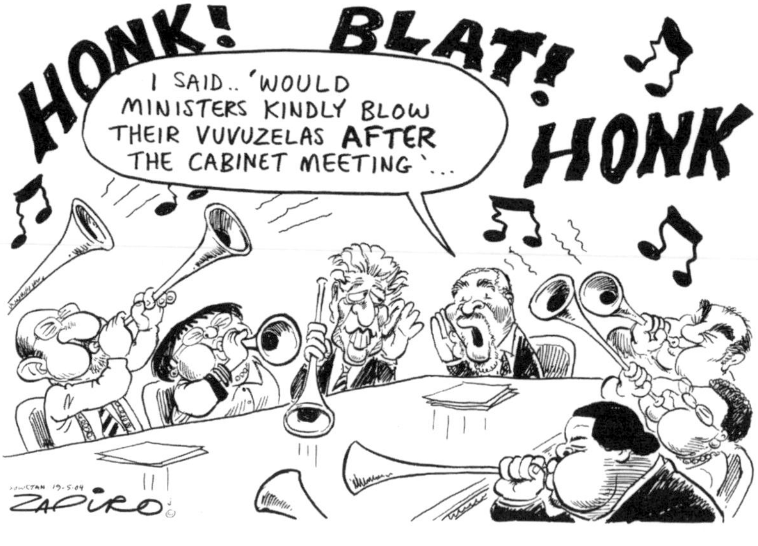
HONK!
BLAT!
I SAID.. 'WOULD MINISTERS KINDLY BLOW THEIR VUVUZELAS AFTER THE CABINET MEETING'...
HONK
ZAPIRO

Triumph quickly turned to despair in June 2004 when Operation Dribble, a police investigation into local soccer match-fixing, led to the arrest of 33 people, including 19 referees.

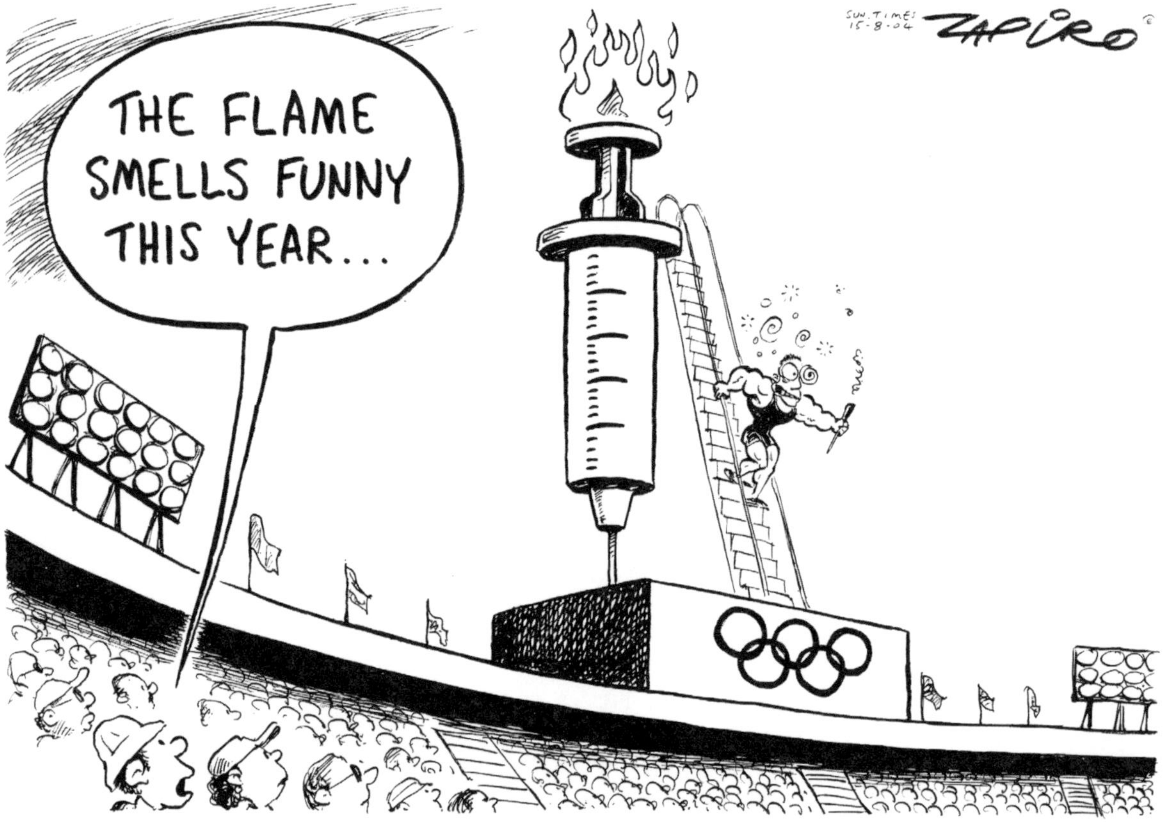
SUN. TIMES 15-8-04 ZAPIRO
THE FLAME SMELLS FUNNY THIS YEAR...

The 2004 Olympics were held in "Athens se ma se". Greece might have been the spiritual home of the ancient games but the defining narrative was a very modern one – debt and drugs.

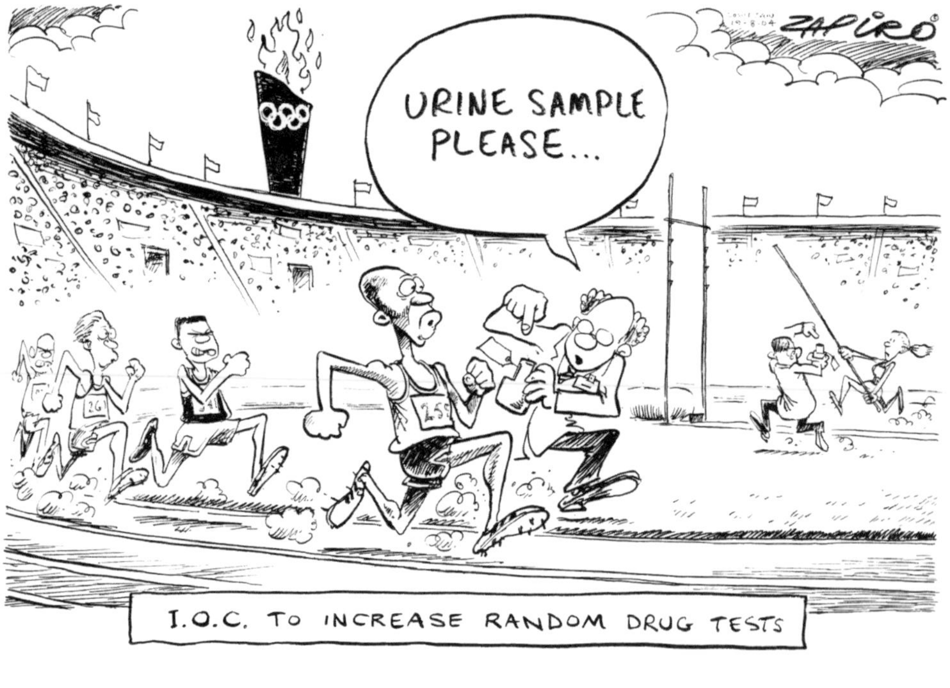
ZAPIRO
URINE SAMPLE PLEASE...
I.O.C. TO INCREASE RANDOM DRUG TESTS

South Africa's only gold came in the pool with the epic 4 x 100 m men's freestyle relay but it was becoming a sporting tradition that our Paralympians would lead the way to Olympic glory. Ernst van Dyk in the wheelchair, with three medals in Athens, was one of the standard-bearers. He went on to win a record nine Boston marathons and six Paralympic medals across three games.

One of our successful Olympians, triple-medallist Roland Schoeman, was soon flirting with a lucrative switch of nationalities. He later declined the offer from Qatar.

Things were not going smoothly with the world cup. Danny Jordaan had spearheaded the successful bid but Pirates' boss Irvin Khoza, not for nothing known as "The Iron Duke", wanted to run the organising committee.

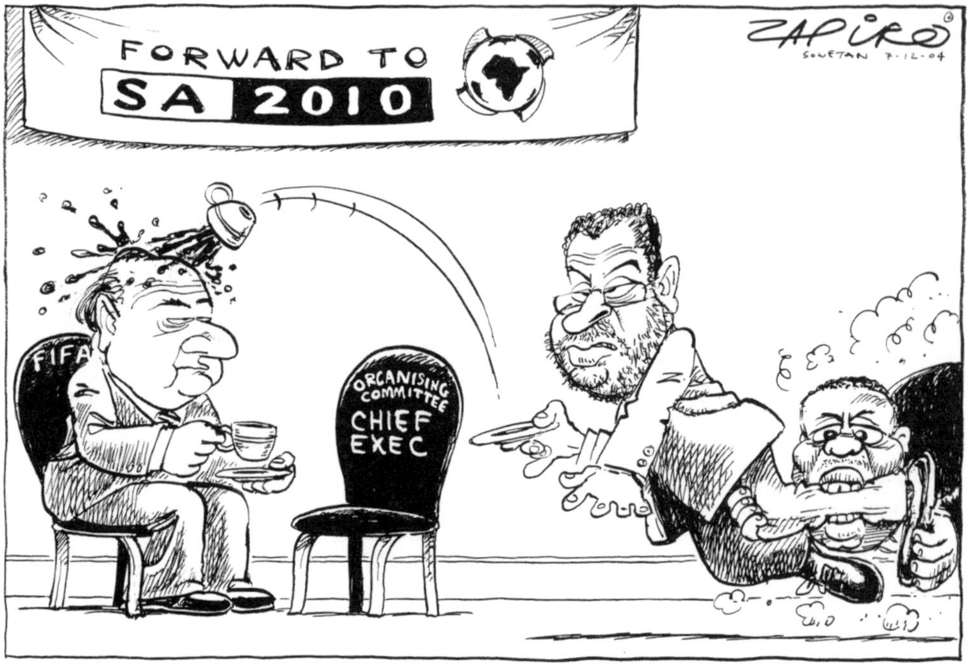
FORWARD TO
SA 2010
ZAPIRO
SOWETAN 7-12-04
FIFA
ORGANISING COMMITTEE
CHIEF EXEC

As we were soon to discover about everything to do with the world cup, FIFA President Sepp Blatter's opinion was the only one that ever counted on anything.

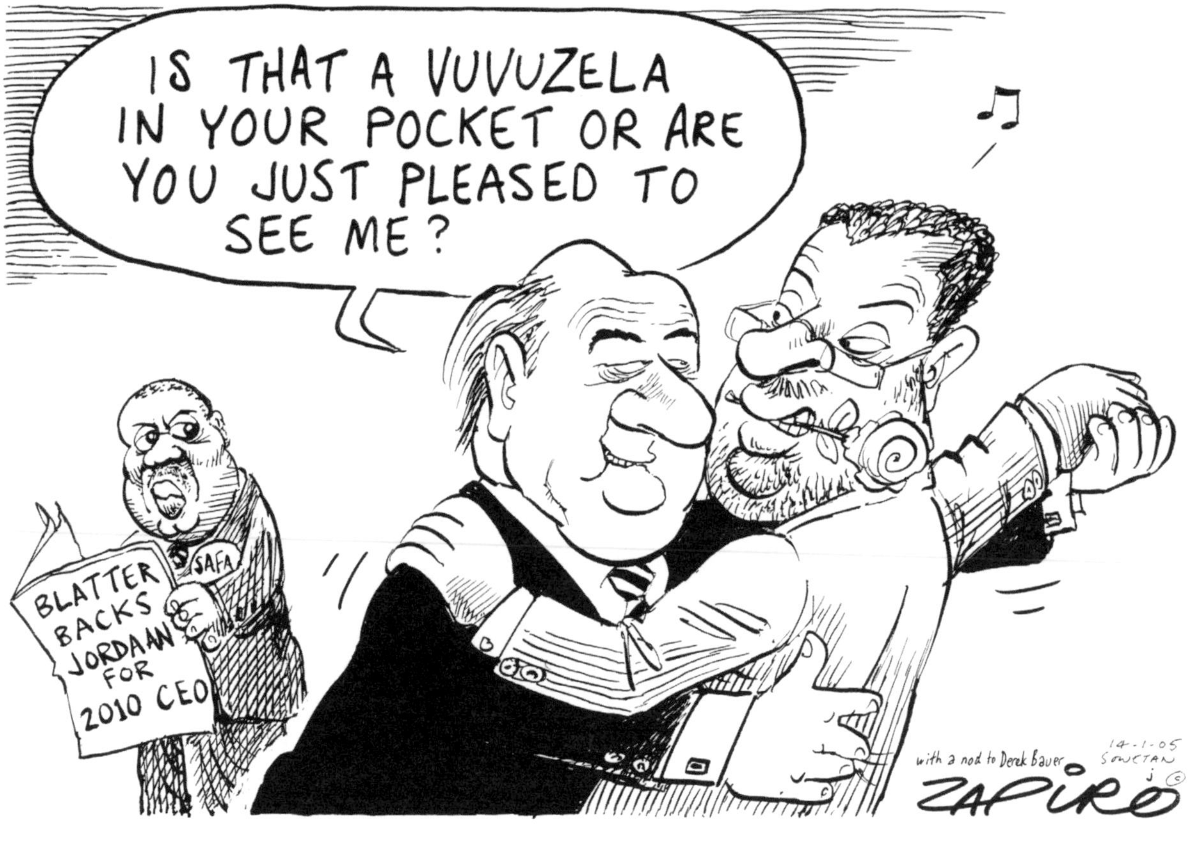
IS THAT A VUVUZELA IN YOUR POCKET OR ARE YOU JUST PLEASED TO SEE ME?
SAFA
BLATTER BACKS JORDAAN FOR 2010 CEO
with a nod to Derek Bauer
14-1-05 SOWETAN
ZAPIRO

The Proteas were in the Caribbean for the first time since the dope tour and, after a limp performance in the first test, Makhaya Ntini smashed records and the West Indians in the second. Suddenly no one remembered ever labelling him as a quota player.

On the rugby front, it was situation (ab)normal for the new Sports Minister Makhenkesi Stofile.

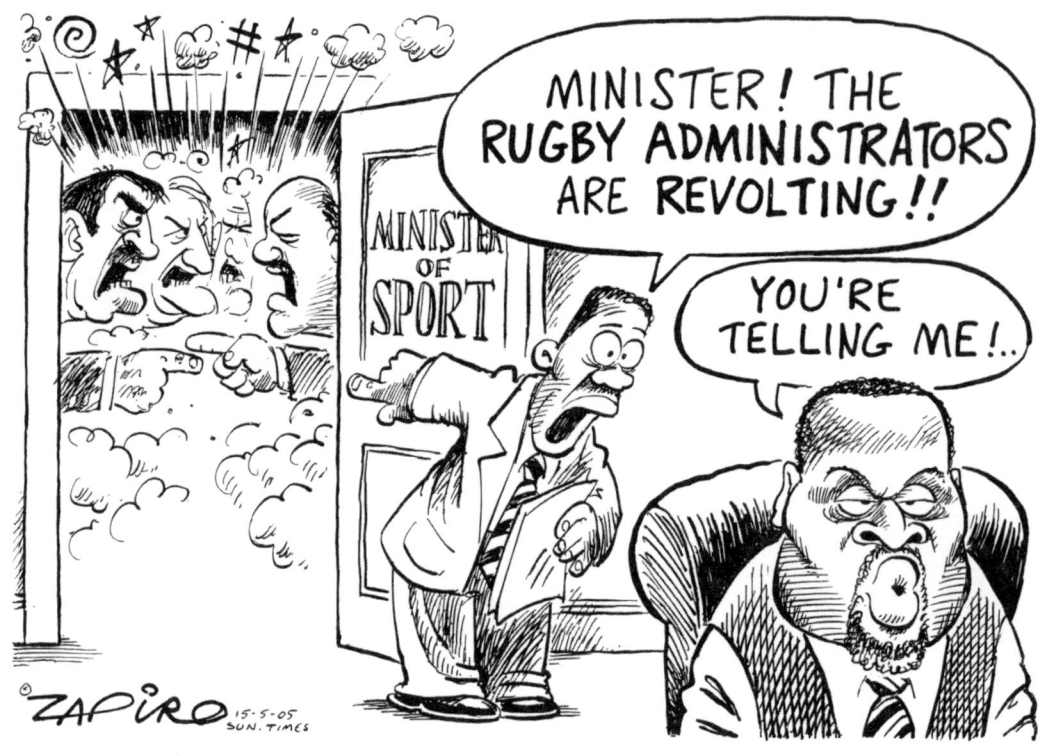

Things were also very familiar with Bafana Bafana as Englishman Stuart Baxter got his marching orders after the team failed to qualify for the 2006 world cup finals. He would surprisingly return in 2012 as coach of Kaizer Chiefs.

The eccentric Romanian Ted "The Professor" Dumitru took charge of Bafana Bafana for AFCON 2006. The team, led by Sibusiso Zuma, returned home in humiliation without scoring a single goal.

With a home world cup looming, SAFA were desperate for a successful coach. They found themselves a former world cup winner in the veteran Brazilian Carlos Alberto Parreira, for whom they paid a preposterous sum.

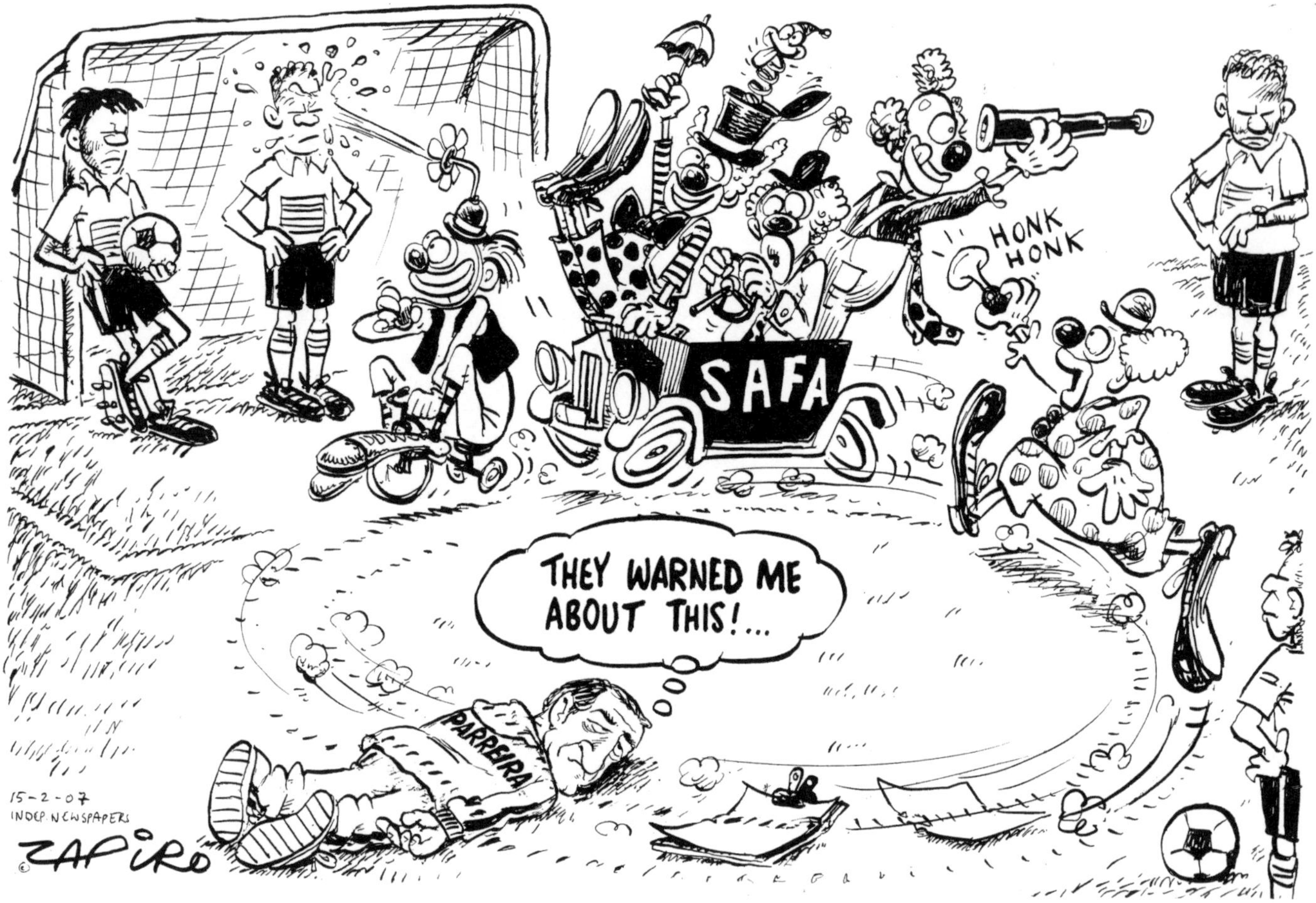
HONK
HONK
SAFA
THEY WARNED ME ABOUT THIS!...
PARREIRA
15-2-07
INDEP. NEWSPAPERS
ZAPIRO

Soon enough Parreira would feel that he was earning his money.

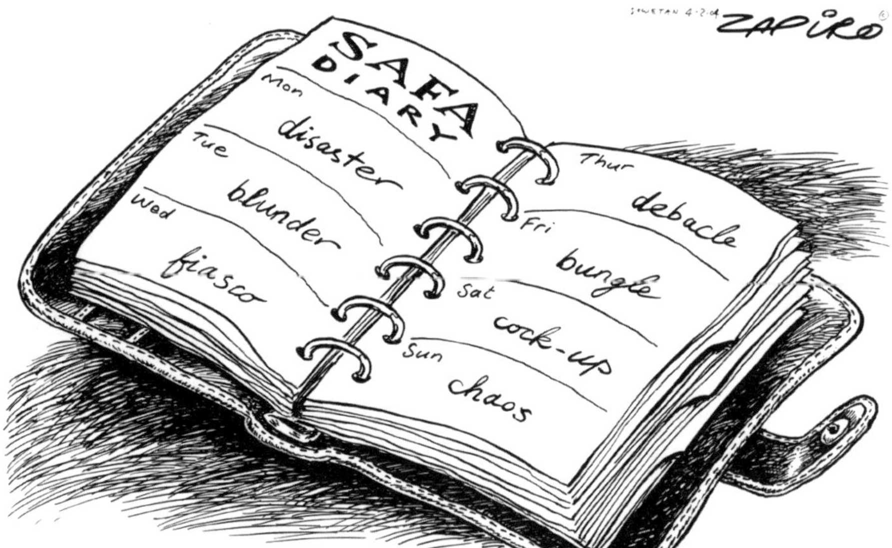
ZAPIRO
SAFA DIARY
Mon
disaster
Tue
blunder
Wed
fiasco
Thur
debacle
Fri
bungle
Sat
cock-up
Sun
chaos

On the cricket field the Ricky Ponting-led Australians still gave the Proteas nightmares until one dream day at the Wanderers in 2006 when the number 438 entered South African sporting folklore. Led by an inspired Herschelle Gibbs, the home side gunned down a preposterous ODI target and handed the Australians a painful and unforgettable defeat.

Globally the shadow of drugs fell over just about every event involving power or stamina. The 2006 Tour de France champion Floyd Landis and the world 100m sprint record-holder Justin Gatlin both tested positive.

Seven-times Tour de France winner Lance Armstrong was still six years away from his Oprah confession but suspicions about him and anyone else who could win the torturous tour were widespread.

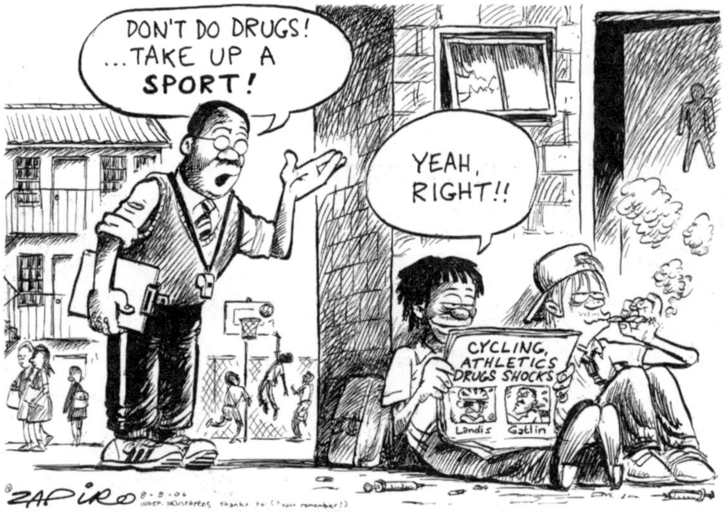
DON'T DO DRUGS! ...TAKE UP A SPORT!
YEAH, RIGHT!!
CYCLING, ATHLETICS DRUGS SHOCKS
Landis
Gatlin
ZAPIRO 8-8-06

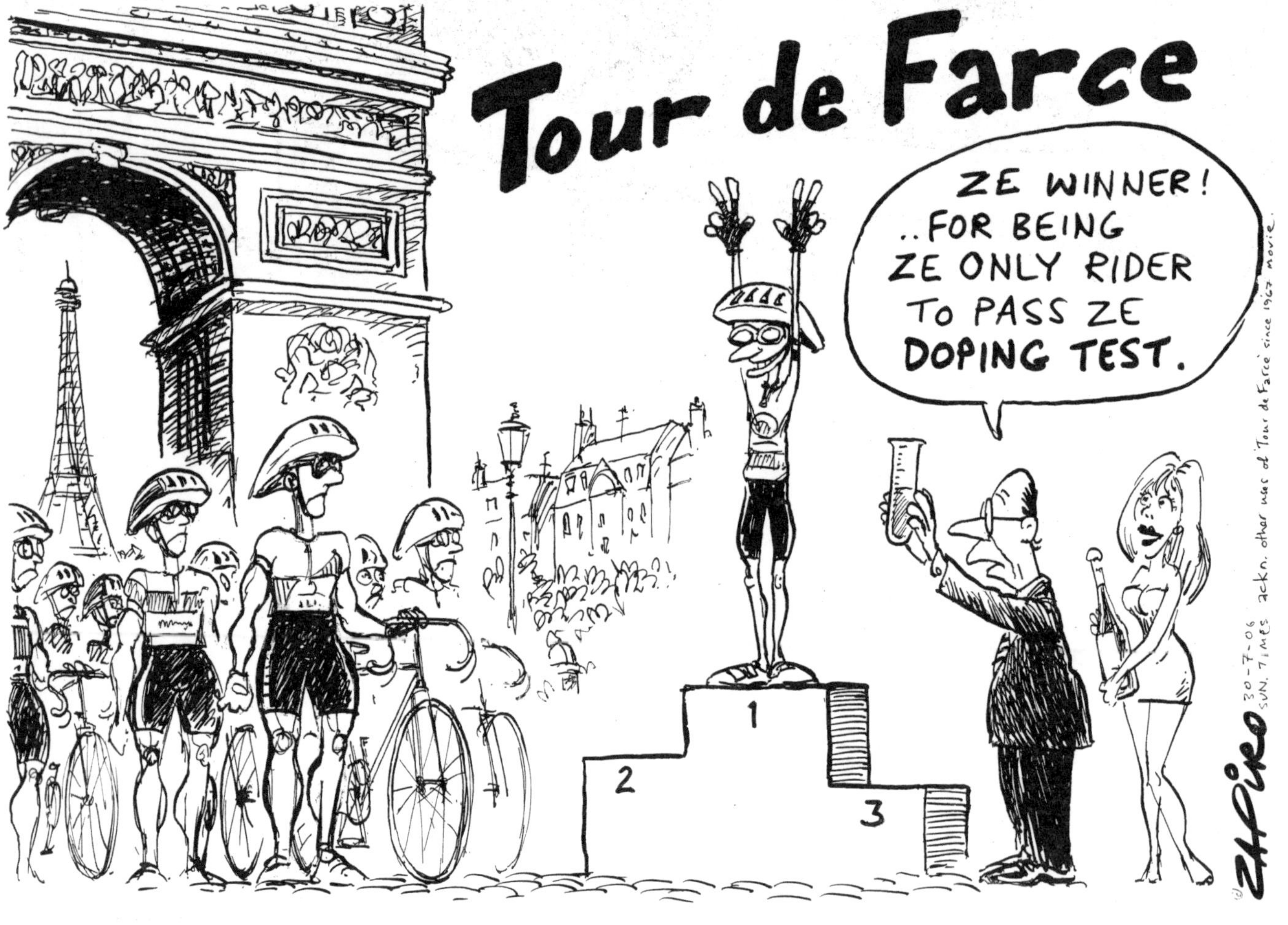
Tour de Farce
ZE WINNER! ..FOR BEING ZE ONLY RIDER TO PASS ZE DOPING TEST.
1
2
3
ZAPIRO 30-7-06 SUN. TIMES

TOUR DE FRANCE
START
PARIS
Steroidville
Syringe
Amphetamine
Le-Grand-Pillpoppage
St-Stimulant
Plateau-de-Urineswitch
T'estosterone
Anabolique
Eau Verdose
I MISS ZE OLD RACE...
CAFE
INDEP. NEWSPAPERS © 26-7-07
ZAPIRO

2006

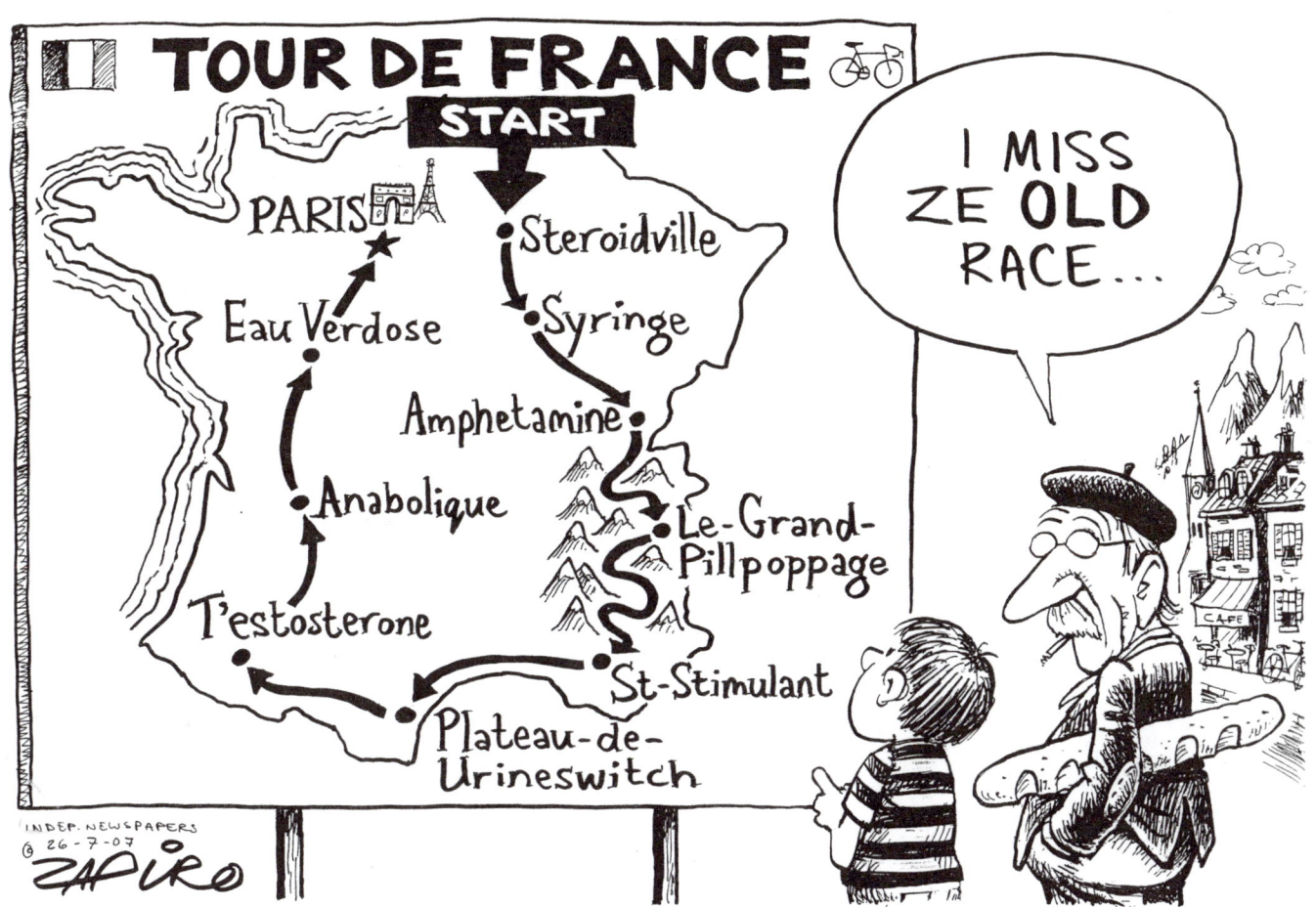

The 2007 cricket world cup was rocked by the death in a Jamaican hotel room of the highly-respected former Proteas' coach Bob Woolmer, who was at the tournament with the Pakistanis.

On the field, Herschelle hit six 6s in an over against Holland and the Proteas blitzed their way through the tournament until the semi-final where, inevitably, they ran into the Australians. In the blink of an eye the no.1-ranked SA were 27–5 and out of the contest. The dreaded c-word was once again being bandied about.

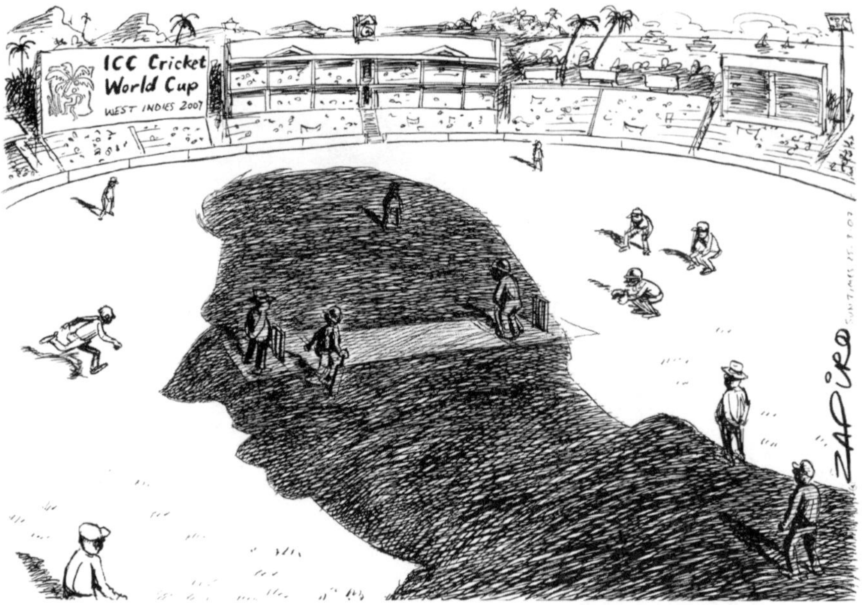

ICC Cricket World Cup
WEST INDIES 2007
ZAPIRO

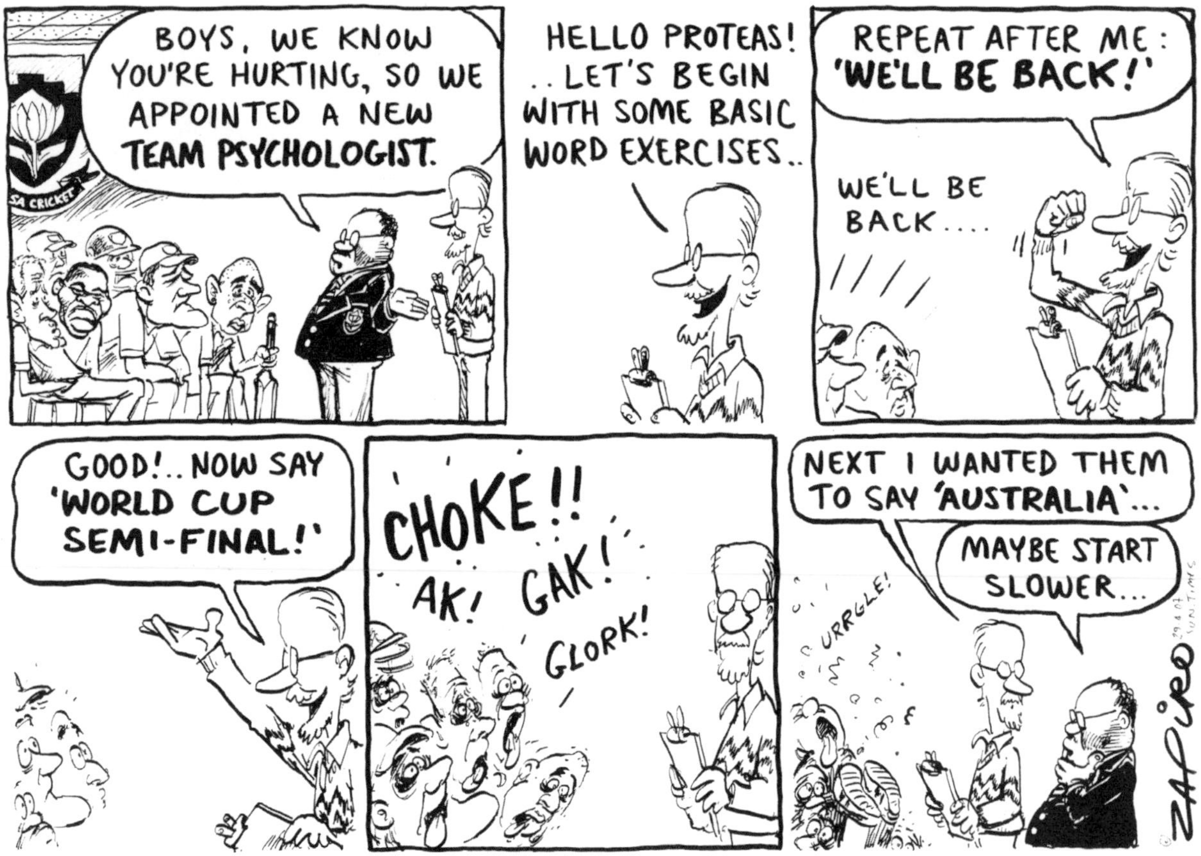

BOYS, WE KNOW YOU'RE HURTING, SO WE APPOINTED A NEW TEAM PSYCHOLOGIST.
SA CRICKET
HELLO PROTEAS! .. LET'S BEGIN WITH SOME BASIC WORD EXERCISES..
REPEAT AFTER ME: 'WE'LL BE BACK!'
WE'LL BE BACK....
GOOD!.. NOW SAY 'WORLD CUP SEMI-FINAL!'
CHOKE!!
AK!
GAK!
GLORK!
NEXT I WANTED THEM TO SAY 'AUSTRALIA'...
MAYBE START SLOWER...
URRGLE!
ZAPIRO

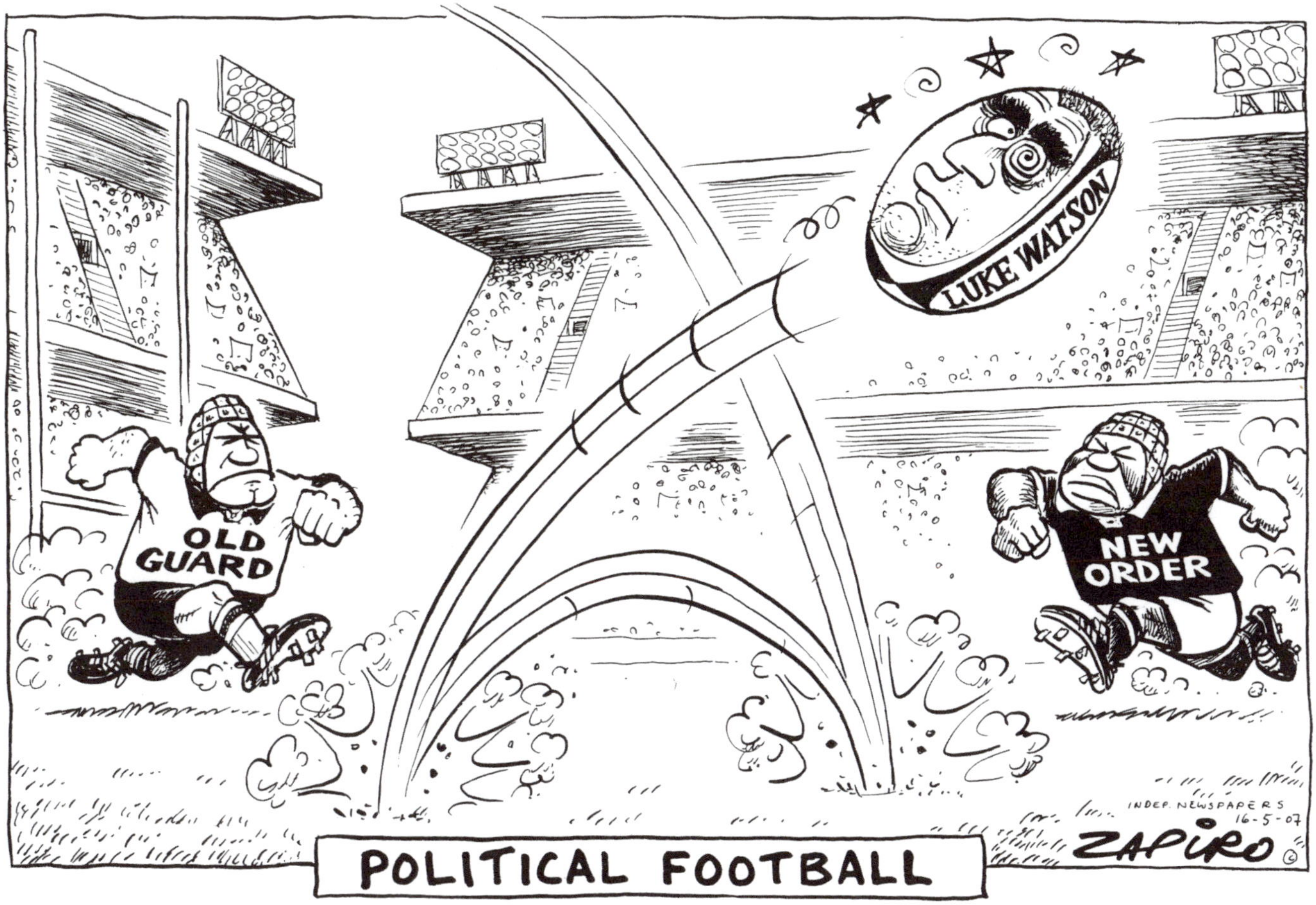
LUKE WATSON
OLD GUARD
NEW ORDER
INDEP. NEWSPAPERS 16-5-07
ZAPIRO
POLITICAL FOOTBALL

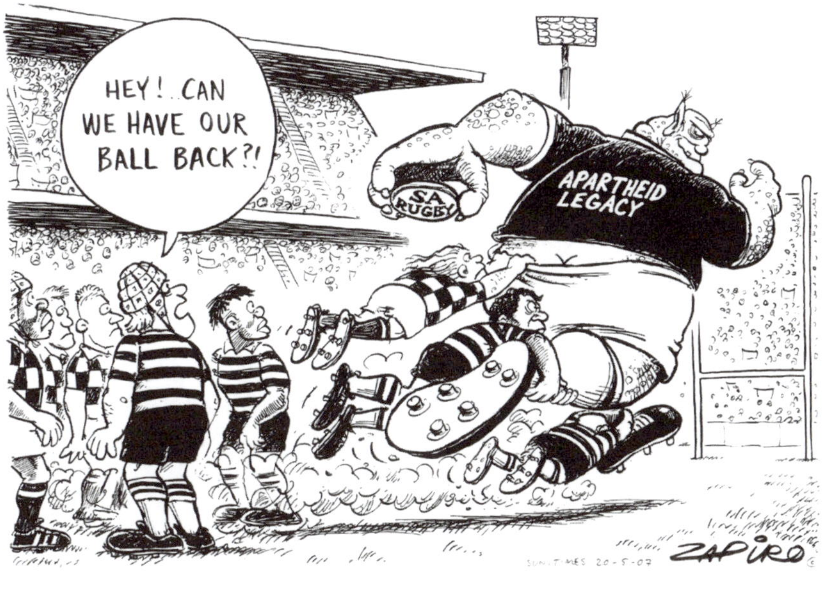
HEY!..CAN WE HAVE OUR BALL BACK?!
SA RUGBY
APARTHEID LEGACY
ZAPIRO

During 2007 Springbok rugby was dominated by the Luke Watson saga. The son of one of the few rugby-connected struggle heroes, the strident Watson had a stellar Super-14 in the Stormers' back row but the national selectors ignored him.

2007

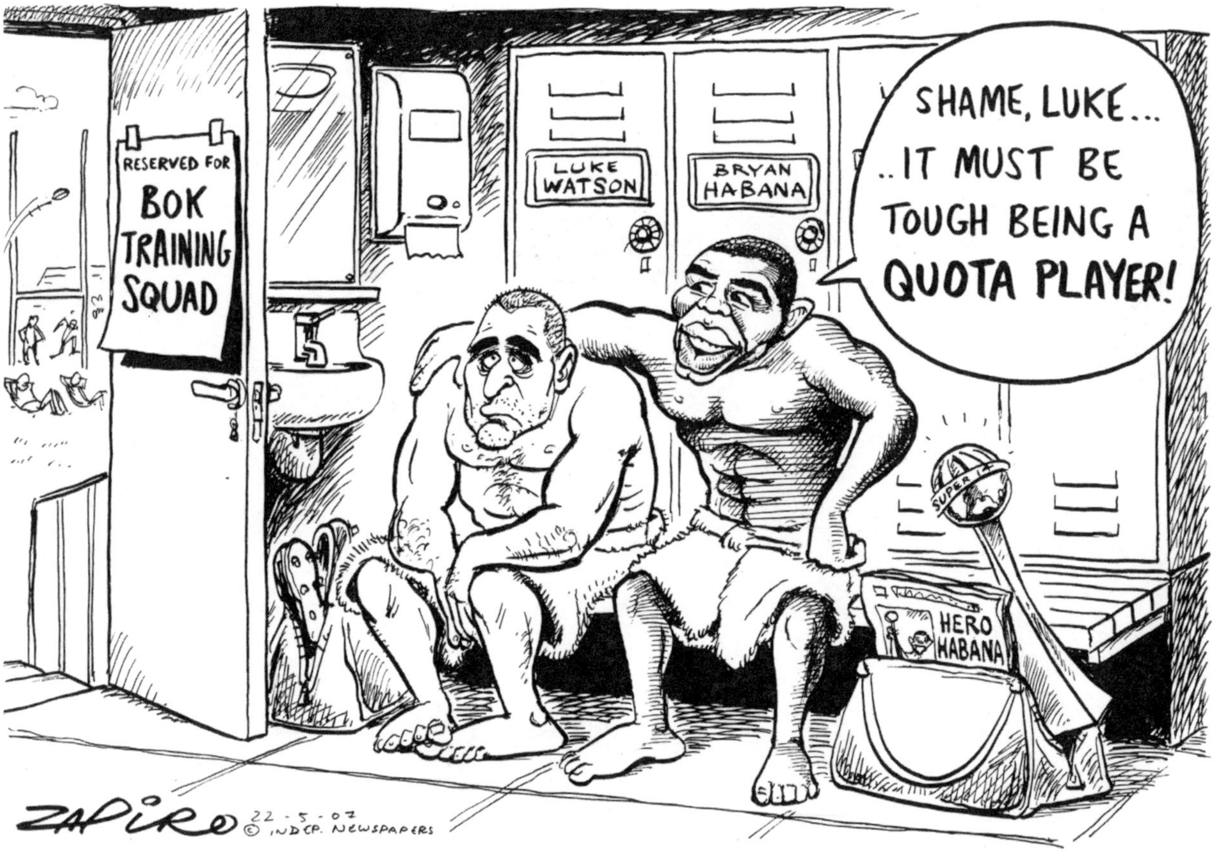
RESERVED FOR
BOK
TRAINING
SQUAD
LUKE
WATSON
BRYAN
HABANA
SHAME, LUKE...
..IT MUST BE
TOUGH BEING A
QUOTA PLAYER!
HERO
HABANA
SUPER 14
ZAPIRO 22-5-07 © INDEP. NEWSPAPERS

After politicians and administrators bayed for his inclusion, coach Jake White grudgingly (and briefly) assented to Watson's presence in the team but he was not part of the 2007 world cup squad.

The Boks managed to leave the politics behind and thumped England 36-0 in the tournament opener. They then reprised that performance with a controlled 15-6 win in the final.

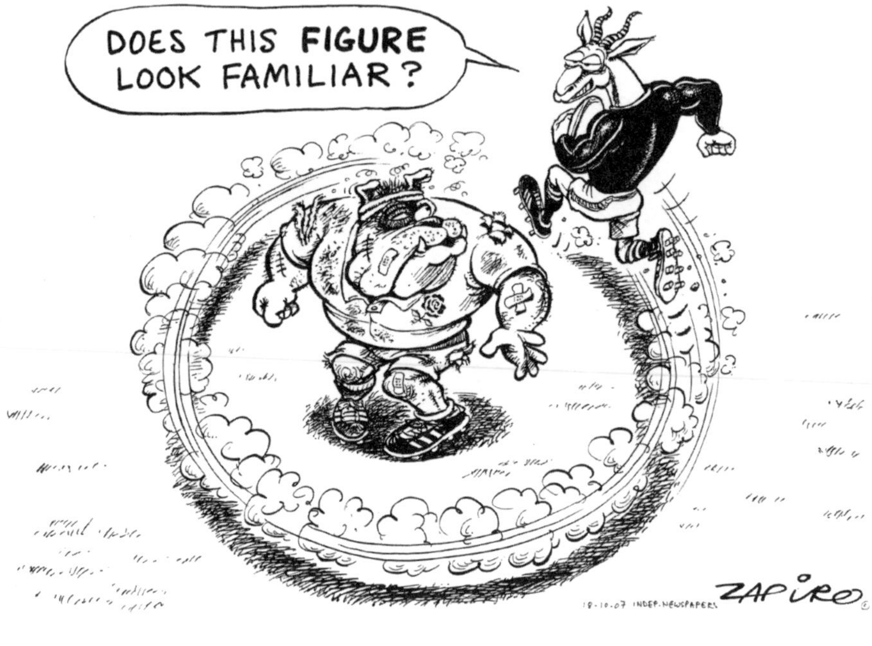
DOES THIS **FIGURE**
LOOK FAMILIAR?
ZAPIRO

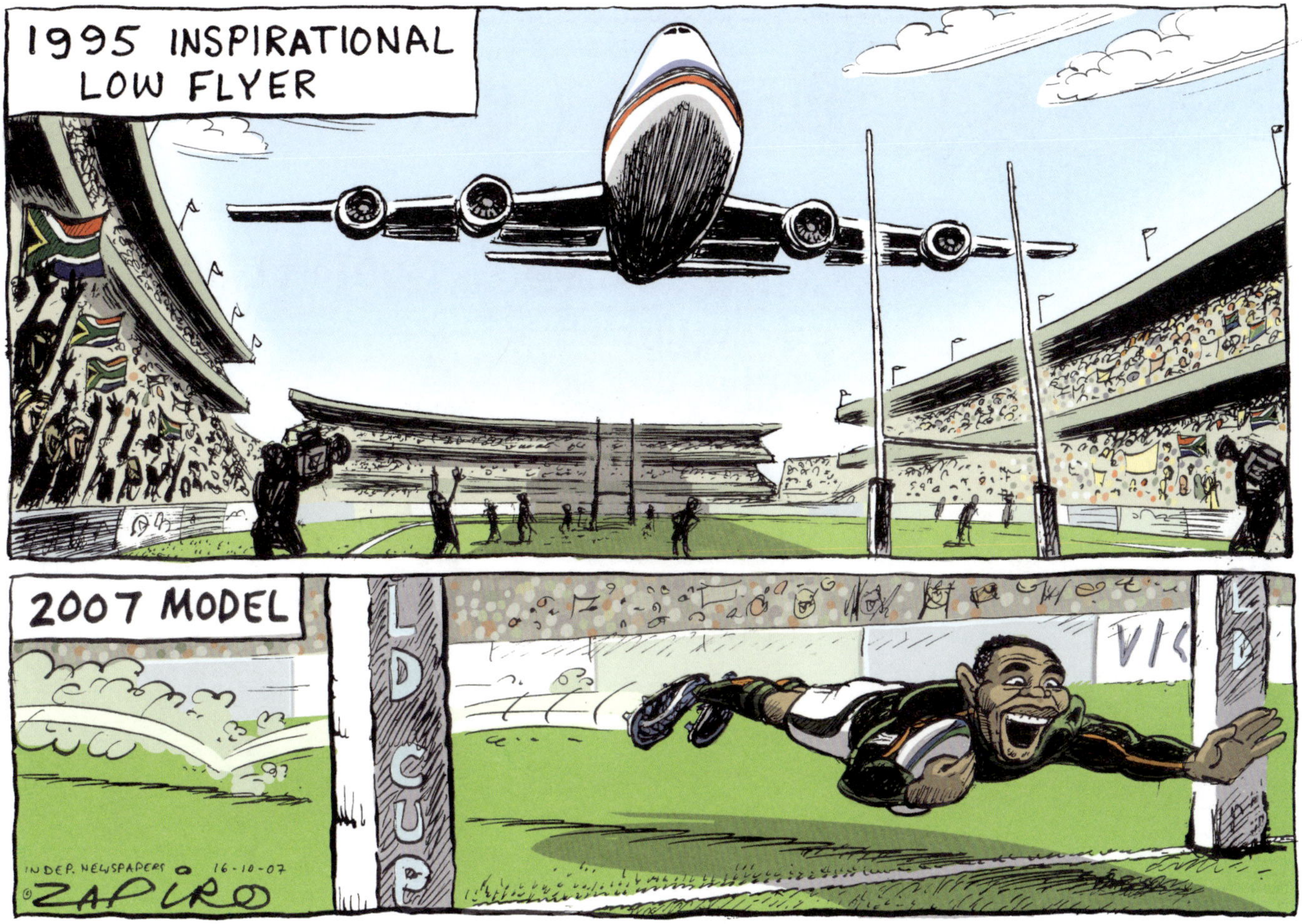
1995 INSPIRATIONAL LOW FLYER
2007 MODEL
LD CUP
LD CUP
INDEP. NEWSPAPERS 16-10-07
©ZAPIRO

2007

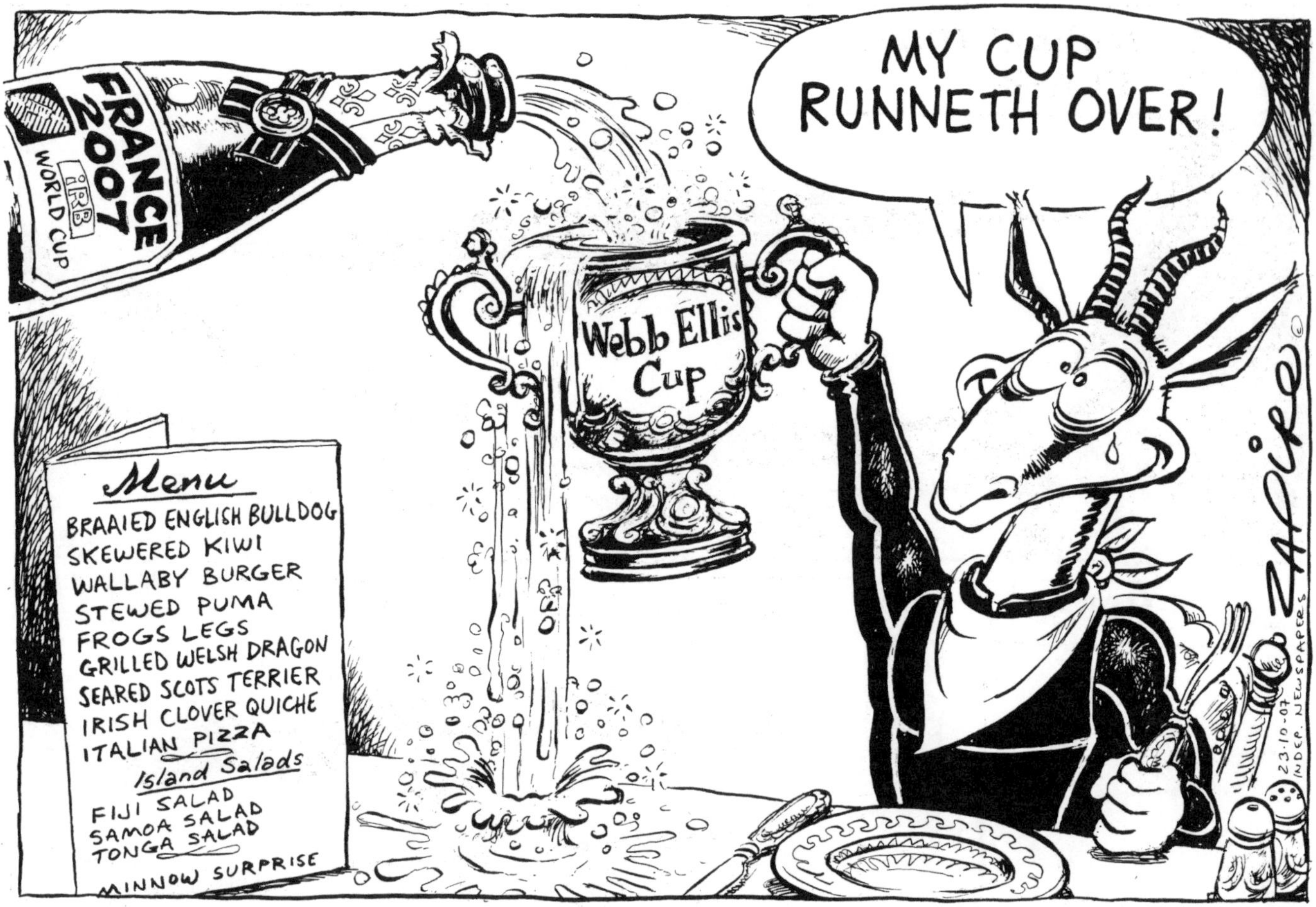
FRANCE 2007
IRB WORLD CUP
MY CUP RUNNETH OVER!
Webb Ellis Cup
Menu
BRAAIED ENGLISH BULLDOG
SKEWERED KIWI
WALLABY BURGER
STEWED PUMA
FROGS LEGS
GRILLED WELSH DRAGON
SEARED SCOTS TERRIER
IRISH CLOVER QUICHE
ITALIAN PIZZA
Island Salads
FIJI SALAD
SAMOA SALAD
TONGA SALAD
MINNOW SURPRISE
ZAPIRO
23-10-07 INDEP. NEWSPAPERS ©

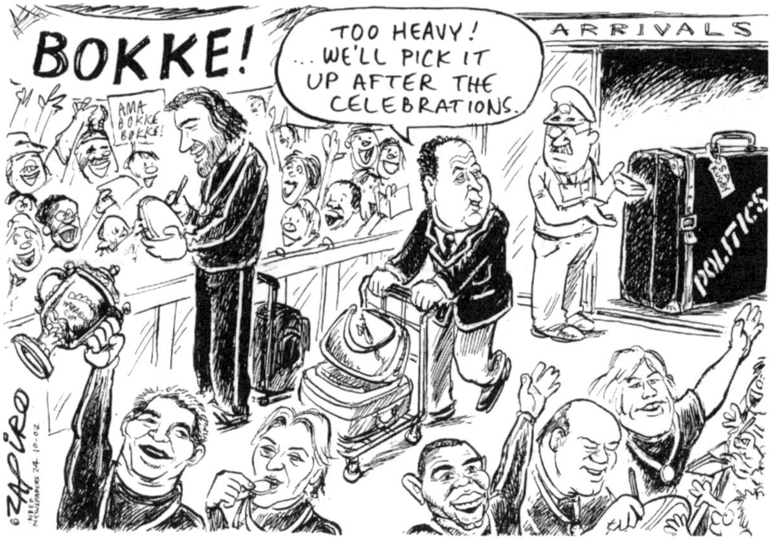
BOKKE!
TOO HEAVY! ...WE'LL PICK IT UP AFTER THE CELEBRATIONS.
ARRIVALS
AMA BOKKE BOKKE!
SA RUGBY
POLITICS
© ZAPIRO INDEP. NEWSPAPERS 24-10-07

Coach Jake White's reward for the historic victory, ultimately, was to not have his contract renewed.

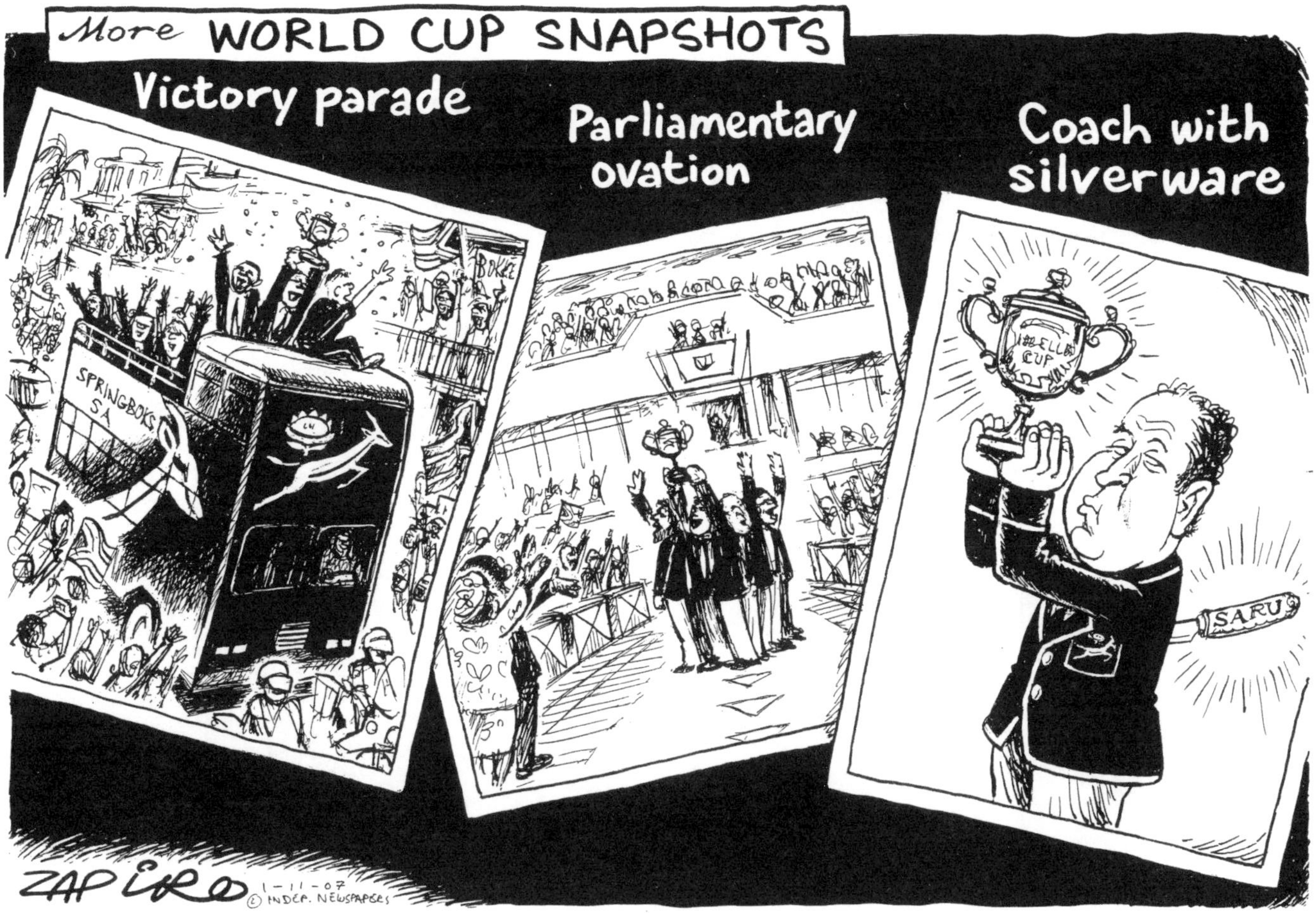
More WORLD CUP SNAPSHOTS
Victory parade
Parliamentary ovation
Coach with silverware
SPRINGBOKS SA
SARU
ZAPIRO 1-11-07 © INDEP. NEWSPAPERS

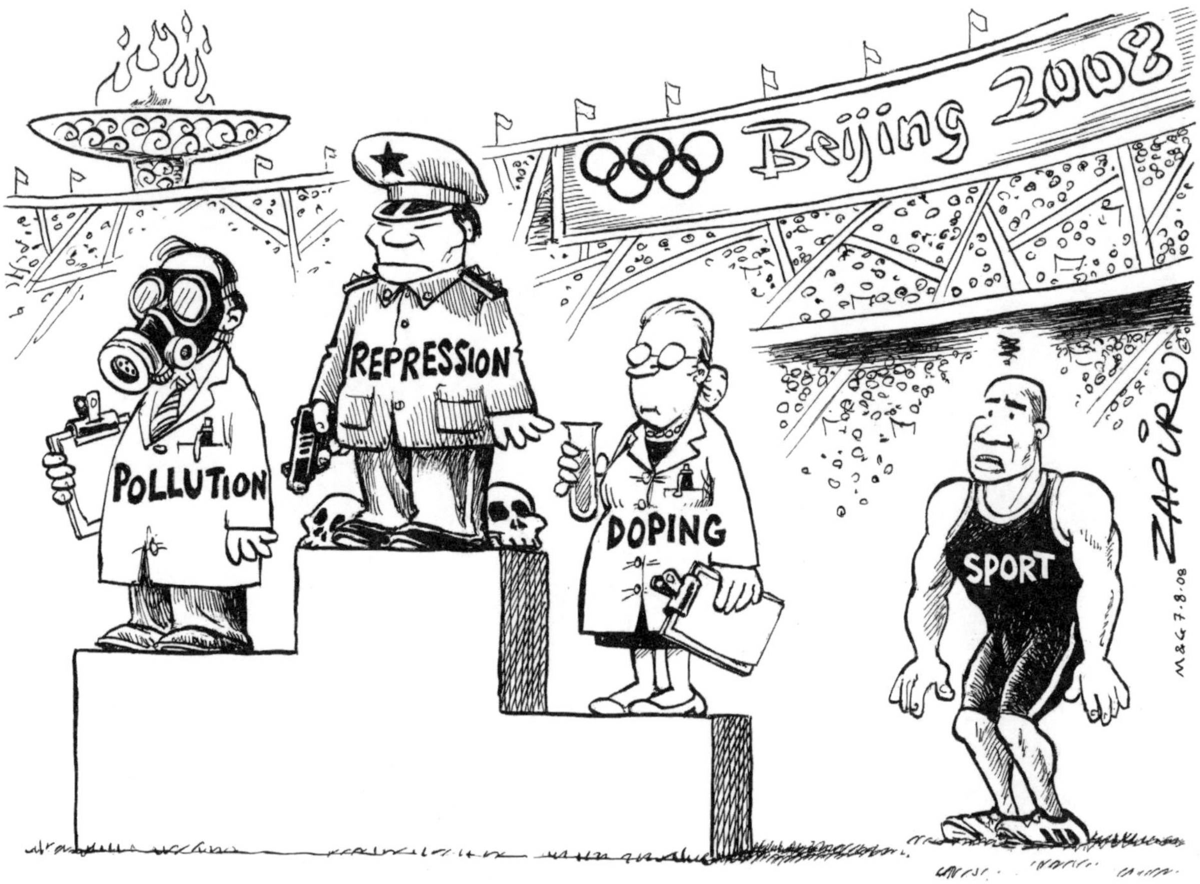
Beijing 2008
REPRESSION
POLLUTION
DOPING
SPORT
ZAPIRO
M&G 7.8.08

The 2008 Beijing Olympics were held in a controversial political environment comparable only to Berlin in 1936 and Moscow in 1980.

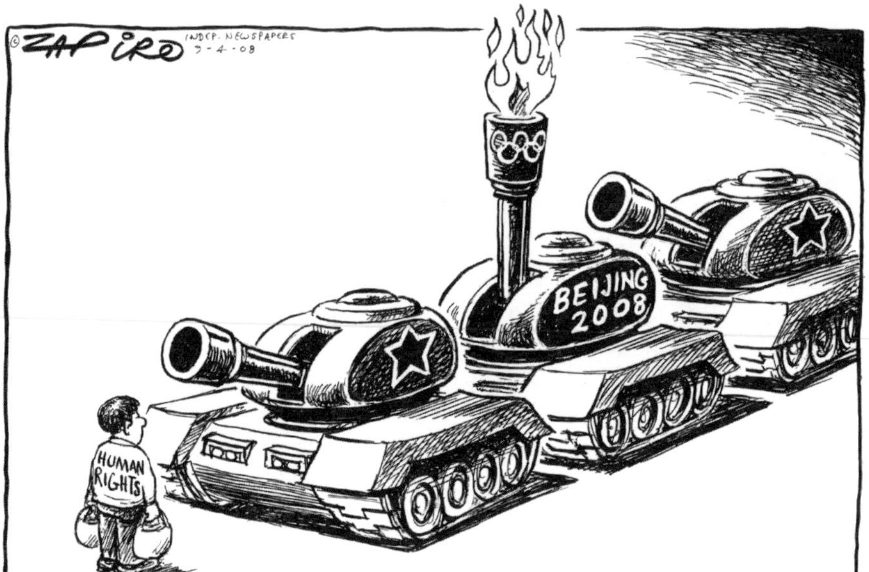
© ZAPIRO
INDEP. NEWSPAPERS
3-4-08
BEIJING 2008
HUMAN RIGHTS

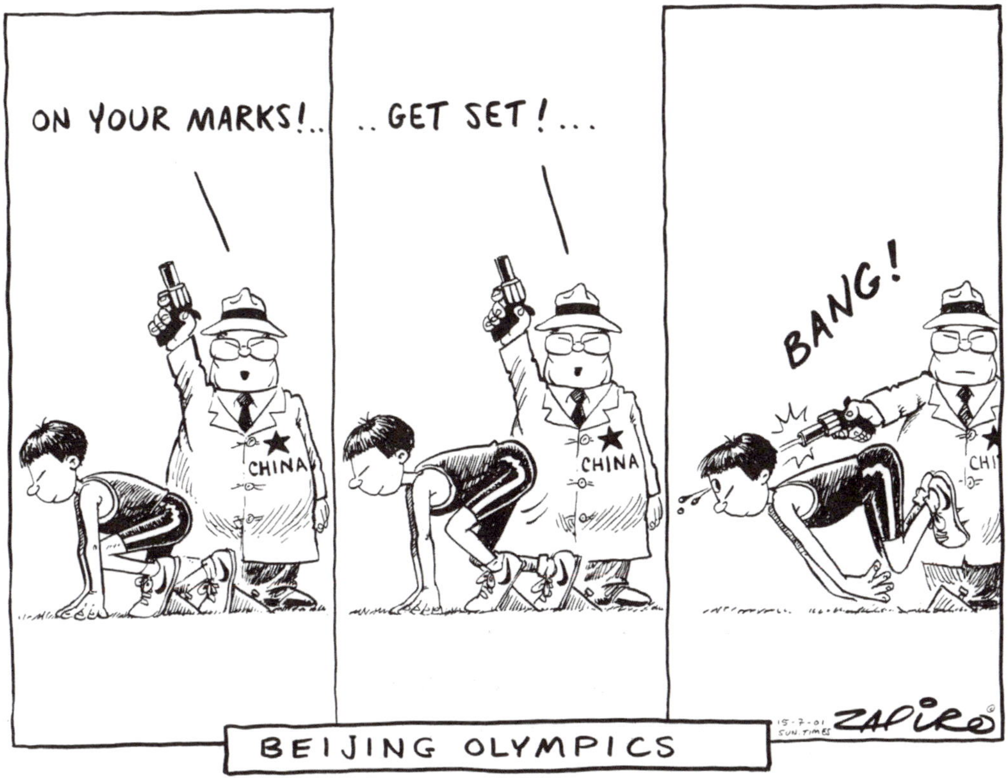
ON YOUR MARKS!..
CHINA
..GET SET!...
CHINA
BANG!
CHI
15-7-01 SUN. TIMES
ZAPIRO
BEIJING OLYMPICS

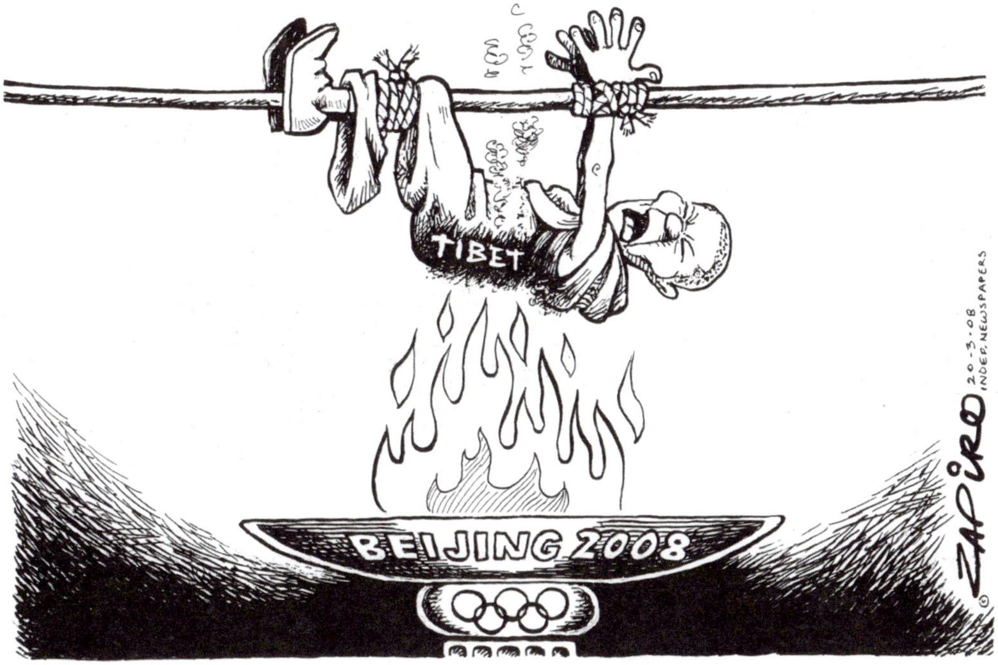
TIBET
BEIJING 2008
ZAPIRO
20-3-08 INDEP. NEWSPAPERS

2008

The Chinese hosted an administratively impeccable games, which were somewhat soulless until Usain Bolt struck and set new world records in the finals of both the 100m (even though he eased up before the finish) and the 200m (even though he ran into a headwind).

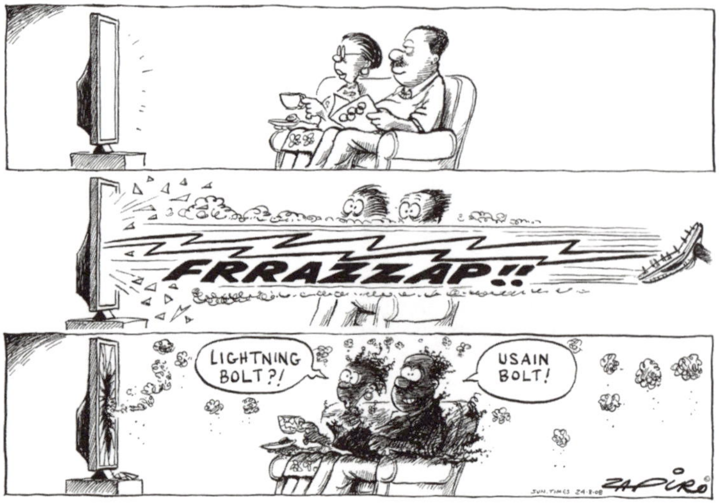
FRRAZZAP!!
LIGHTNING BOLT?!
USAIN BOLT!
ZAPIRO

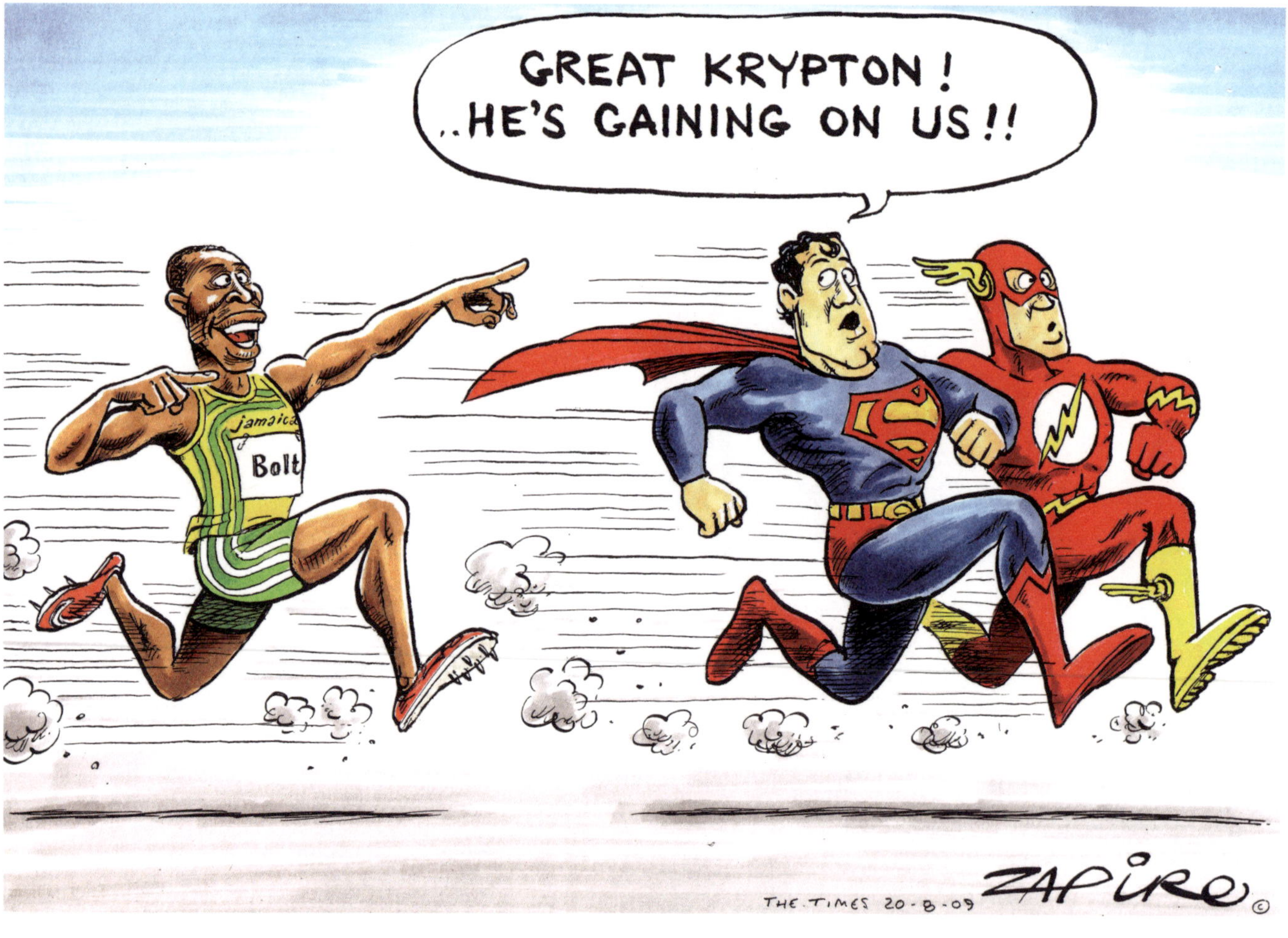
GREAT KRYPTON! ..HE'S GAINING ON US!!
jamaica
Bolt
THE TIMES 20-8-09
ZAPIRO©

The Beijing Games were another disappointment for Team SA with a solitary silver but, by 2009, we had finally found a new world beater on the track. However, almost as always with us, there were complications and politics. The 18-year-old Caster Semenya from Limpopo powered to victory in the 800m at the world championships in Berlin and was immediately the subject of rumour, gossip, testing and incompetent administration over her gender status.

2009

Semenya's case was appallingly mishandled by both Athletics SA, headed by its Loose-Cannon-in-Chief Leonard Chuene and the IAAF. Another even looser cannon, Julius Malema, did not miss a chance to racialise the entire episode.

The return home to OR Tambo of the bewildered Semenya was intensely politicised by Chuene, Malema and Winnie Madikizela-Mandela.

The hurt for Semenya deepened when highly personal biological details from an unverified IAAF test were shamefully revealed in an Australian newspaper before the athlete herself had been informed of them.

We were now one year away from the FIFA world cup, and the successful hosting of the Confederations Cup tournament was a big boost for the organisers and for Bafana who performed creditably against both Brazil and Spain.

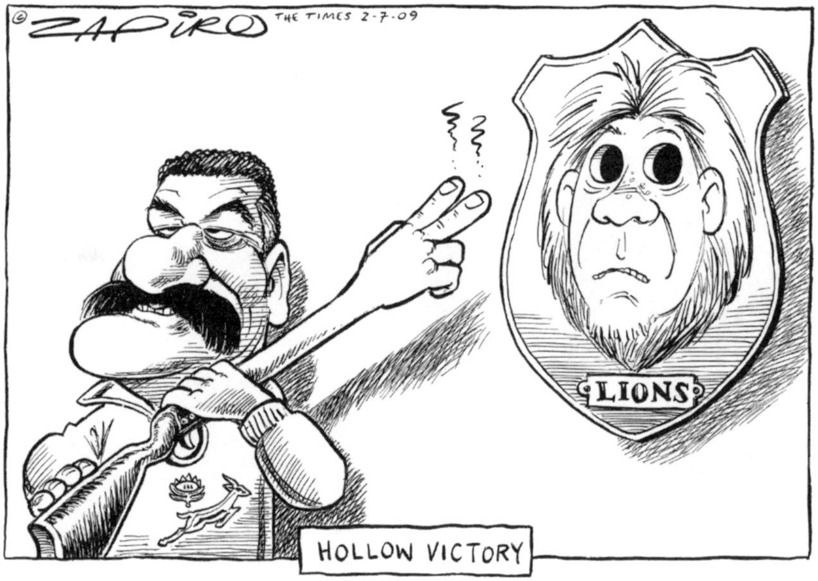
©ZAPIRO THE TIMES 2-7-09
LIONS
HOLLOW VICTORY

The South African rugby authorities in 2008 had provided us all with a bit of light relief (and Zapiro with a goldmine of material) by appointing the unconventional, and usually incomprehensible, Peter de Villiers as Springbok coach.

A dramatic series win in 2009 over the British & Irish Lions was marred by his comments dismissing eye-gouging; "If you are going to complain about every incident we might as well go to a ballet shop and all get tutus."

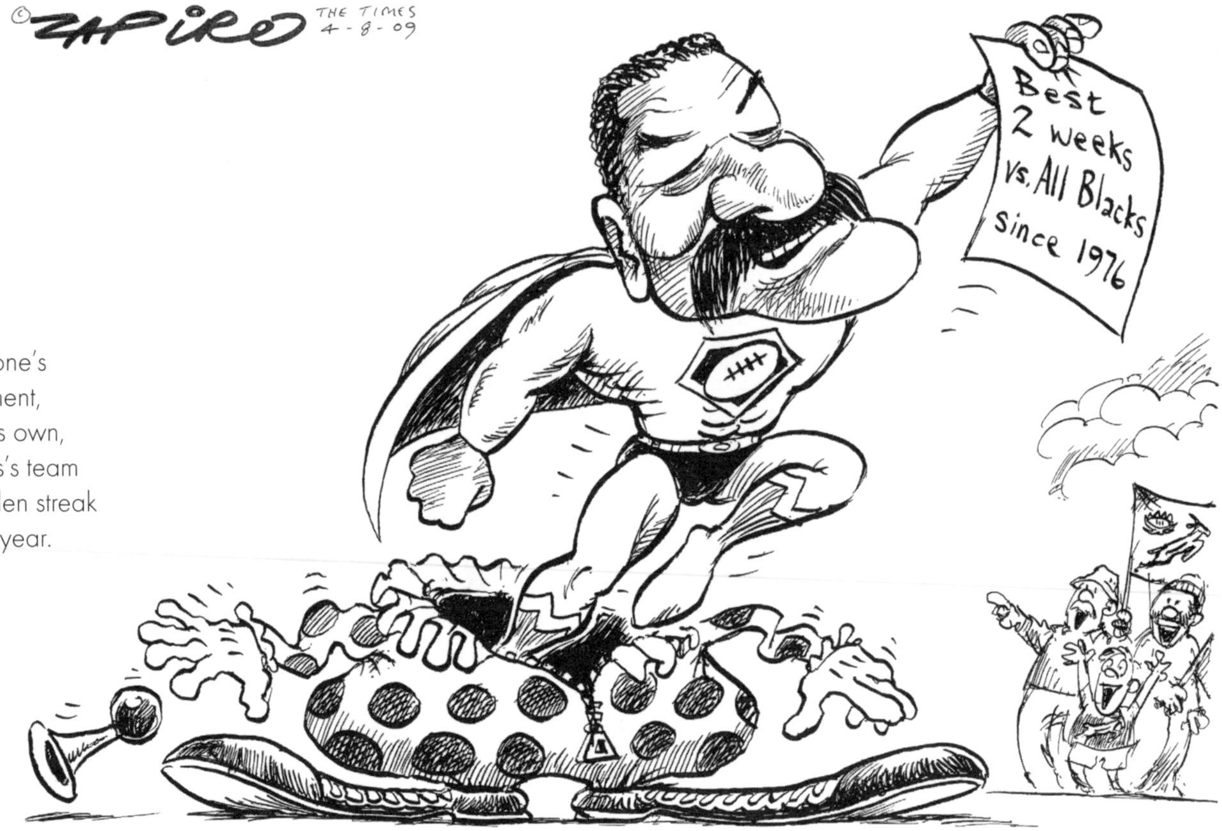
©ZAPIRO THE TIMES 4-8-09
Best 2 weeks vs. All Blacks since 1976

To everyone's astonishment, except his own, De Villiers's team hit a golden streak later that year.

It couldn't last, of course. The Springboks managed to find a new way to lose – thrown off track before the kick-off against France in Toulouse by an awful reggae version of the national anthem "sung", to the accompaniment of two mis-timing bongo drummers, by the previously unknown Ras Dumisani.

Bafana Bafana coach Parreira had gone back to Brazil to be with his sick wife and had persuaded a gullible SAFA to appoint his friend and compatriot, the linguistically challenged and under-qualified Joel Santana, to the coaching position in his place, with the usual ludicrously inflated salary.

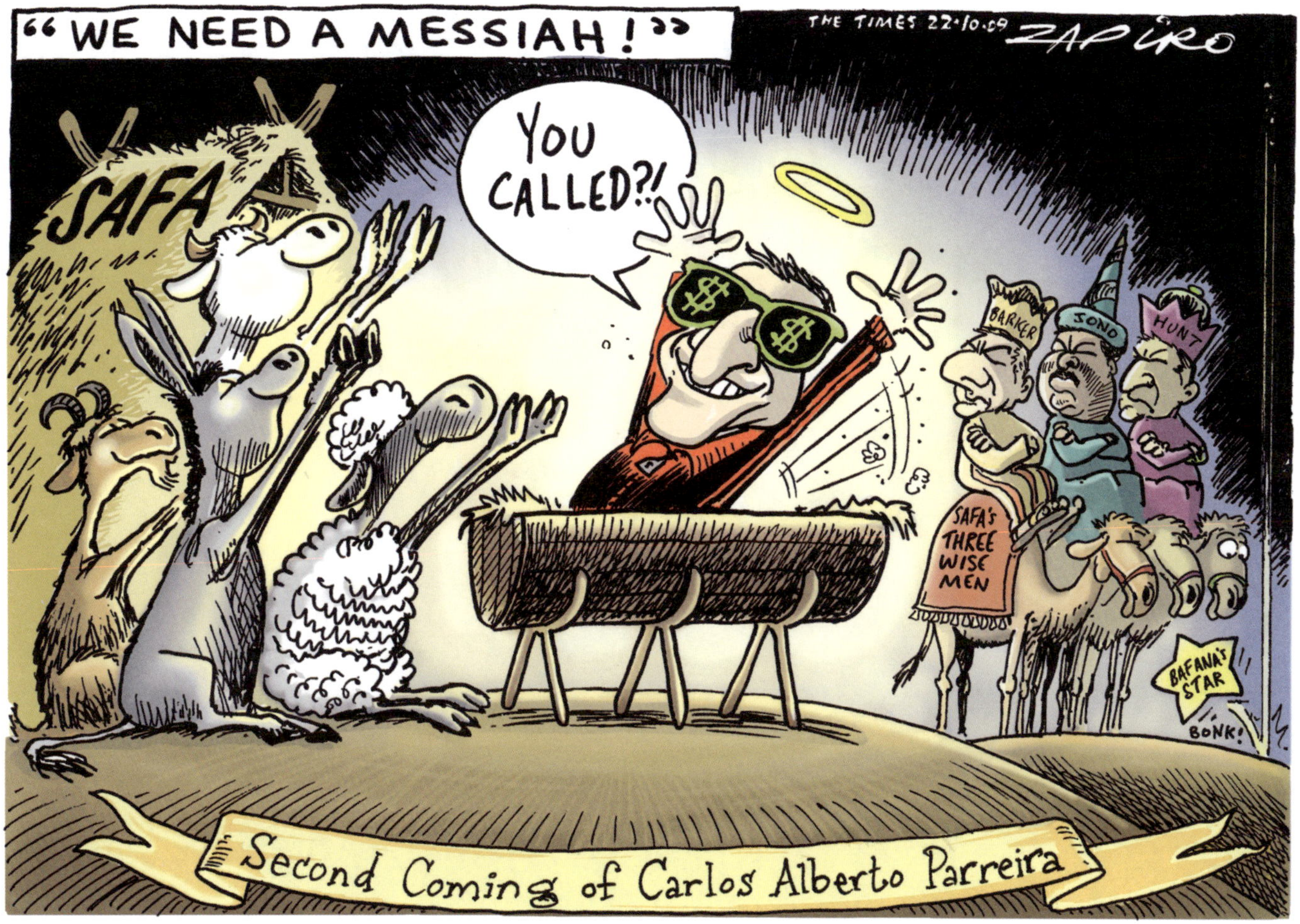
"WE NEED A MESSIAH!"
THE TIMES 22·10·09 ZAPIRO
YOU CALLED?!
SAFA
BARKER
SONO
HUNT
SAFA'S THREE WISE MEN
BAFANA'S STAR
BONK!
Second Coming of Carlos Alberto Parreira

The Santana era was brief and shambolic, even by SAFA standards, and Parreira, his wife now recovered, answered the call for a return to the cash-laden trough.

As for the cricketers, another early exit from an ICC event – this time at the 2010 World T20 in the Caribbean – saw an old theme re-emerge, sadly not for the last time.

Herschelle Gibbs then distracted everyone with an indiscreet autobiography, *To the Point*, which rocketed off the shelves. Herschelle's long-suffering school teachers are still recovering from hearing that he had produced any kind of book, let alone a bestseller.

The whole of 2010 was dominated by the world cup as the imperious Sepp Blatter became president of South Africa as well as of FIFA.

For all the grumbling about Septic Bladder, the vibe was good and we were ready for action, if not exactly bursting with optimism about Bafana's prospects.

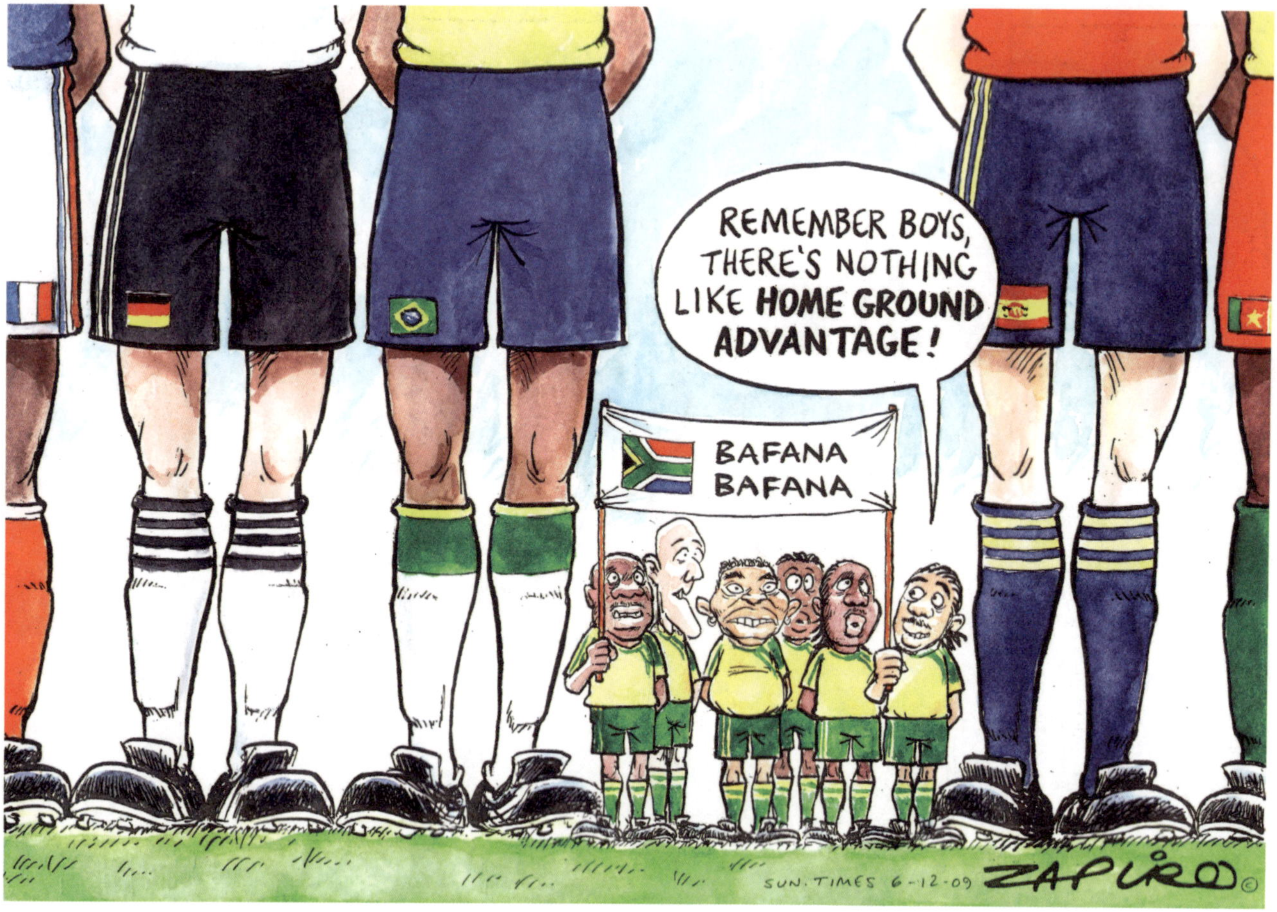
REMEMBER BOYS, THERE'S NOTHING LIKE HOME GROUND ADVANTAGE!
BAFANA BAFANA
SUN. TIMES 6-12-09
ZAPIRO ©

There were some niggling concerns around threats of industrial action ...

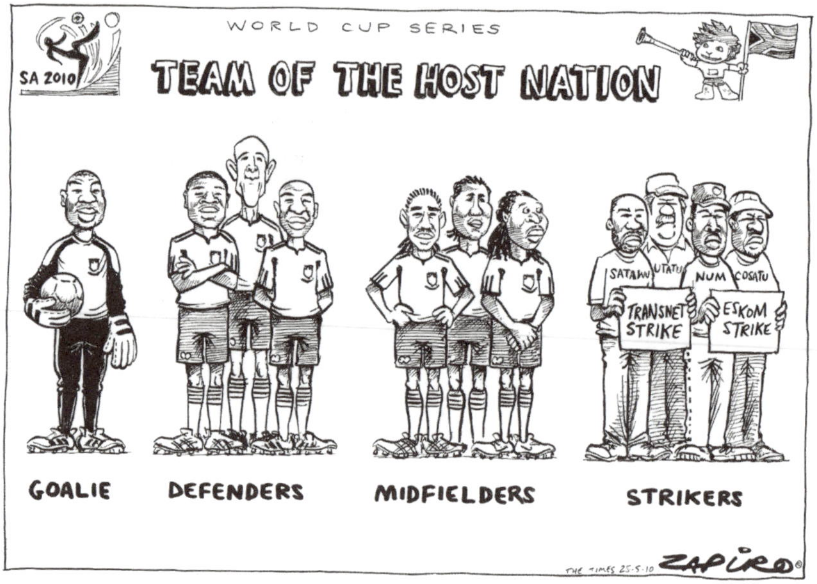
WORLD CUP SERIES
SA 2010
TEAM OF THE HOST NATION
SATAWU
UTATU
NUM
COSATU
TRANSNET STRIKE
ESKOM STRIKE
GOALIE
DEFENDERS
MIDFIELDERS
STRIKERS
THE TIMES 25-5-10
ZAPIRO ©

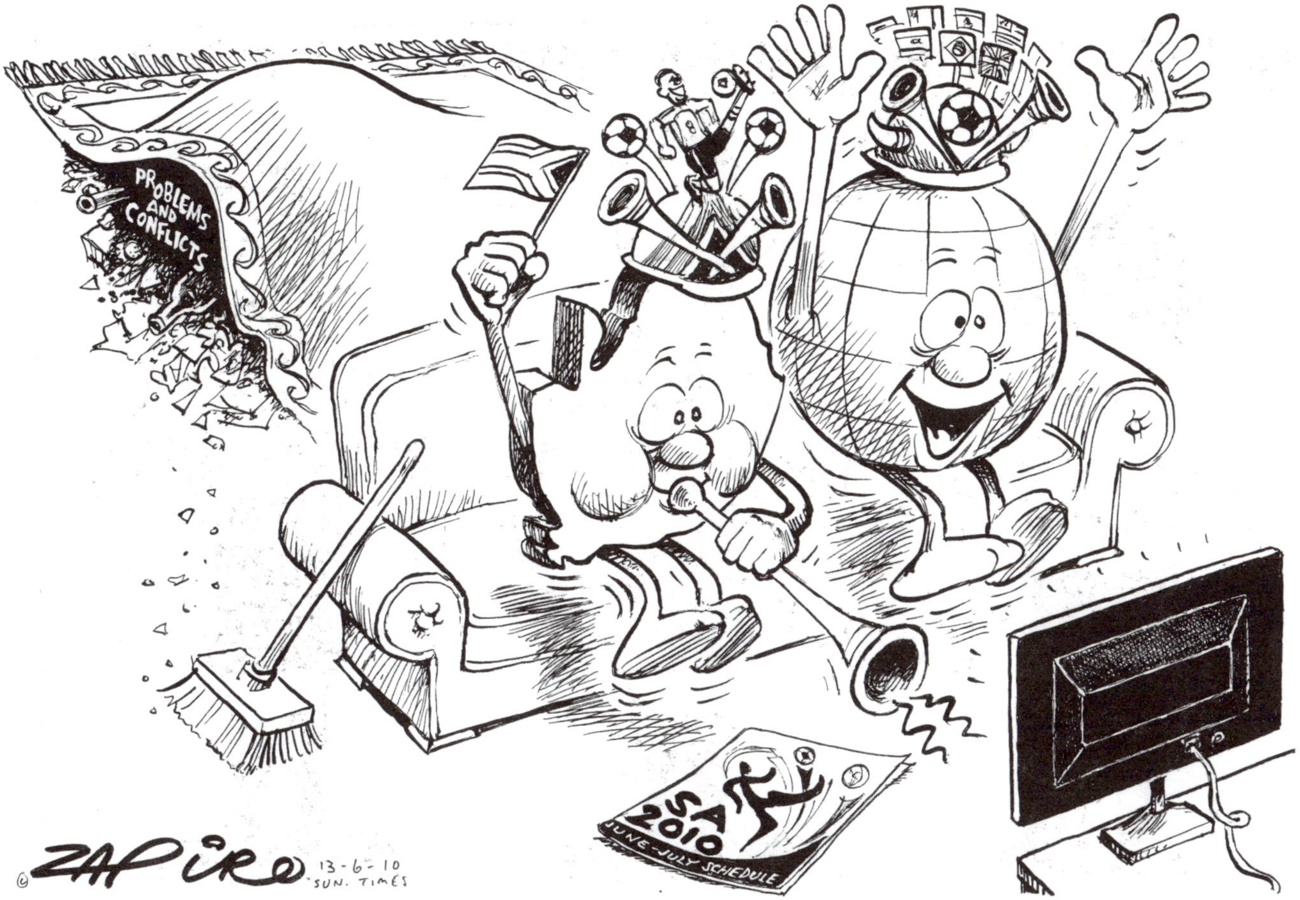
PROBLEMS AND CONFLICTS
SA 2010
JUNE-JULY SCHEDULE
ZAPIRO
13-6-10
SUN. TIMES

... but, once the tournament began, the nation was transformed and transfixed for five weeks.

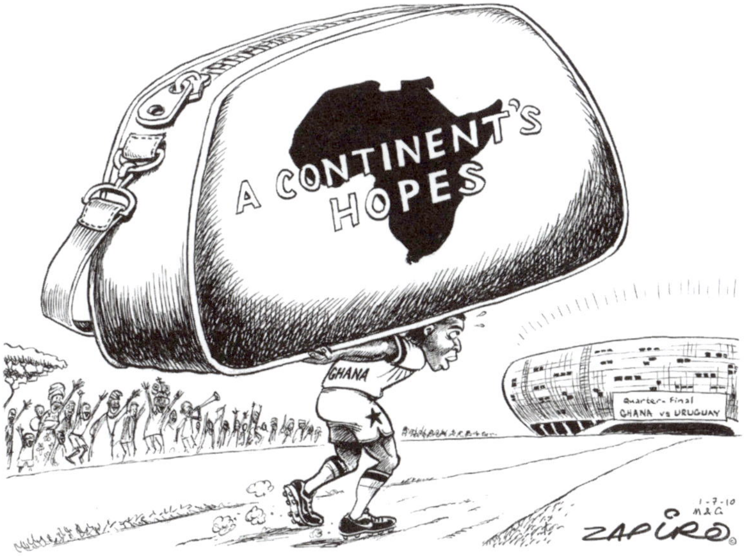
A CONTINENT'S HOPES
GHANA
Quarter-Final
GHANA vs URUGUAY
1-7-10
M&G
ZAPIRO

Bafana Bafana did reasonably well in holding Mexico and beating former champions France but became the first host country not to reach the knockout phases. The entire nation, and most of Africa, swung behind Ghana as they took on Uruguay in the quarter-finals.

2010

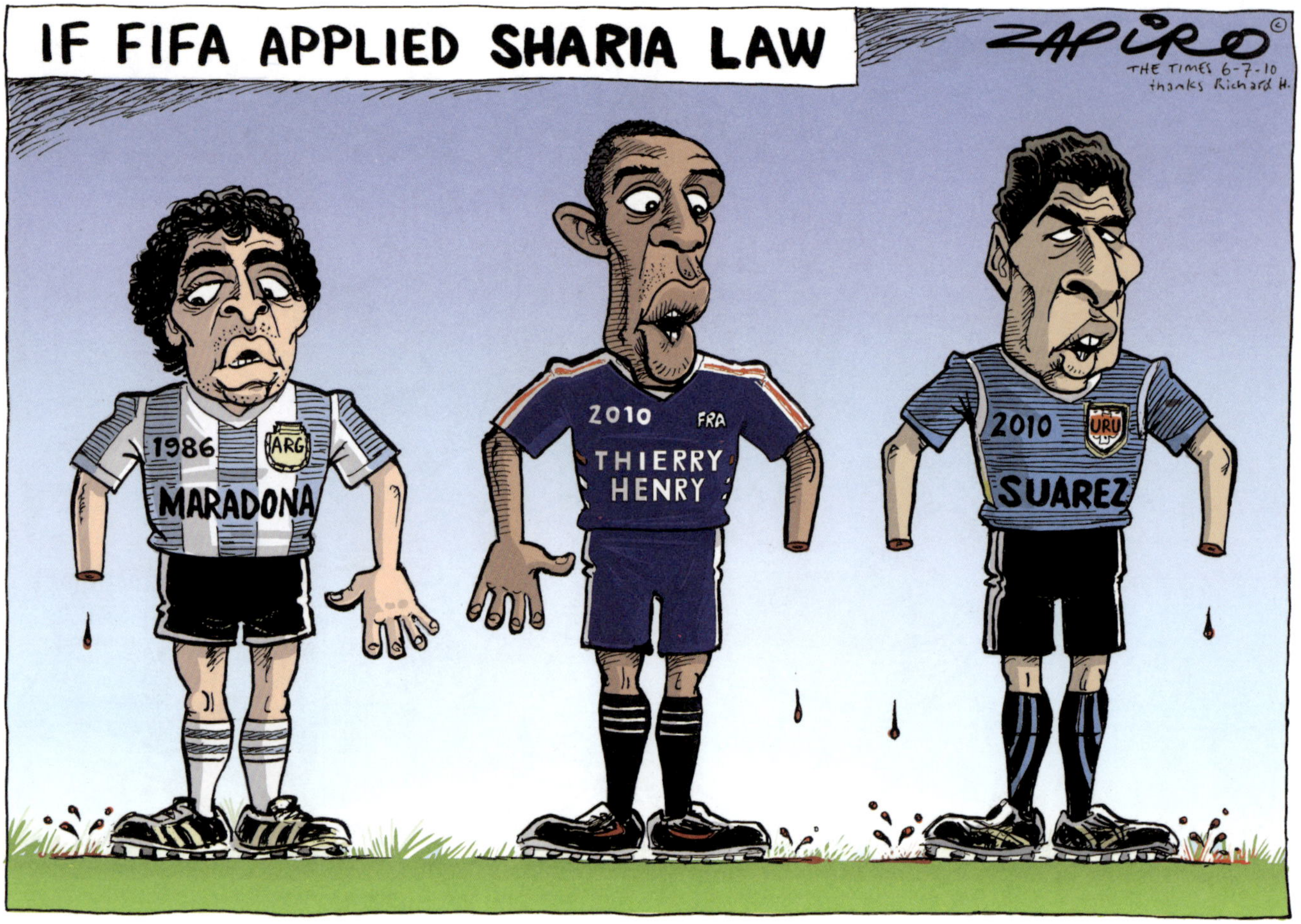
IF FIFA APPLIED SHARIA LAW
ZAPIRO
THE TIMES 6-7-10
thanks Richard H.
1986
ARG
MARADONA
2010
FRA
THIERRY
HENRY
2010
URU
SUAREZ

Ghana was cynically denied glory by the deliberate handball of Luis Suarez in the final minute. The Uruguayan entered a hall of shame which already included Diego Maradona, for his 'Hand of God' goal against England in 1986, and Thierry Henry, for his unpunished handball which earned France qualification for the 2010 finals over the Irish.

Events during the world cup – especially a Frank Lampard 'ghost goal' for England in Bloemfontein against the Germans – increased the pressure on FIFA to enter the 21st century.

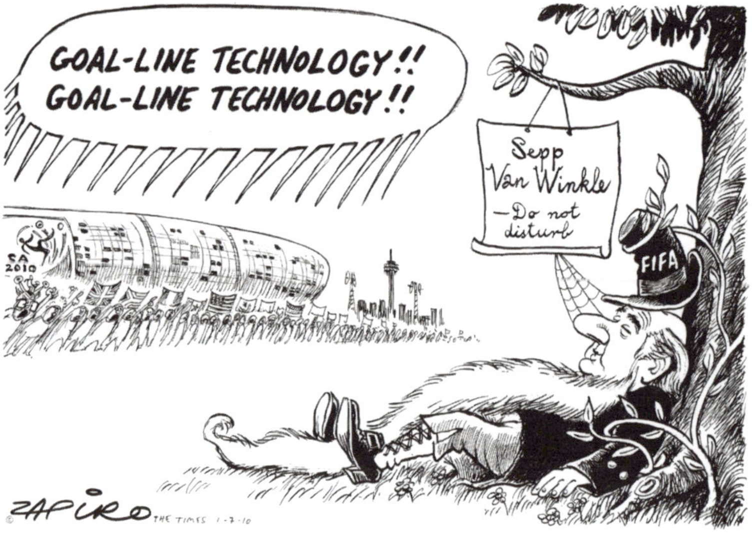
GOAL-LINE TECHNOLOGY!!
GOAL-LINE TECHNOLOGY!!
Sepp
Van Winkle
–Do not
disturb
FIFA
SA
2010
ZAPIRO THE TIMES 1-7-10

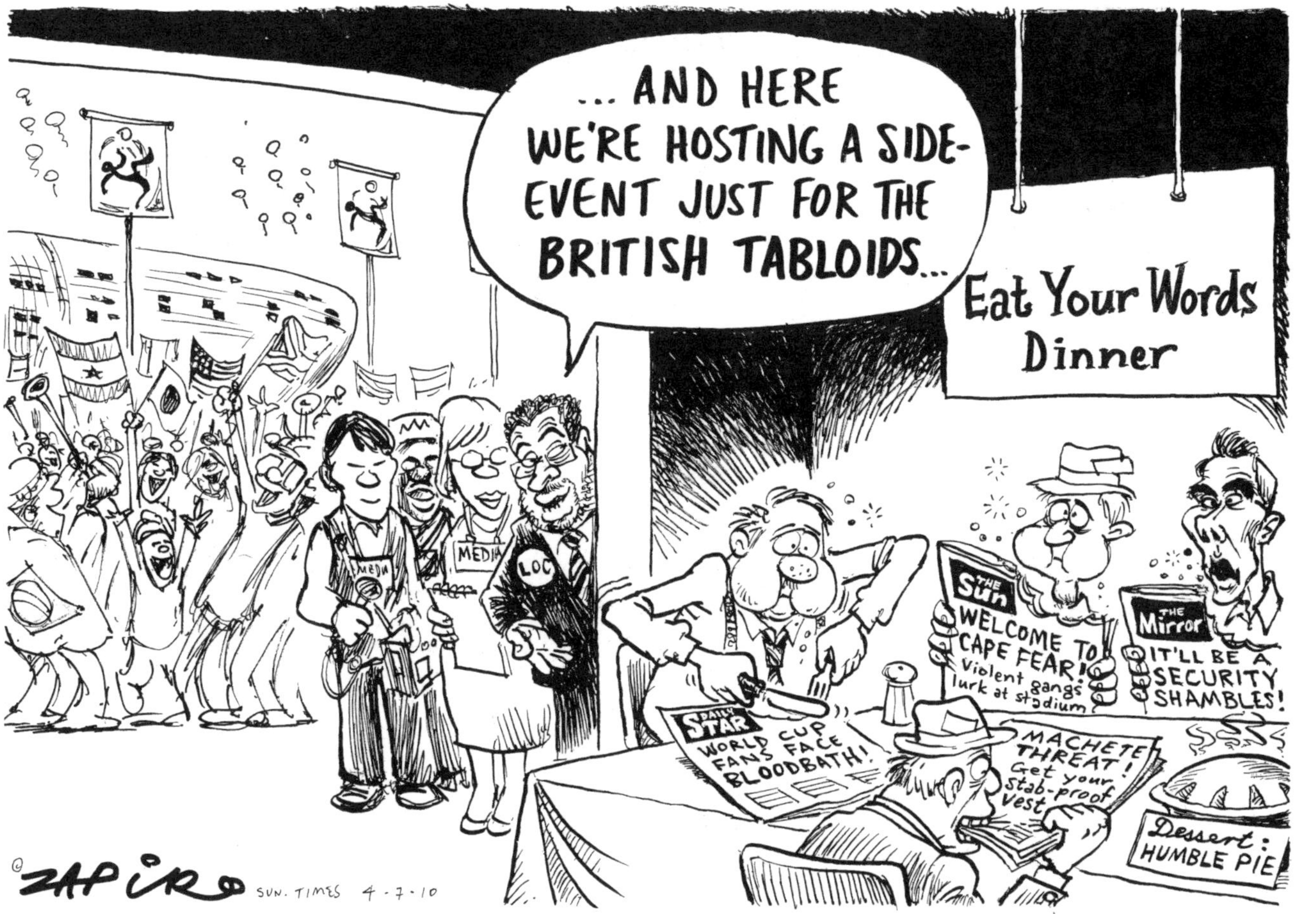
... AND HERE WE'RE HOSTING A SIDE-EVENT JUST FOR THE BRITISH TABLOIDS...
Eat Your Words Dinner
MEDIA
MEDIA
LOC
THE Sun
WELCOME TO CAPE FEAR! Violent gangs lurk at stadium
THE Mirror
IT'LL BE A SECURITY SHAMBLES!
DAILY STAR
WORLD CUP FANS FACE BLOODBATH!
MACHETE THREAT! Get your stab-proof vest
Dessert: HUMBLE PIE
©ZAPIRO SUN. TIMES 4-7-10

Spain ultimately lifted the cup but South Africa was the biggest winner with an exuberant and efficient hosting effort which proved the London tabloids spectacularly wrong.

The world cup left us with a surplus of strange, noisy plastic instruments and the tough challenge of returning to normal life.

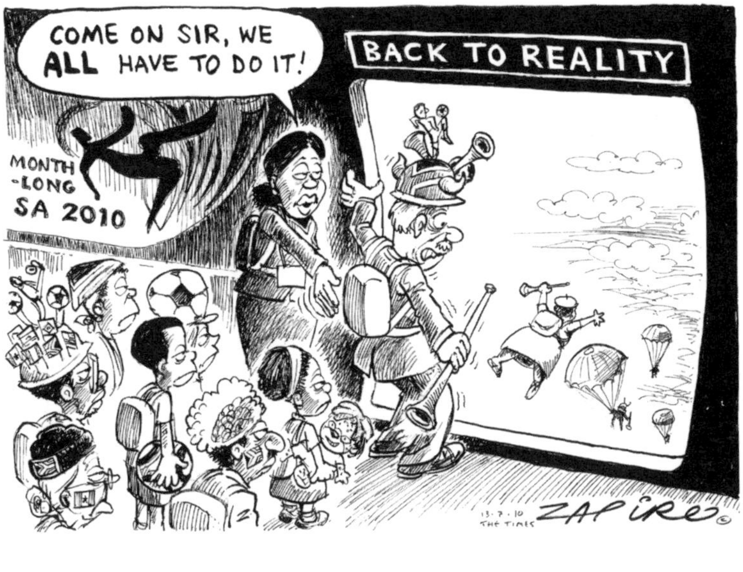
COME ON SIR, WE ALL HAVE TO DO IT!
BACK TO REALITY
MONTH-LONG SA 2010
13-7-10 THE TIMES ZAPIRO©

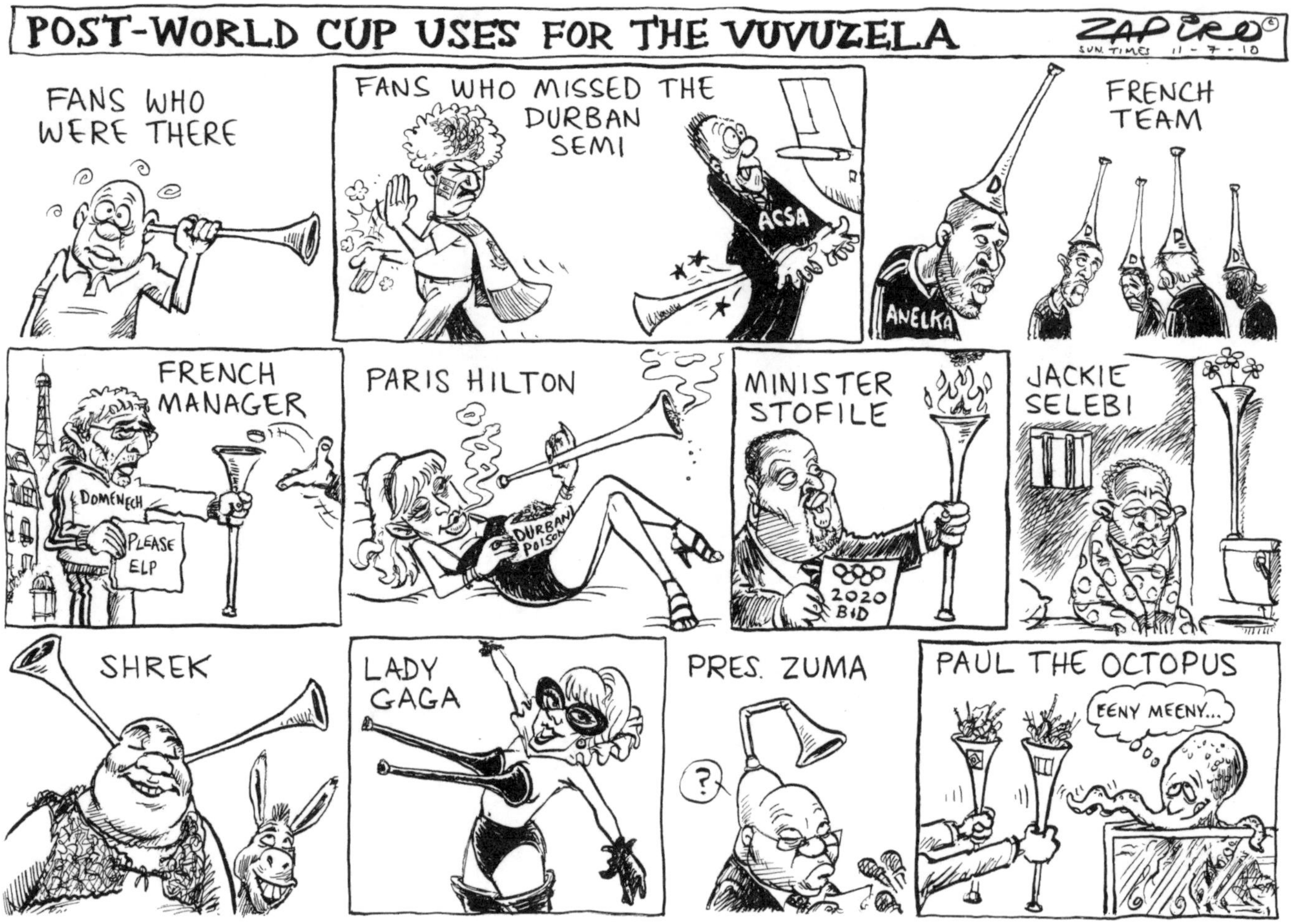
POST-WORLD CUP USES FOR THE VUVUZELA
ZAPIRO©
SUN. TIMES 11-7-10
FANS WHO WERE THERE
FANS WHO MISSED THE DURBAN SEMI
ACSA
FRENCH TEAM
ANELKA
FRENCH MANAGER
DOMENECH
PLEASE ELP
PARIS HILTON
DURBAN POISON
MINISTER STOFILE
2020 BID
JACKIE SELEBI
SHREK
LADY GAGA
PRES. ZUMA
?
PAUL THE OCTOPUS
EENY MEENY...

Sepp and his FIFA flunkeys scurried back to Zurich taking with them most of the profits and none of the problems. They had moved on to Russia & Qatar, the next desperate suitors for their favours.

The promised world cup payoff for South Africa was both remarkably small and remarkably slow in materialising.

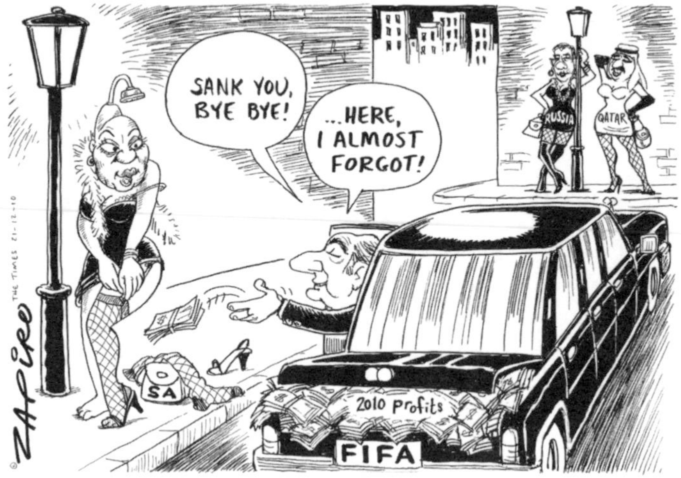
SANK YOU, BYE BYE!
...HERE, I ALMOST FORGOT!
RUSSIA
QATAR
SA
2010 Profits
FIFA
ZAPIRO
THE TIMES 21-12-10

Blatter's main legacy was a raging row over the future use of the expensive FIFA vanity projects which now littered the landscape.

2010

Back on the rugby field, Peter de Villiers continued to innocently wade into chaos, instinctively expressing his (and his team's) support for Blue Bulls player and murder-accused Bees Roux.

De Villiers, like Jake White before him, held fast to his belief that the number of test caps mattered most.

The 2011 RWC campaign came to a grinding halt in a quarter-final against the Australians. John Smit's team played the Wallabies off the park but spent the entire game on the wrong side of a controversial performance from Kiwi ref Bryce Lawrence who took out the Boks in a way that reminded Zapiro of a massively popular viral video of a mountain biker being flattened by a buck.

After the game, which effectively ended his Bok career, Div was his usual clear self.

De Villiers did indeed move on, no doubt to a career sometime in stand-up comedy, and the dour Heyneke Meyer era began. The cartooning community went into mourning.

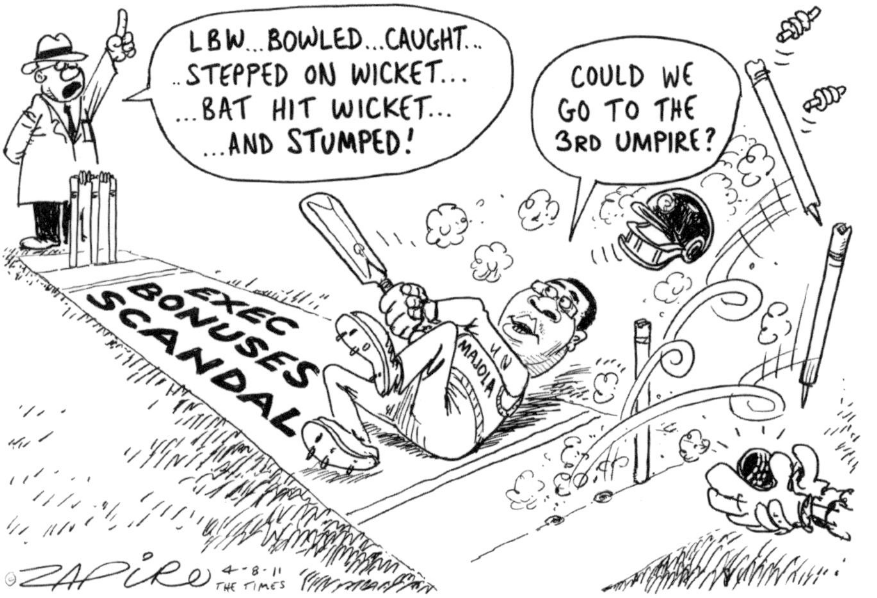
LBW... BOWLED... CAUGHT...
..STEPPED ON WICKET...
...BAT HIT WICKET...
...AND STUMPED!
COULD WE GO TO THE 3RD UMPIRE?
EXEC BONUSES SCANDAL
MAJOLA
ZAPIRO 4-8-11 THE TIMES

2011 was a rough year for cricket. There was more ICC world cup torment for the Proteas – this time at the hands of the Kiwis – and Cricket SA CEO Gerald Majola clung tenaciously to his position in the face of constant appeals for his departure after several damning reports and inquiries into a major governance scandal which arose in part from allegations by Cricket SA president Mtutuzeli Nyoka.

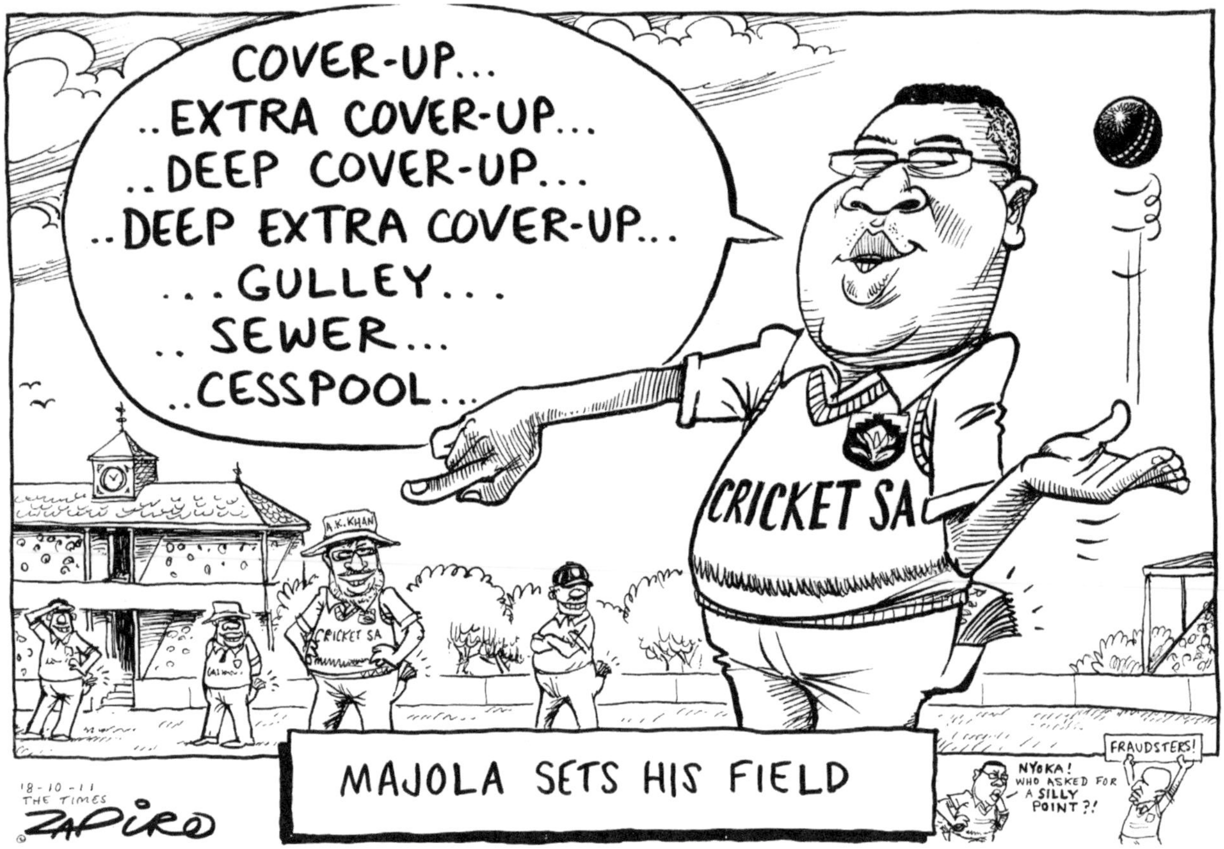
COVER-UP...
..EXTRA COVER-UP...
..DEEP COVER-UP...
..DEEP EXTRA COVER-UP...
...GULLEY...
..SEWER...
..CESSPOOL...
CRICKET SA
A.K.KHAN
CRICKET SA
MAJOLA SETS HIS FIELD
NYOKA! WHO ASKED FOR A SILLY POINT?!
FRAUDSTERS!
18-10-11 THE TIMES ZAPIRO

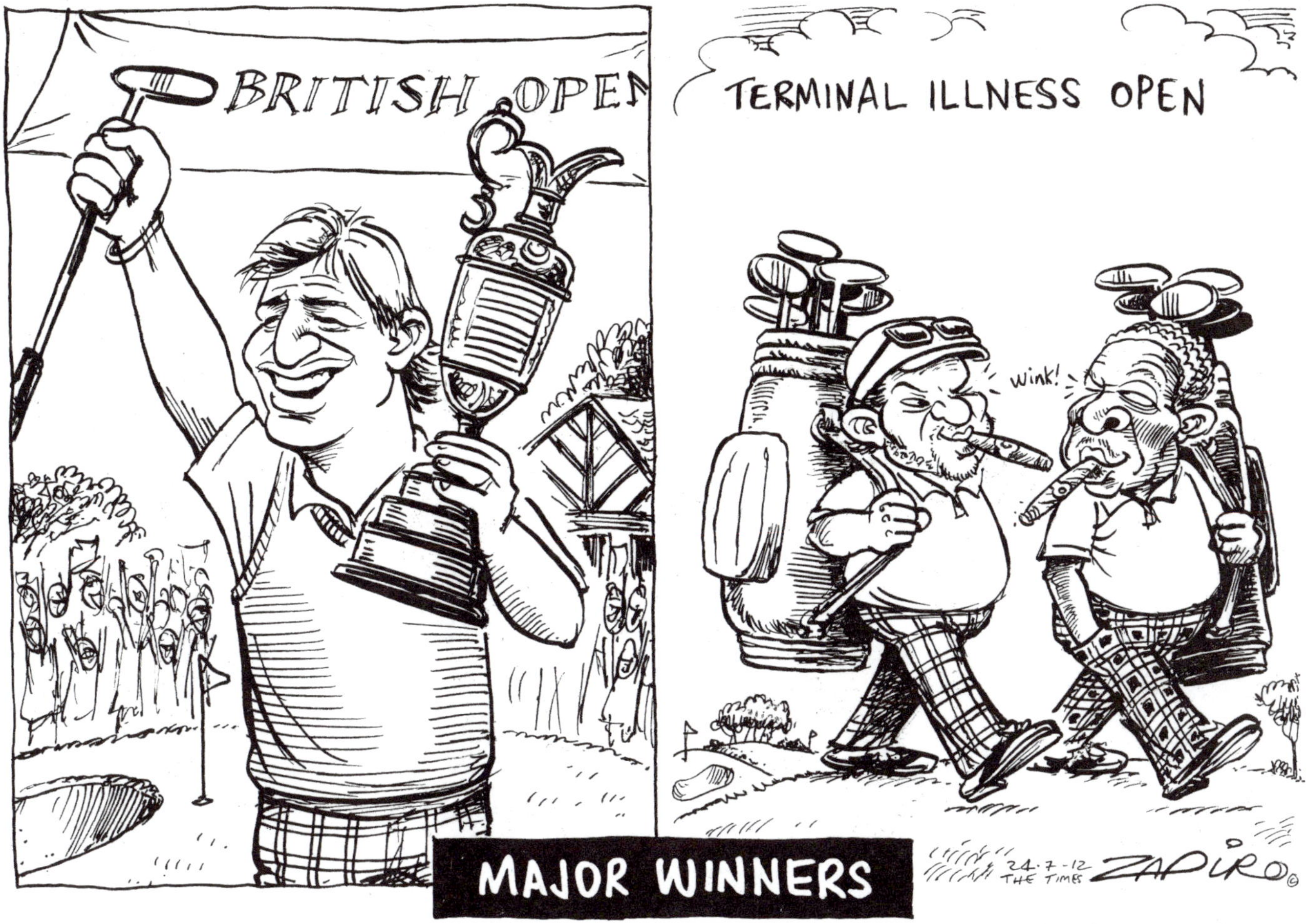
BRITISH OPEN
TERMINAL ILLNESS OPEN
Wink!
MAJOR WINNERS
24.7.12
THE TIMES
ZAPIRO ©

South Africa had consistently prospered on the world stage in golf. The new generation of Trevor Immelman, Louis Oosthuizen and Charl Schwartzel had all won majors but many had written off the ageing, belly-putting Ernie Els. The Big Easy came back with a bang in 2012 when he won the British Open at Royal Lytham.

Golf was also a preoccupation for the convicted fraudster and "terminally ill" parolee Schabir Shaik, who could have been joined in a round by another medically paroled convict, disgraced former national police commissioner Jackie Selebi.

2012

At the Euro 2012 soccer tournament the quarter-final in Gdañsk between Greece and Germany was played against the grim backdrop of a huge monetary crisis in which Greek prime minister Antonis Samaras desperately needed the reluctant German Chancellor Angela Merkel to bail out his impoverished nation. The footballing fortunes reflected the fiscal ones - Germany won 4-2.

Post-world cup, Bafana Bafana turned to Pitso Mosimane as coach. He didn't read the rules properly and we went out of the AFCON qualifiers after manically and erroneously celebrating a lame draw at home to Sierra Leone. Steve Komphela replaced Mosimane ... but not for long.

Gordon Igesund, a four-time PSL winner and owner of many suits, was finally handed the job which many felt should have been his years ago. He had little time to prepare his side for a home AFCON in 2013.

The London 2012 Olympics were a raging success on the couch and in the water.

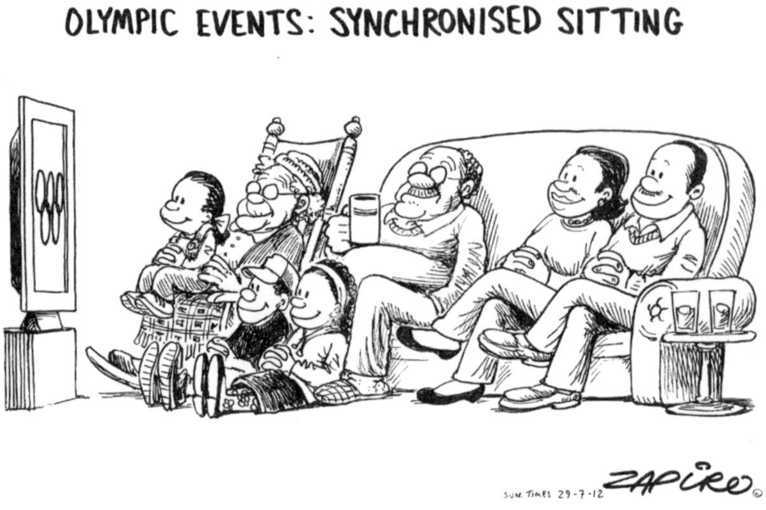
OLYMPIC EVENTS: SYNCHRONISED SITTING
SUN. TIMES 29-7-12
ZAPIRO

Cameron van der Burgh won the nation's first gold in eight years when he took the 100m breast-stroke.

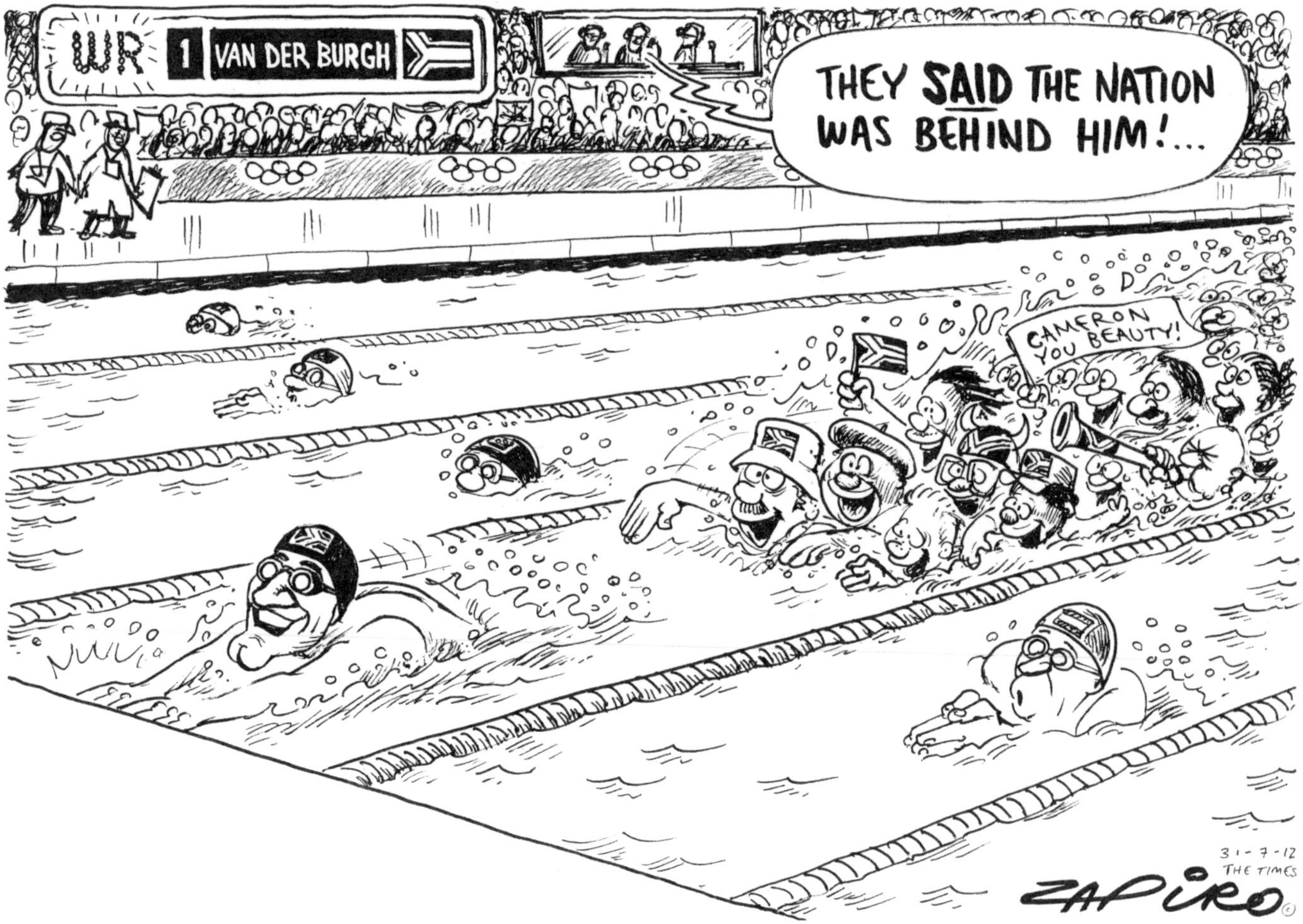
WR
1
VAN DER BURGH
THEY SAID THE NATION WAS BEHIND HIM!...
CAMERON YOU BEAUTY!
31-7-12
THE TIMES
ZAPIRO

Two days later, Chad le Clos got his finger-tips past Olympic legend Michael Phelps on the final stroke to win gold in the 200m butterfly.

These performances gave the lie to claims being made from the dock in the interminable Boeremag trial in Pretoria.

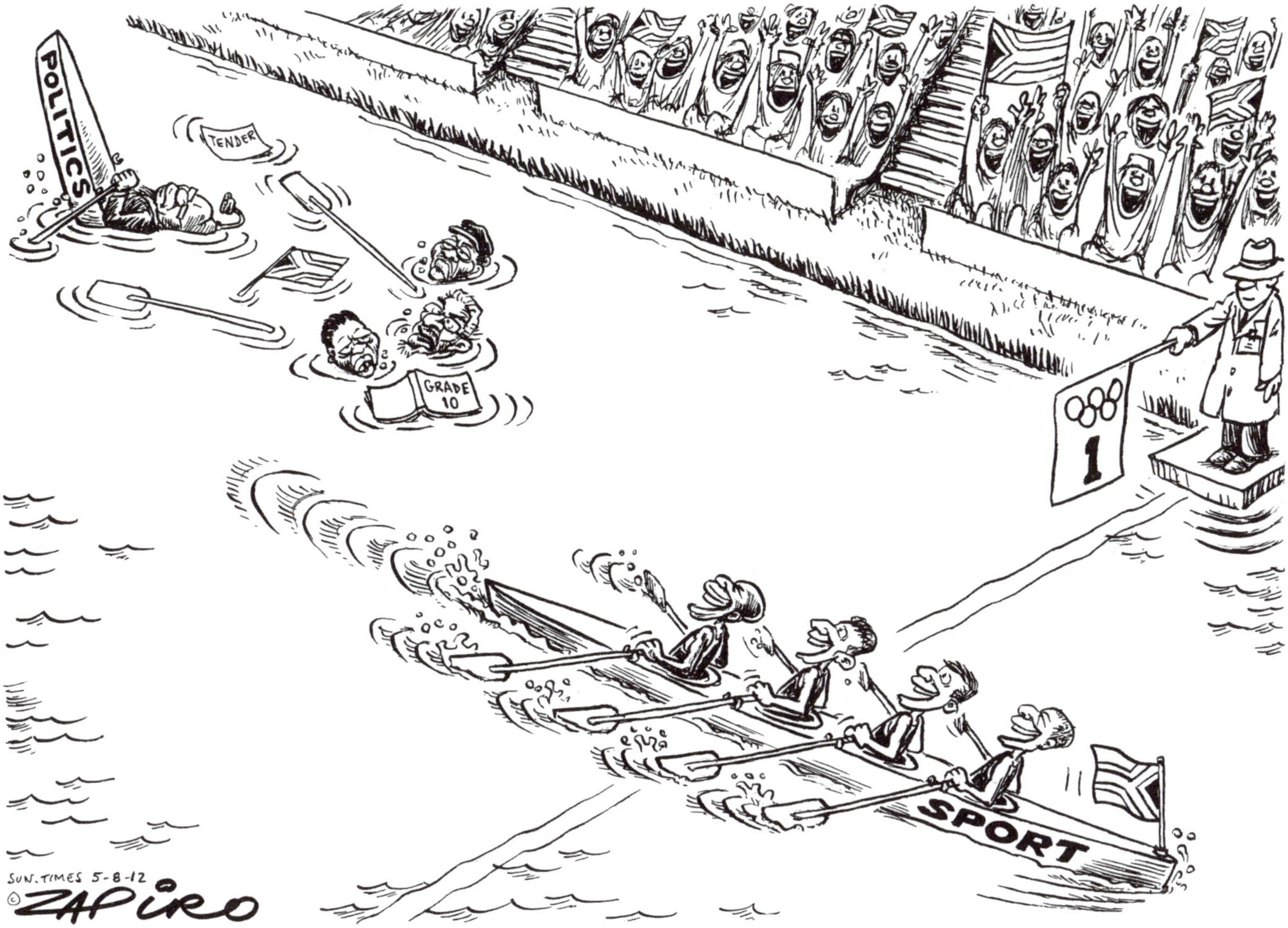
POLITICS
TENDER
GRADE 10
1
SPORT
SUN.TIMES 5-8-12
© ZAPIRO

There had been a degree of expectation around Van der Burgh and Le Clos but there was none around the lightweight men's four in the rowing. Sizwe Ndlovu, James Thomson, Matthew Brittain and John Smith defied logic, powerful opposition and the nation's haphazard politics to claim an astonishing gold medal.

Blade Runner Oscar Pistorius became the first track and field athlete to compete in both the Olympics and the Paralympics. His star was to fall catastrophically the following year but he bestrode these games as one of its biggest names.

The entire South African Paralympian team once again performed creditably and the growing significance (and television ratings) of the Paralympics changed perceptions of the whole Olympic concept.

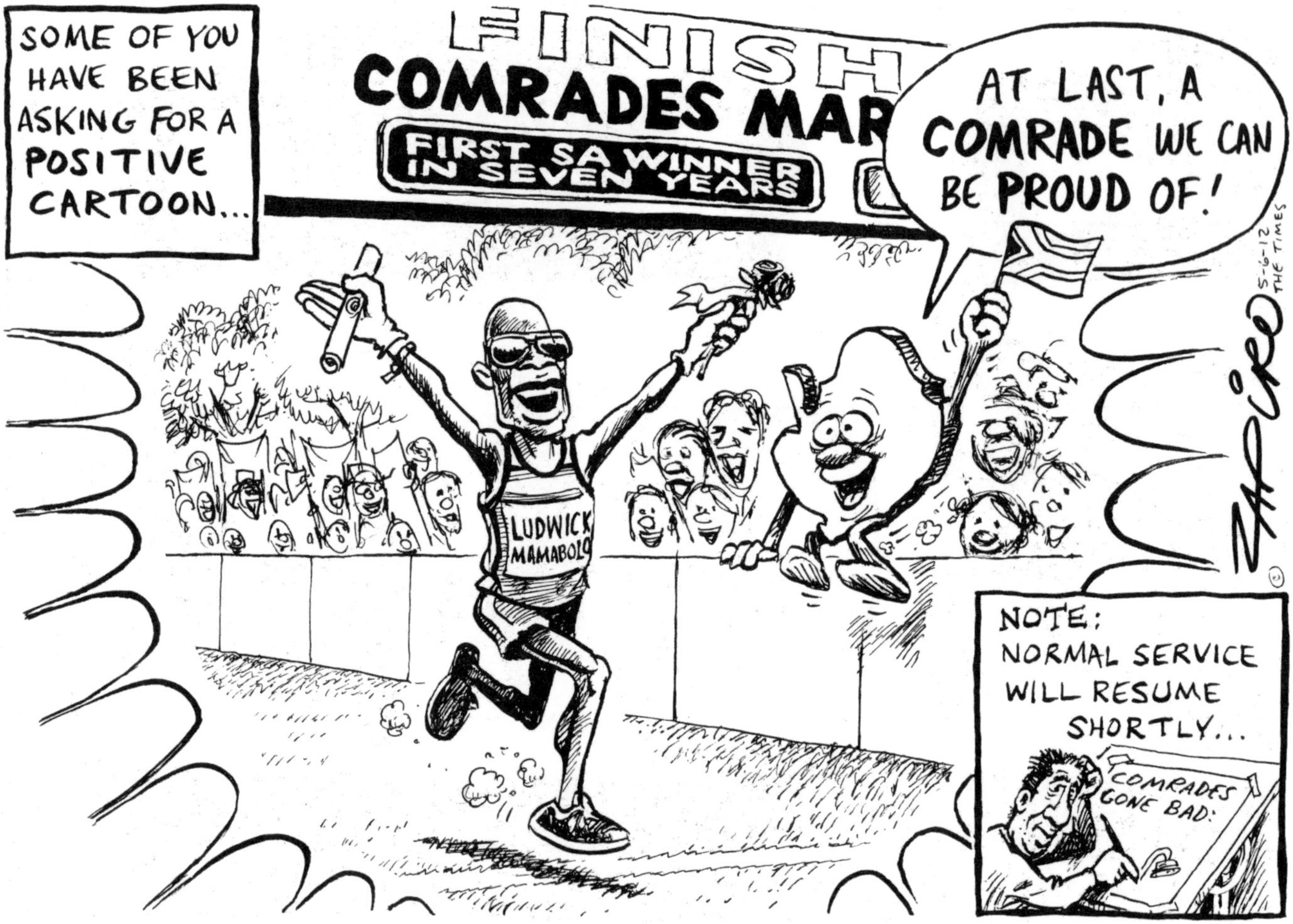
SOME OF YOU HAVE BEEN ASKING FOR A POSITIVE CARTOON...
FINISH
COMRADES MAR
FIRST SA WINNER IN SEVEN YEARS
AT LAST, A COMRADE WE CAN BE PROUD OF!
LUDWICK MAMABOLO
5-6-12 THE TIMES
ZAPIRO
NOTE: NORMAL SERVICE WILL RESUME SHORTLY...
COMRADES GONE BAD:

The ANC comrades in power were often disappointing the nation but the Comrades on the road had always inspired, except for the lack of recent local winners. The women's race was dominated by interchangeable Russian twins while Zimbabweans and Russians had ruled the men's event for six years. Ludwick Mamabolo from Limpopo changed all that with a great down run to Durban.

Zapiro's side panel proved remarkably prophetic. Two weeks after the race it was reported that Mamabolo had tested positive for a banned substance.

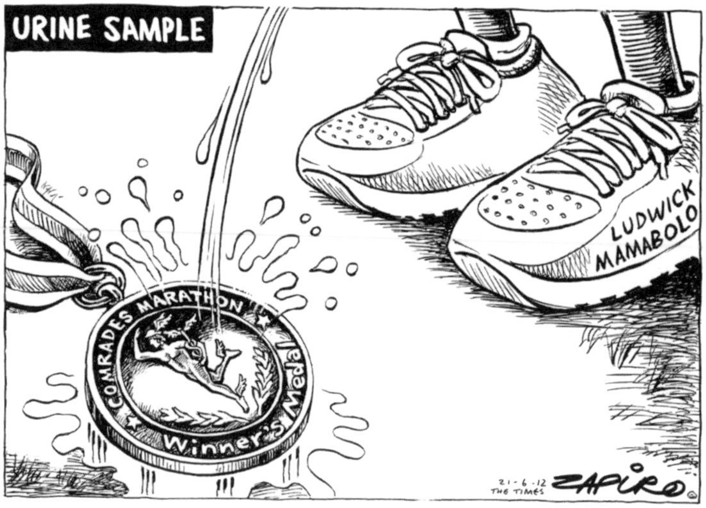
URINE SAMPLE
LUDWICK MAMABOLO
COMRADES MARATHON
Winner's Medal
21-6-12 THE TIMES
ZAPIRO

Speaking of drugs, Lance Armstrong finally caved in and admitted that he had cheated during each of his seven Tour de France wins, although Lance told Oprah he wasn't actually cheating; "it was levelling the playing field".

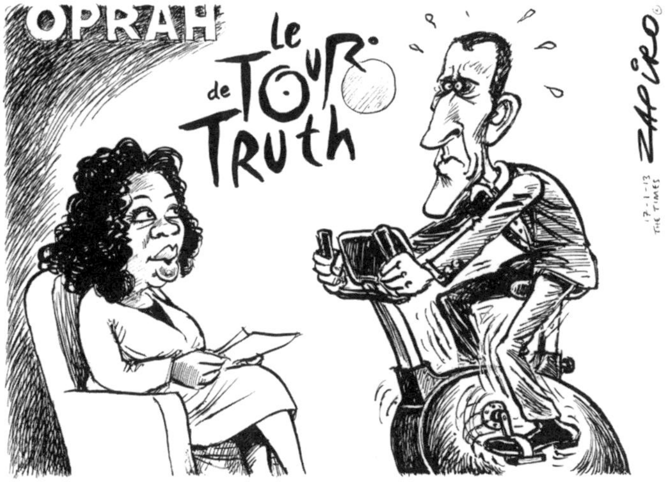
OPRAH
le de TOUR TRUTH
ZAPIRO
17-1-13 THE TIMES

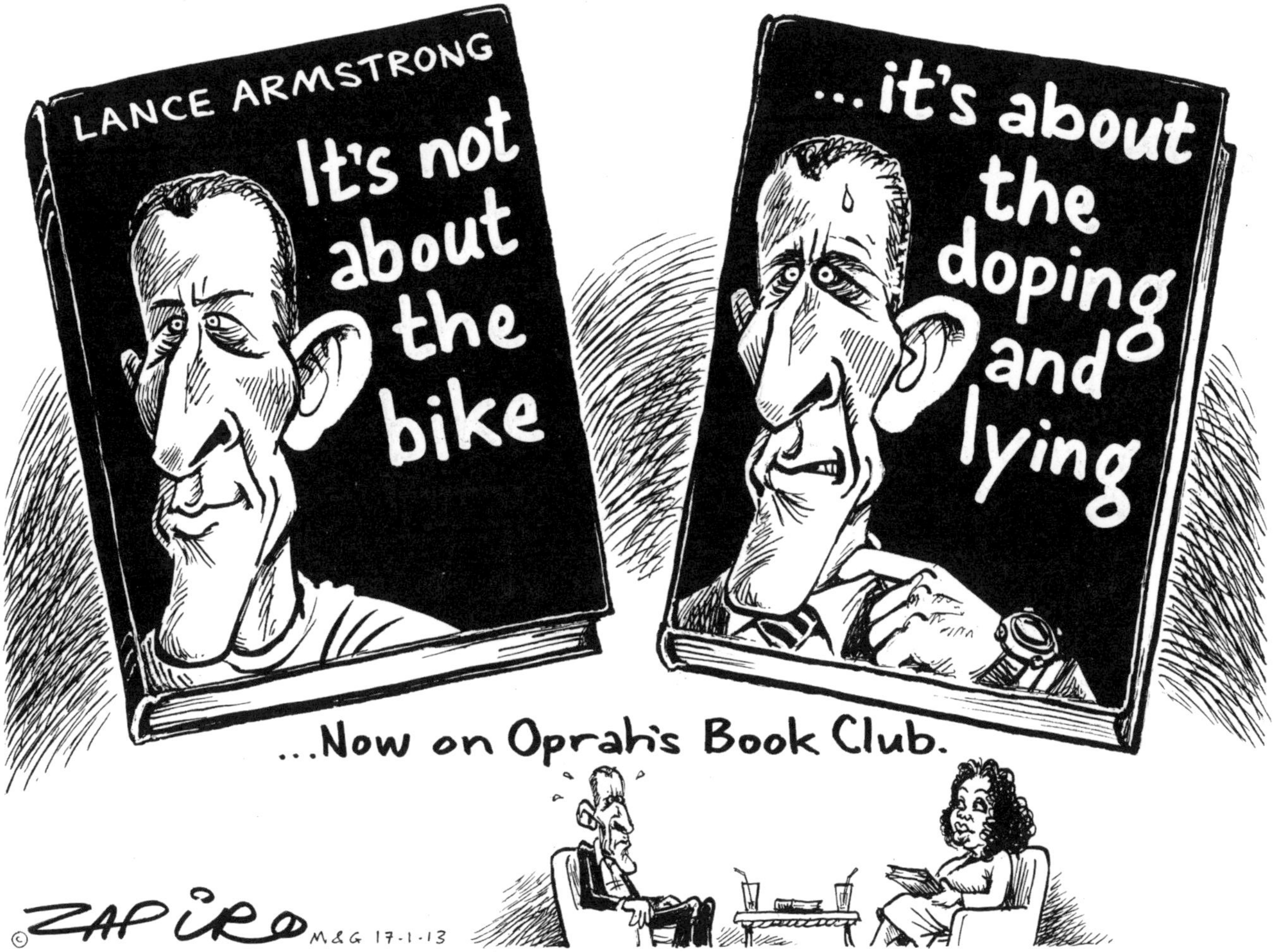
LANCE ARMSTRONG
It's not about the bike
...it's about the doping and lying
...Now on Oprah's Book Club.
© ZAPIRO M&G 17-1-13

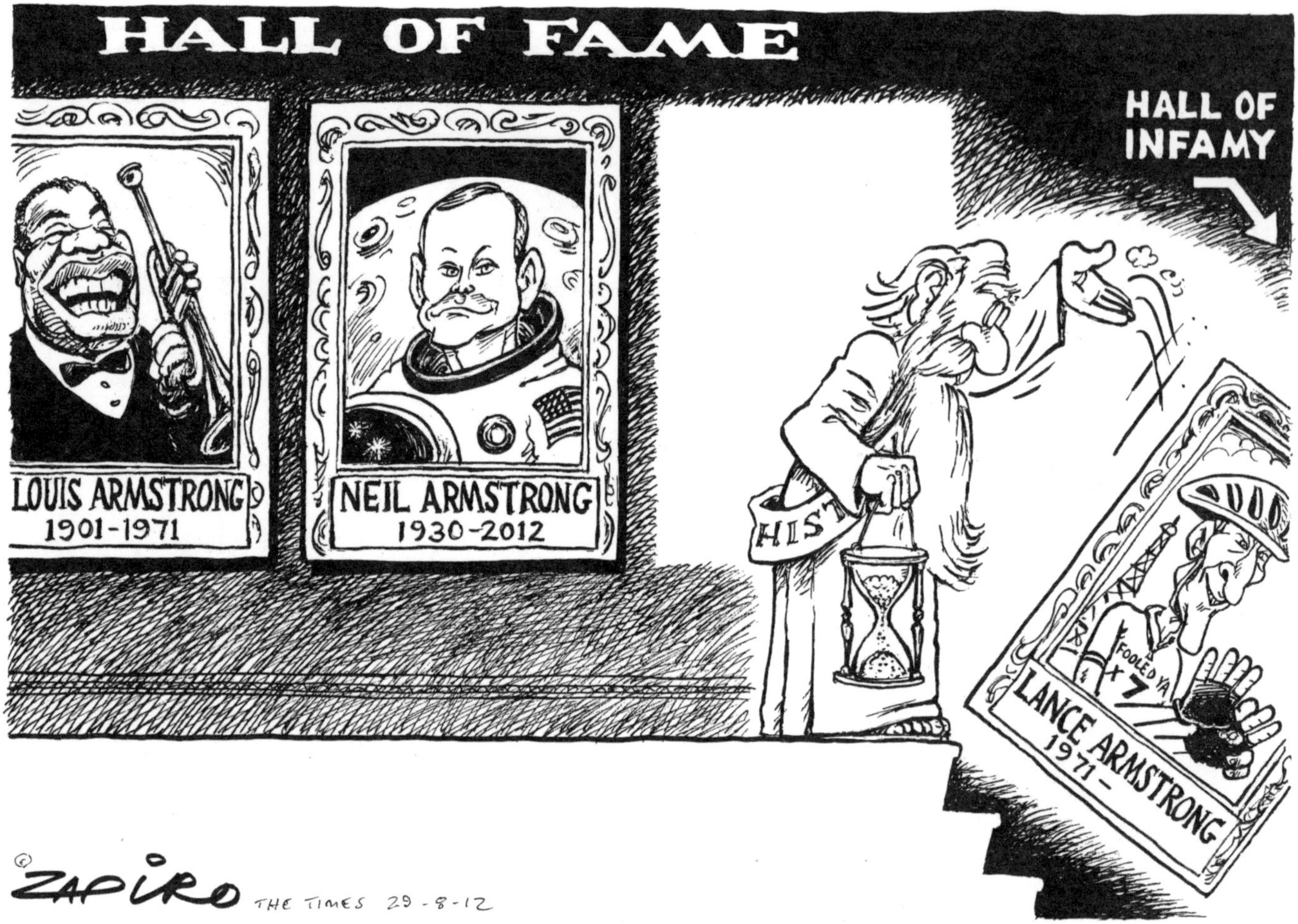
HALL OF FAME
HALL OF INFAMY
LOUIS ARMSTRONG
1901-1971
NEIL ARMSTRONG
1930-2012
HIST
FOOLED YA
×7
LANCE ARMSTRONG
1971-
© ZAPIRO THE TIMES 29-8-12

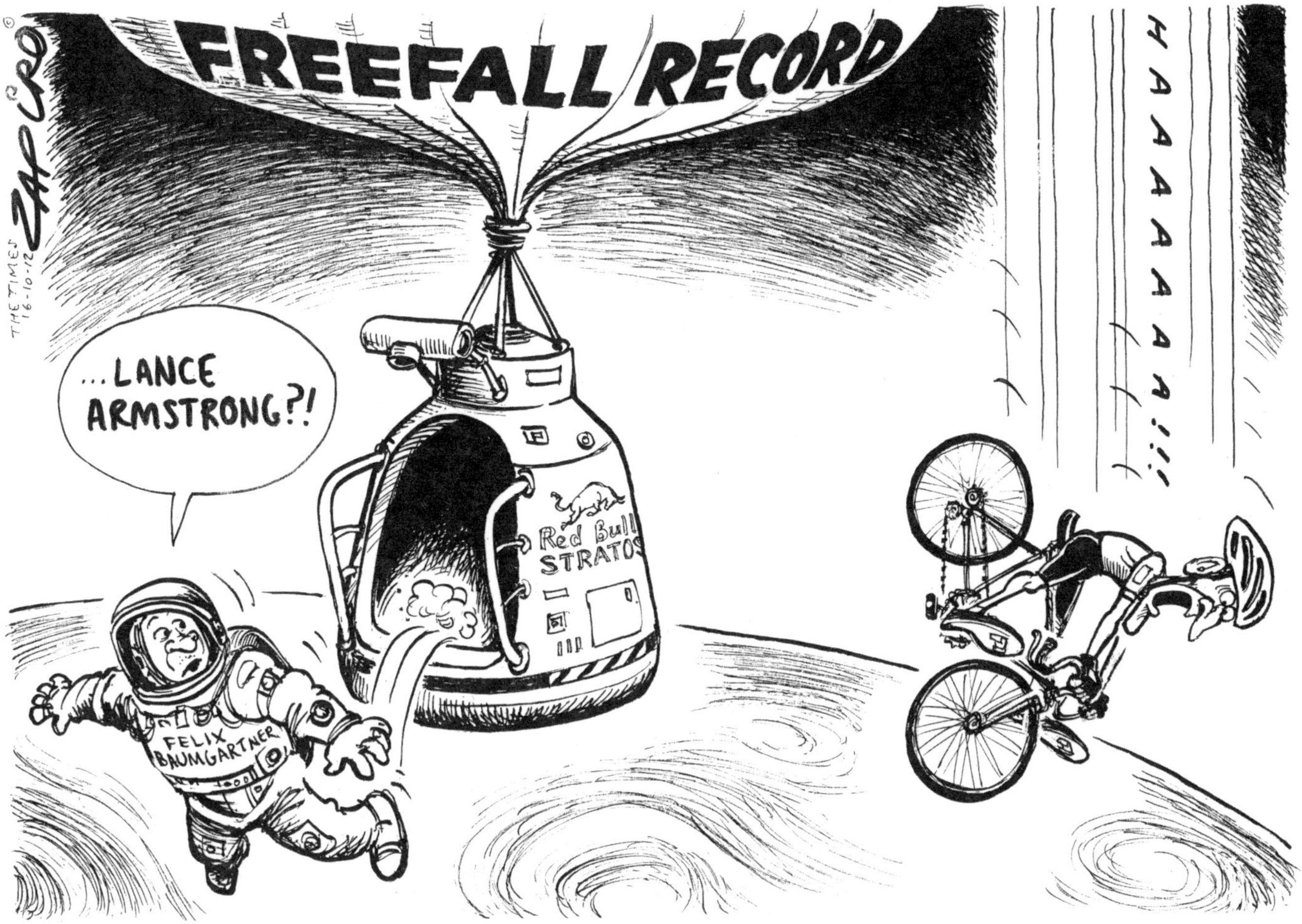
FREEFALL RECORD
ZAPIRO ©
THE TIMES 16-10-12
...LANCE ARMSTRONG?!
Red Bull STRATOS
FELIX BAUMGARTNER
AAAAAAAAAA!!!

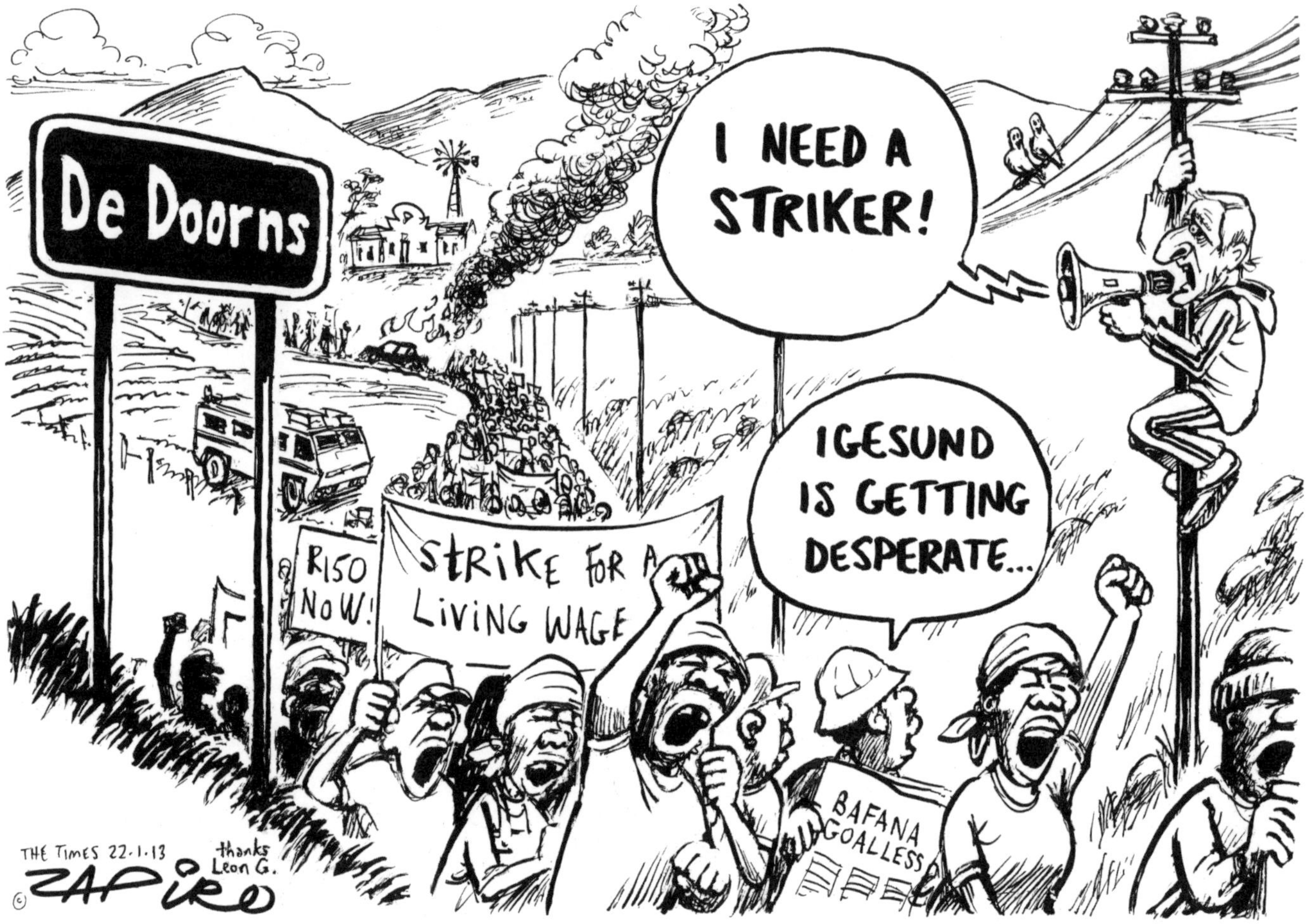
De Doorns
I NEED A STRIKER!
IGESUND IS GETTING DESPERATE...
R150 NOW!
STRIKE FOR A LIVING WAGE
BAFANA GOALLESS
THE TIMES 22.1.13
thanks Leon G.
ZAPIRO

For Bafana Bafana, AFCON on home soil loomed and the coach was looking everywhere for someone who could score a goal.

The competing finalists arrived to the backdrop of more serious matters than football – a French military intervention in the Malian civil war.

Ultimately it was Mali who knocked Bafana Bafana out of the tournament on penalties in the quarter-finals but the fact that the team managed to score five goals in four matches was cause for national celebration.

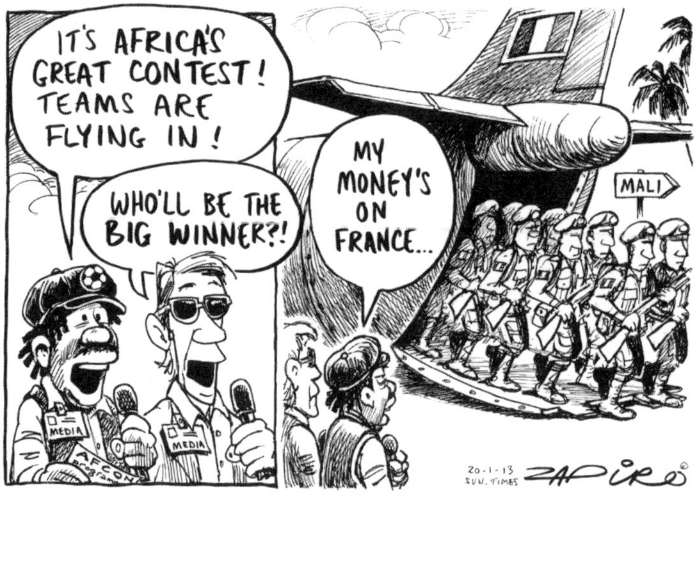
IT'S AFRICA'S GREAT CONTEST! TEAMS ARE FLYING IN!
WHO'LL BE THE BIG WINNER?!
MY MONEY'S ON FRANCE...
MALI
MEDIA
MEDIA
AFCON
20-1-13 SUN. TIMES
ZAPIRO

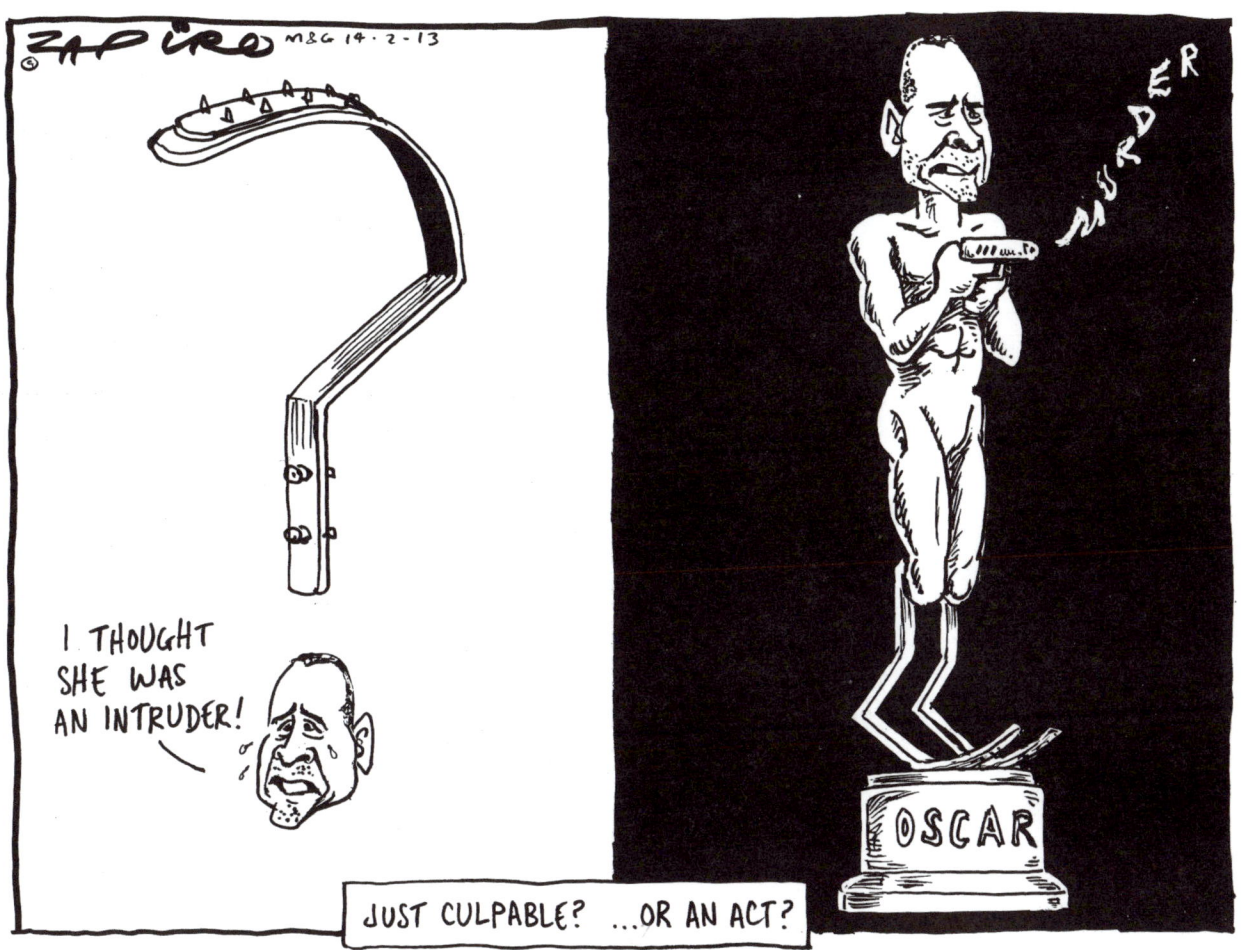

A cause for national shock and shame was the Valentine's Day 2013 arrest of Oscar Pistorius on a charge of premeditatedly murdering his girlfriend Reeva Steenkamp.

Yet another local sporting hero had bitten the red dust of Southern Africa.

2013

IT'S OSCAR WEEK!
BEST ACTOR:
Oscar, for "I thought she was an intruder!"
BEST SCRIPTING:
Oscar's spin team
BEST COMEDY PERFORMANCE:
Investigator Hilton Botha
EVIDENCE
BEST NON-PERFORMANCE:
Police brass who hand-picked Botha
H. BOTHA
ATTEMPTED MURDER CHARGES
ZZZ
BEST PROPS:
Oscar's armoury
BEST DOCUMENTARY:
Twitter, where it's all happening
BEST PICTURE:
Oscar's perp walk
BEST EXTRAS:
Billions of us — all legal experts!
LIVE
© ZAPIRO 24-2-13 SUN. TIMES
And the Oscar goes to... jail.
apology to Trevor Noah

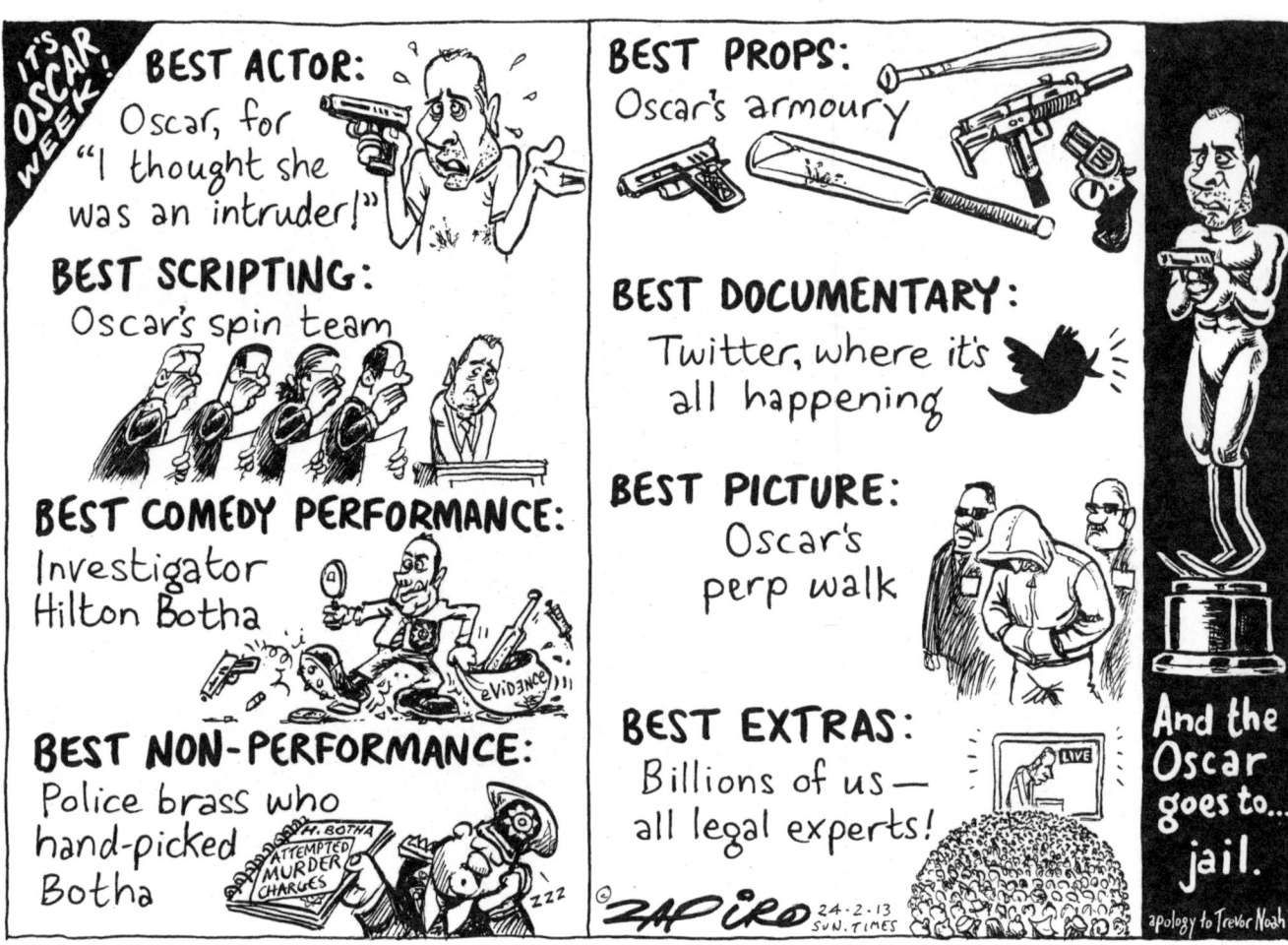

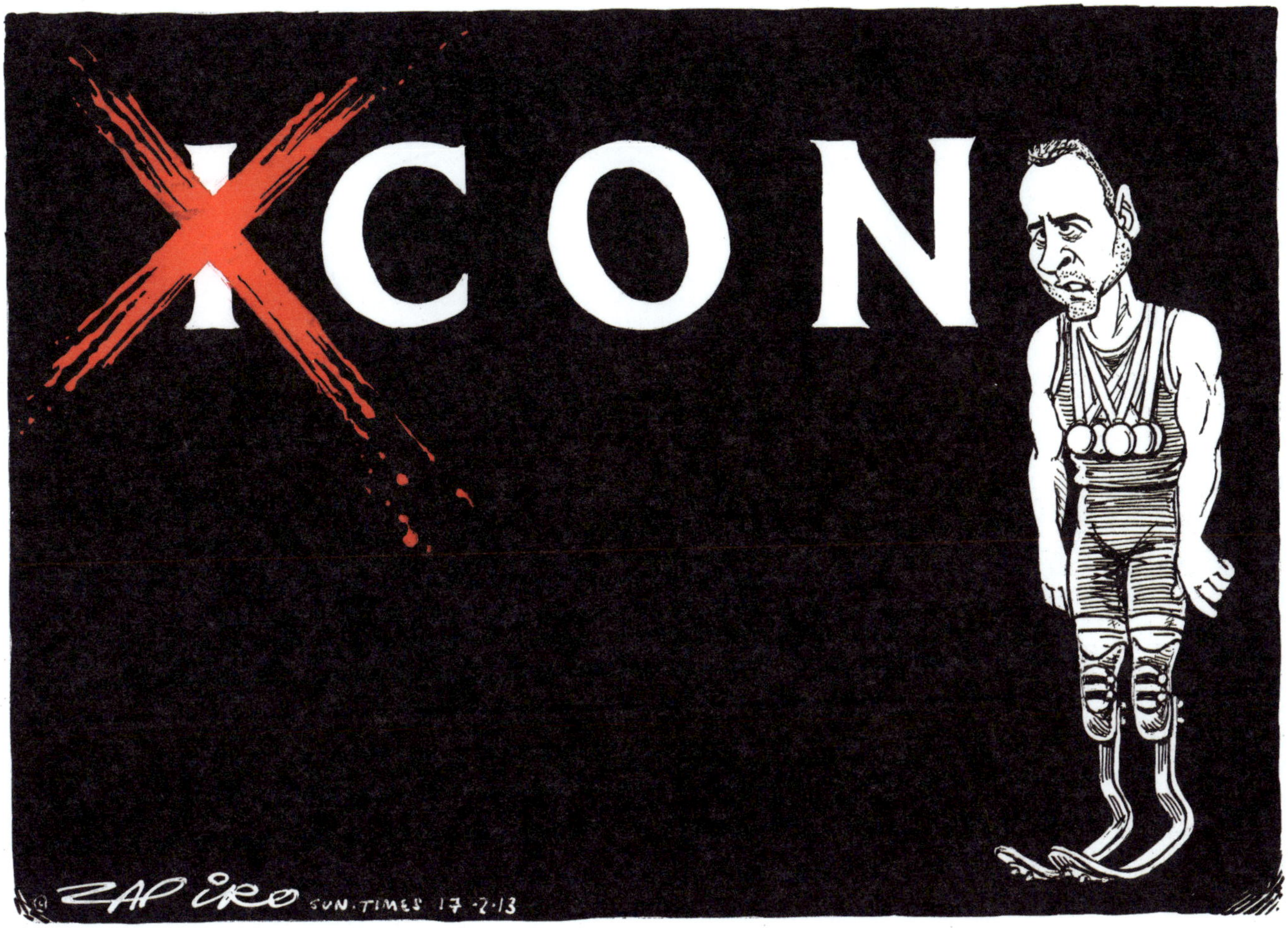
ICON
© ZAPIRO SUN.TIMES 17-2-13

CARTOON ANNUALS BY ZAPIRO

The Madiba Years (1996)
The Hole Truth (1997)
End Of Part One (1998)
Call Mr Delivery (1999)
The Devil Made Me Do It! (2000)
The ANC Went in 4X4 (2001)
Bushwhacked (2002)
Dr Do-Little and the African Potato (2003)
Long Walk to Free Time (2004)
Is There a Spin Doctor In the House? (2005)
Da Zuma code (2006)
Take Two Veg and Call Me In the Morning (2007)
Pirates of Polokwane (2008)
Don't Mess With the President's Head (2009)
Do You Know Who I Am?! (2010)
The Last Sushi (2011)
But Will It Stand Up in Court? (2012)

PUBLISHED IN LARGE-FORMAT HARDCOVER
The Mandela Files (2008)

10 Orange Street
Sunnyside
Auckland Park 2092
South Africa
+27 11 628 3200

In association with

© Jonathan Shapiro, 2013
Text © Mike Wills, 2013

All rights reserved

ISBN 978-1-4314-0164-2

Cover design by Jonathan Shapiro

Page layout by MR Design

Colourists are
Roberto Milano: p25, p34, p42, p63, p65, p78, p97, p103, p115, p122, p132, p139; Andrew Putter: p9; the rest by Jonathan Shapiro

Printed by Ultra Litho
Job no. 001986

See a complete list of Jacana titles at
www.jacana.co.za